America's Nation-Time:
1607-1789

BOOKS BY BENJAMIN W. LABAREE
IN THE NORTON LIBRARY

America's Nation–Time: 1607–1789 N821

*Patriots and Partisans: The Merchants of
Newburyport, 1764–1815* N786

America's Nation-Time: 1607-1789

Benjamin W. Labaree

The Norton Library

W·W·NORTON & COMPANY·INC·

NEW YORK

Books That Live

The Norton imprint on a book means that in the publisher's
estimation it is a book not for a single season but for the years.
W. W. Norton & Company, Inc.

Library of Congress Cataloging in Publication Data
Labaree, Benjamin Woods.
    America's nation-time, 1607-1789.
    The Norton Library)
    Includes bibliographies and index.
    1.   United States—History—Colonial period, ca. 1600-
1795.   2.   United States—History—Revolution, 1775-1783.
3.   United States—History—Confederation, 1783-1789.
I.   Title.
E188.L28   1976   973.2   76-16573
ISBN 0-393-00821-5

1 2 3 4 5 6 7 8 9 0

For
Mary Ellen and Sarah

Contents

Author's Preface

This is a history of those men and women who transformed America from a geographical expression into a new nation in less than two hundred years. I have attempted at the outset to show how the New World appeared to the first of these settlers because the shape of the land and the temper of climate profoundly affected the early patterns of settlement. I have also endeavored to remind the reader that, because these were English colonies, conditions and attitudes in the mother country often influenced the lives of settlers in this New World. But most important, I have tried to emphasize that while the majority of colonists were of English stock and most of their institutions were English too, many other Europeans also joined in the new venture. Still another people — the Africans — contributed their labor and their lives under the most inhumane of institutions — slavery. Living and working together these people made the period 1607 to 1789 America's "nation-time," to borrow the phrase of LeRoi Jones. But the most casual observer of today's divided society must realize that the job of nation-building in America will not be complete until all our citizens are accorded the respect due them as dignified human beings.

With hope for the future and in recognition of the diverse origins of all Americans, this book is dedicated to Mary Ellen and Sarah, one a daughter of Africa and the other a daughter of Europe. May we all learn to give our love to one another as freely as they do.

Williamstown, Massachusetts

Part I

The Seventeenth Century

1

A New World

The vast North American continent lay like a sleeping giant. A few thousand Indians had trekked across its broad plains and through its mountain valleys. A handful of Scandinavians had probed at its northeastern coast, and later, Europeans fished along the banks that lay far off its Atlantic shores. The Spaniards came to plunder the islands and continent to the south. But until the seventeenth century no other peoples from the Old World had succeeded in establishing a permanent settlement in the New World. Then and only then did the English, driven by poverty, persecution, and perhaps curiosity, begin what would in time rank as one of the greatest migrations in the history of mankind. Within three hundred years, more than forty million people from Europe, Africa, and Asia found new homes in America, many for better, and many for worse, but all with some sense of wonder about what the New World would mean for them.

Exploration

Through the misty northern seas Bjarni Herjolfsson steered his rugged knorr steadily westward. Along with his companions Bjarni had set out in the summer of 986 A.D. from his home in Iceland to join his father in the Norse colony recently established on the eastern coast of Greenland. But the forces of nature that have ever imperiled the lives of mariners in these waters fell upon the small vessel and its crew. First a raging northeaster drove them far to the south of their intended route. Then a deep fog closed in, and without the advantage of a compass, the men could only sail aimlessly on until at last the sun broke through. Shortly the first signs of land appeared — the abundance of birds, bits of vegatation in the water, and perhaps a change in the heave of the shoaling water. Although none of the men had even seen Greenland, they were told to expect high snow-topped peaks. When instead a low, heavily wooded coastline, probably Newfoundland, gradually stretched across the horizon before them, Bjarni and his companions became, as far as we know, the first Europeans to gaze upon the New World.

A voyage of discovery was far from Bjarni's intention, however, and he put his vessel about to continue his search for Greenland. Upon his arrival, the story of his discovery spread through the colony. Bjarni himself never went to sea again, but a few years later a Norseman named Lief came to him to learn all he could about the lands to the west. Lief, the son of Erik the Red, was determined to discover distant lands as his father had done. Soon he assembled a band of thirty-five men, bought Bjarni's knorr, and sailed toward the setting sun. Although the exact route of Lief's voyage in 1001 A.D. remains in dispute, modern archeology suggests that he and his men, like Bjarni before them, eventually landed on the northern tip of Newfoundland, where they wintered possibly at L'Anse aux Meadows. Lief returned to Greenland the following spring full of enthusiasm for the land he called Vinland because of the abundance of wild grapes and other vegetation found there.

Such tales stirred other Norsemen to colonize the new lands, as Iceland and Greenland had been settled by earlier generations. In the most ambitious expedition, Thorfinn Karlsefini assembled a company of 250 men and women with livestock and other necessities and set off in 1009 to establish a permanent colony in Vinland. With a planting harvested and shelters constructed, the settlers survived their first winter with little apparent difficulty. To their surprise, they had discovered inhabitants — Skrellings, they called the native Americans. Relations were friendly at first, and the Norsemen traded their produce for the fine furs trapped by the Indians. Before the second winter had passed, however, quarrels broke out; the Indians attacked the colony and were driven off only after a desperate battle. But the newcomers realized how great were the odds against them, and the will to continue the settlement slowly drained away. By spring they climbed aboard their vessels and returned to Greenland. The first European settlement in the New World was at an end.

What finally destroyed the Norse colonies in Newfoundland, and in Greenland too, were some of the same problems that confronted later settlers as well — how to survive in a distant land with little material support from home, how to attract new settlers to provide needed manpower, and how to get along with native inhabitants without exploiting them or becoming locked in wars of extinction. In spite of their impressive settlements in Iceland, the Norse proved unable to solve these problems for their colonies in Greenland and North America. Their exploits are thus noted more as a legend than as a legacy for those who followed.

For at least four centuries after the last of the Norse voyages to North America, Europeans remained ignorant of the vast continents of the New World that lay beyond the Western Sea. Various commentators have recently claimed that Italian, Portuguese, Irish, or Welsh adventurers rediscovered America, but evidence for such exploits is at best circumstantial. More reliable is the claim that around 1400 French, Basque, and perhaps German fishermen began to frequent the banks off Newfoundland, but if they saw the mainland beyond, they left no written record of their discovery.

One reason for the long pause in European exploration of the western Atlantic was a preoccupation with the Orient in the years that followed Marco Polo's return from the fabled East in 1295. Ultimately, however, the search for a water route to China by a succession of Portuguese and Spanish expeditions led the way to the rediscovery of America. Only because he miscalculated the earth's circumference did the Genoese navigator, Christopher Columbus, conclude that he could reach the East most easily by sailing west. Fortunately for Spain, Queen Isabella agreed to underwrite his scheme, and in the late summer of 1492 he embarked on one of the most famous voyages in history. Despite three subsequent expeditions into the Caribbean Sea and along the South American coast, Columbus never learned that he had discovered a new continent, although he did come to refer to the region as an "Other World."

Word of Columbus' first voyage spread rapidly through the European world, and in the next decades other nations scurried to send out expeditions of their own. In 1497 Henry VII of England sent another Italian navigator, John Cabot, due west in an effort to find a route to the Orient that would stay clear of the area already pre-empted by his archrivals, the Spaniards. Lands of the New World once more intervened, Cabot making his landfall somewhere along the coast of Newfoundland or Nova Scotia, where he promptly went ashore to stake a claim for his English master. Upon his return, Cabot spoke enthusiastically of the dense forests of trees suitable for ships' masts and of the codfish that were so plentiful that his men had hauled them out of the ocean in buckets. Both fish and timber would in time become staple products of the New World. Three years later Gaspar Corte Real claimed Newfoundland for the King of Portugal, and within a decade fishing fleets from England, France, and Portugal spent the summers working the offshore banks while some of the crew lived ashore and fished the nearby grounds.

Thus far the European knowledge of North America was confined to what later became the Maritime Provinces of Newfoundland and Nova Scotia. It remained for Giovanni Verrazano, sailing for France in 1524, to grasp the extent of the mainland coast. Ranging north from Cape Hatteras to the Strait of Belle Isle, he discovered New York harbor, Narragansett Bay, and numerous other landmarks of significance, which led to a fairly accurate chart of the coast to guide those who followed. When Jacques Cartier claimed the St. Lawrence River valley for France in 1533, the fourth European nation joined the American scene, and on the strength of Hendrik Hudson's discoveries at the beginning of the seventeenth century, the Dutch entered the competition for empire too.

Spain was the only nation strong enough to exploit its claims to New World territory in the first hundred years after Columbus and Cabot. With but token opposition from the Portuguese, the Spaniards established a string of settlements from Peru, in the south, to Santa Fe and St. Augustine, in the north. Expeditions of soldiers conquered the native Indians and put them to work in the silver and gold mines. By mid-century, Spain had carried away from the New World vast treasures, leaving behind two European institutions of enduring strength, the Christian religion and the university. In addition to strengthening Spain's position as the world's leading power, at least temporarily, the wealth pouring out of South America whetted the appetite of other Europeans. Some searched in vain for "Norumbega," the legendary city of gold somewhere in the North. Other adventurers — like the English sea dogs, Gilbert, Raleigh, and Drake — found the capture of Spanish plate fleets a more practical road to wealth. Before the end of the sixteenth century, England at last seemed ready to follow up its American claims on a serious scale.

Topography

To the Europeans exploring the coastline, North America was not only a new world, it was a land more lavishly endowed by nature than any they had seen before. Its scenic splendors inspired many voyagers to lyrical praise. Some spoke of the abundant vegetation and the land's potential for cultivation, while mariners like Cabot could not fail to note the stands of oak and pine suitable for ship's timbers and masts.

One factor that accounted for much of this praise was of course the virginal nature of the American continent. Among people now living only those who have viewed the northern woods of Canada or parts of interior Alaska can imagine what the great American forest was like. But where can we now find duplicates of the rich, ripe shores of Chesapeake Bay, the inviting Hudson River Valley, and the isolated, unspoiled granite boldness of the Maine coast? We can only guess at the awe and the sense of newness which overcame these visitors to America.

Yet the North American continent was no less old than Europe and Asia, from a geological standpoint. So important are the shape and natural growth of the land to an understanding of America's historical beginnings that we must find out why the New World looked as it did to those who would come to make it their home. The basic structure of eastern North America had its beginnings in pre-Cambrian times, more than 500 million years ago. During this earliest of geological periods, the Appalachian Highlands took form. This chain of mountains ranges from the Acadian Highlands of maritime Canada, through the White and Green Mountains of New England, the Highlands of New York and New Jersey, thence by the Blue Ridge from southern Pennsylvania through Virginia, and it terminates in the Great Smoky mountains of the Carolinas. After their initial uplifting, these mountains underwent millions of years of folding, compression, and finally erosion from wind, rain, and river, until they acquired the rounded, subdued appearance they have today. Some miles to the west, meanwhile, across the Great Appalachian Valley, rose an even more formidable barrier, the Newer Appalachians. While not so high as some of the peaks to the east, this second chain of mountains was more sharply defined. Altogether, the Appalachian Highlands would prove to be an effective western boundary for Colonial America.

South of New York, the land slopes eastward from the Appalachians toward the Atlantic Ocean, making a broad region which nature has divided into two distinct zones. The Piedmont Upland is an area of gently rolling foothills and varies in width from about fifty miles at its northern end to over 100 miles in the Carolinas. Bounded on the west by the Blue Ridge and Smoky Mountains, its eastern edge follows the line of waterfalls and rapids in the major rivers of the region. This "fall line" runs through the present cities of Trenton, Philadelphia, Washington, Richmond, Columbia, and Macon, and it represents the head of deep-water navigation. East of the fall line stretches the Coastal Plain, deeply indented with broad river mouths, bays, and sounds, all the result of alternate sinking of the land and rising of the sea level, a process which continues today.

North of New Jersey and Pennsylvania, an additional force of nature has brought a rather different shape to the face of the land. On top of the foundations of mountain ranges, plateaus, and plains already established in New York and New England came what one scientist has called "the scenery maker." Beginning about 600,000 years ago, a series of glaciers moved down across the face of the land, especially the last, "Wisconsin Stage" of activity, whose final wave receded barely 10,000 years ago. Before it left, however, the last glacier had covered the highest mountain tops, strewn the countryside with ground rock and stone, and by its sheer weight depressed the level of the land, especially along the shore. Only the ocean waters, warmed by the Gulf Stream, could stem the onward tide of ice.

The terminal moraine — the line of furthest advance — runs across the top of Pennsylvania, out the length of Long Island, and through the islands of Martha's Vineyard and Nantucket. This moraine, and other deposits caused by temporary pauses in the glacier's retreat, account for the general shape of the southern New England coast from Cape Cod to Connecticut. As the ice sheet constantly melted, the waters running off etched river valleys more deeply into the landscape. Thus, the Delaware, Hudson, Connecticut, Merrimack, and Kennebec, among others, became major waterways for future development. At the same time, this meltwater gradually raised the level of the ocean. Up the river valleys the sea advanced, "drowning" much of the coastal plain that during the height of the glacial period had reached as far out as 200 miles from today's shore and is the present-day continental shelf. Major bays, well suited for harbors, formed at the river mouths. By about 10,000 B.C. the "scenery maker" retreated inland, leaving the northern portion of the continent much as we know it today.

The advance and retreat of polar ice have suggested to scientists that the earth's climate does not remain constant. Whether because of changes in the sun's heat, as some claim, or the change in ocean currents, as others maintain, it is apparent that the climate of North America has long been subject to cyclical patterns. The Norse voyages and settlements seemingly came during a warming trend, between 500 and 1000 A.D. Hence the abundant grass and other vegetation in "Vinland." By 1400 the cycle had reversed itself and the Norse colonies in Greenland disappeared without trace, perhaps partly because of increasingly severe climate conditions. In the first century of European settlement of North America, winter weather was reportedly severe, with harbor freeze-ups and heavy snowfalls a commonplace. But soon a new warming trend began. Even as early as 1800 newspapers described a blizzard as an "old-fashioned" snowstorm. Scientists expect this warming trend to continue for several more centuries.

Within these long cycles, however, the climate of North America has, during the short historical period, remained relatively stable. We can therefore characterize the regions settled by European immigrants with reasonable accuracy. Influenced by the Gulf Stream, as well as by latitude, the warm and humid semitropical plains of Georgia and South Carolina give way gradually to the more temperate bays and sounds of North Carolina, but even here winter snows are a rarity. Off Cape Hatteras, the Gulf Stream bends eastward into the Atlantic. As a result, the Chesapeake Bay area, while often subjected to the steaming hot spells of the Carolina summer, is occasionally blanketed with one-foot snowfalls in the winter. Throughout most of the year, however, a belt of moderate weather stretches from North Carolina well into southeastern Pennsylvania. Not until one passes east of the mouth of the Hudson River, and particularly north of Cape Cod, do winters become severe, for here the Labrador current adds its chilly waters to the influence of northern latitudes. Looking at it another way, we might say that much of the North American coast shares in common a warm summer with ample rainfall and occasional hot spells, which are more frequent of course in Georgia and the Carolinas. What makes the major difference between the regions are the severe New England winters, along with the early autumns and late springs. These force dramatic changes on the landscape and on those who live there.

Climate has of course determined in large measure the ecology of the land. The entire region settled by Europeans during the colonial period was at that time covered with what naturalists have called the Great American Woods. Nowhere in Europe was there such an extensive virgin forest, and many of the trees themselves were to be found only in the New World. As monarch of these woods stood the white oak, with roots planted deeply in the soil to support its thick, short trunk and broad mantle of sturdy limbs. South of the Chesapeake the live oak ranged along the Coastal Plain all the way to Texas. The elm, its profile a fountain of limbs and branches against the sky, could be found at both northern and southern ends of the continent. The pine too was common throughout the Great American Forest. In the north, the white pine predominated, tall and straight, with trunks sometimes three feet through or more. Its southern counterparts have been called collectively yellow pine, and they were found in the most extensive pine forest of all, stretching from the Atlantic coast to the Mississippi in a band nearly 300 miles wide in places. Added to these were a variety of maples, birches, nut trees of several kinds, and a score of other major families. Small wonder, then, that the explorer and early settler alike spoke with awe about the forests of the New World.

The American forest consisted of far more than its trees, for of course the dense growth supported a range of other living things as well. Berries of all sorts, grasses for livestock, and a myriad of wild flowers carpeted the open spaces between the stands of trees. Most of the species of birds and animals were familiar to European settlers, but there were indigenous varieties too, like the turkey and beaver, both of which became valuable quarry for the huntsman. In the lakes and rivers throughout the forest lived salmon, bass, sturgeon, and trout in abundance, and along the edge of the sea were lobsters, clams, and other shellfish in quantities quite unknown to Europeans.

How could an observant explorer escape being struck by the virgin beauty of the New World? "We stood awhile like men ravished at the beauty and delicacy of this sweet soil," wrote John Brereton, in 1602, of the view from atop a hill overlooking Buzzards Bay. "Besides divers clear lakes of fresh water (whereof we saw no end), meadows very large and full of green grass; even the most woody places . . . do grow so distinct and apart, one tree from another, upon green grassy ground, somewhat higher than the plains, as if Nature would show herself above her power, artificial."

The Indian

The North American continent was not, in actuality, a virgin world when the earliest Europeans arrived at the end of the fifteenth century A.D. The land had been inhabited ever since the first immigrants crossed the land bridge over the Bering Sea, perhaps as early as 30,000 B.C. Most early groups apparently migrated southward through Mexico and over the isthmus of Panama, for within a few thousand years Asians had reached nearly to the tip of South America. Subsequently, other groups worked eastward across the North American continent, bringing with them the Stone Age culture of Eurasia. Artifacts found at Bull Brook, in Ipswich, Massachusetts, suggest that man reached the east coast as early as 10,000 B.C., closely behind the retreating ice sheets.

Perhaps the inhabitants encountered in Central and South America by the Spanish explorers were directly descended from the first immigrants, or possibly their ancestors were among subsequent invaders who brought a more advanced stage of civilization from the Old World, before the land bridge had receded beneath the rising seas. In any case, the Mayans, Aztecs, and Incas had made remarkable progress through the millennia of isolation from the Old World. Their accomplishments included urban construction and community organization. They also mastered the mysteries of developing an accurate calendar, and they made pottery, wove cloth, and worked precious metals. These men also learned how to domesticate animals like the llama, and to cultivate such crops as potatoes, corn, and beans, in irrigated fields where water was scarce.

On the eve of European colonization, approximately 125,000 Indians lived along the eastern seaboard of North America from Canada to Florida. The Chesapeake Bay region and Southern New England held a greater concentration of natives than other regions, for many of the same reasons that attracted white settlers to these areas in the coming decades. Three large family groups predominated in the area east of the Mississippi Valley. Along the immediate seacoast were the Algonquians, whose tribes included the Abnaki, the Delaware, and the Powhatan Confederacy. The Five Nations of the Iroquois effectively controlled the interior regions bordering on the Great Lakes, while Creeks, Seminoles, and other tribes of the Muskhogean family ranged through the southeastern region of the continent.

Cultural anthropologists have not fully explained why the Indians who inhabited eastern North America never reached the impressive level of civilization attained by their cousins on the southern continent. The Algonquians and other eastern Indians had not advanced beyond a Stone Age culture when the first whites settled here early in the seventeenth century. They dwelt in domelike wigwams covered with matting or bark, a hearth in the middle for the fire and a low bench around the walls for sitting and sleeping. Perhaps as many as fifty or one hundred families lived together in a village, although communities with more than five hundred members were virtually unknown. Around the cluster of wigwams, they erected a palisade of branches for protection from animals and enemy tribes. The sachem and his council of elders ruled the village by persuasion more often than by fiat. Matters pertaining to impending warfare and other crises had a full airing at a powwow of all the braves, while the medicine men claimed a line of communication with the spiritual world beyond. At best, the Indian village was a loosely organized affair.

Beyond the inhabited area, the Indians made clearings in the forest for cultivation. Usually they cut or burned away the underbrush and girdled the larger trees, planting their first crops as soon as sufficient light filtered through the limbs of the dying trees above. They had no plows, and therefore crops were planted in hills, with fish or some seaweed fertilizer. In addition to corn and beans, the Indians planted squashes, pumpkins, and other crops that could be kept through the winter without spoilage. Since the land was owned communally, it was worked on a communal basis. The women performed almost all the agricultural chores, from first planting to final preparation for storage or consumption. Some tribes, like the Delawares, showed unusual skills as farmers.

The men spent their time hunting, fishing, and occasionally fighting with their neighbors. The woods of Eastern North America abounded in game; the white-tailed deer of course was of particular importance, not only for its venison but also for its skin, which was used for clothing. Other valuable game included rabbit, elk, moose, and bear. The hunter also set out cleverly devised traps and snares for game birds like ducks, and geese, pheasant, partridge, and especially pigeon. Like farming, hunting was generally a community operation, with parties working together to maximize their efficiency in the woods.

Still another important source of food, particularly for the Algonquian tribes of the eastern seaboard, was fishing. In the spring salmon, shad, sturgeon, and other fish came up the coastal rivers to spawn and fell prey to fishermen along the banks. In the summer months, many of the tribes moved their villages to the edge of the sea, where they set their weirs for alewives and herring and dug along the shore for clams and oysters. Often they ventured forth in their birchbark canoes to establish fishing camps on offshore islands along the New England coast. The Penobscots of central Maine distinguished themselves in making good use of the resources of the bay now bearing their name. They dried and stored much of their summer catch for consumption during the winter months. With the coming of autumn, most of the tribes moved into the interior to find a snug valley deep in the forest for protection against the cold winds of winter.

Historians have generally concluded that the Indians fought constantly among themselves, but more recent studies suggest that warfare was only intermittent. Nevertheless, the men devoted much time to martial preparations, and war played an important role in their folklore. Actual battles among hostile tribes quickly devolved into a series of individual scuffles in which it was every man for himself. Bravery rated highest on the Indians' scale of personal values, and therefore much more was at stake than a few square miles of disputed territory. Scalps torn from the heads of a man's victims attested to victory, but if a man had the misfortune to fall captive to the foe, he was expected to endure the most hideous tortures, showing nothing but contempt for his enemies until death released him from his agony.

Obviously there were many aspects of the Indians' way of life that weakened their resistance to the coming invasion of the Europeans. For one thing the fact that their villages were small and were scattered over extensive territory made it almost impossible for them to concentrate large forces against the whites. Petty feuds among the various tribes further hindered efforts to unite against the invaders, and in fact virtually invited the whites to play some tribes off against others. Nor were the Indians prepared for the consequences of losing their lands to the whites. When the English settlers proceeded to exclude the native from lands seized or purchased from him, the Indian could not comprehend why he could no longer hunt and fish in the area. Because his survival depended on extensive woodlands for hunting and trapping, the Indian could not coexist with the white invader along the eastern seaboard of North America. As events would prove, however, the natives' retreat to the west came only after the most stubborn efforts to resist the flood of invaders.

Troubled England

England at the beginning of the seventeenth century was suffering through a major transition from its medieval status of earlier centuries to the modern state it soon became. Not surprisingly the stresses and strains that accompanied this change bore heavily upon the common folk of the realm. Disruption became an important force that by mid-century would drive thousands of Britons from their native land in search of better conditions overseas.

Historians estimate that in 1600 England's population totaled little more than four million people, a figure that by 1640 grew by thirty percent to nearly five and a half million. At the top of a social structure best likened to a pyramid stood the upper classes — the royal family of course, and the nobility, bishops, and landed gentry — numbering altogether in 1640 less than 100,000 people. Next followed the yeomen and merchants. The yeomen were independent freeholders, some of whom were quite wealthy landowners but others were only tenants. Their urban equivalent, the merchants, reflected a similar range of economic well-being. Together this middle group constituted nearly ten percent of the population, or about 500,000 persons. But it was the great mass of Englishmen who formed the broad base of the pyramid — nearly five million peasants and cottagers, day laborers, artificers, and cloth workers.

Three out of four Englishmen lived on the soil at the beginning of the seventeenth century, eighty percent of them crowded into southern England below the line between Bristol Channel and the Wash. Despite a keen attachment for place, Englishmen moved around with surprising frequency although they often settled down at no great distance from their original home. Added to geographical mobility was a steady flow of immigrants from France, the Lowlands, and Ireland especially. The Englishman of the seventeenth century represented a far greater ethnic mixture than imagined by those later Americans who proudly traced their ancestry to so-called pure Anglo-Saxon forebears.

Virtually all political and economic power rested in the hands of the upper and middle groups of society, although evidence suggests that on the local level some tenants and laborers held minor roles in the direction of community affairs. Significantly, the stratification of society went unquestioned by rich and poor alike, for such arrangement seemed natural. The meaner sort, as they were called, gave deference to their "betters" in all matters of leadership. Social distinctions did not altogether bar advancement for some aspiring yeomen and merchants into the ranks of the gentry, but for the lower classes upward mobility remained almost impossible.

For the vast majority of Englishmen, life was at best a precarious undertaking. Infant mortality carried off a frightful proportion of children, and those who survived to adulthood faced death in countless forms. Outright starvation claimed some, while malnutrition left many others at the mercy of tuberculosis, rickets, scurvy, and other diseases. Even the able-bodied fell victim by the thousands to periodic epidemics of plague, such as the one that took the lives of over 35,000 Londoners in 1625. Those who survived smallpox bore the disfiguring marks of their ordeal ever after. Venereal disease, tooth decay, and body sores of various kinds condemned still others to a lifetime of pain or discomfort. Accidents in the field or in town claimed many more people than generally supposed, especially among those engaged in hazardous careers like mining or shipping. In some port towns the women outnumbered the men by nearly thirty percent, and throughout the land widows and their fatherless children remained in acute distress.

Poverty was so widespread in seventeenth century England as to include nearly half the population. By even the most spartan standards, one-fourth of the people lived below the subsistence level, without hope of obtaining land by purchase or lease, and condemned to a hand-to-mouth existence while scrabbling for work as farm or urban laborers. Another quarter of the population eked out a bare livelihood just at the line of subsistence, only to be overcome by poverty during periodic crises. Beggary and petty thievery became a way of life for many people in both these groups, and so inevitably did the pain and horror of corporal punishment and mutilation. Alcohol and sex offered only temporary escape, for excessive indulgence in these pleasures also led to severe penalties.

The rapid growth of population in the first half of the seventeenth century contributed to a major housing shortage that plagued residents of many parts of southern England. Inadequate shelter exposed the population to the damp chill of winter at a time when firewood was doubling in price. For the poorer half of the population, personal privacy became a rarity, as in-laws and other relatives crowded together to share whatever space was available. This condition, added to other strains on traditional family life, contributed to a rise in sexual immorality and a resultant sense of uneasiness throughout the land.

Two long-range developments added disruption to the already discomforted lives of many Englishmen. In the countryside the old open-field system was giving way inexorably to a new wave of enclosures, as landowners sought to rearrange their holdings for sheep and cattle grazing or for specialization in particular market crops. Tenants who previously had scraped out a meager existence on holdings of four acres or less in open fields now found themselves without any land at all and reduced to an uncertain future as agricultural laborers. Village life also changed, as the landowners and tenants who survived the movement took up residence on their new enclosed holdings outside of town. At the same time a marked growth in urban communities began, encouraged by the prosperous cloth trade and the expansion of maritime commerce, and fed also by the surge of uprooted farmers into the cities in search of work. The world of an earlier England — stable, secure, and familiar — seemed to be rapidly disappearing. The simple villager often struggled in vain to find a niche in the strange new world around him.

The lost or discontented Englishman of humble status had nowhere to turn for encouragement or comfort. To be sure, in many communities he might have held a minor consultative role in the administration of local affairs, tasks which included jury duty or perhaps office holding but in no sense could he hope to better the conditions of his own life through political action. The lines of authority came from above, not from his fellow commoners. His parish church, while close at hand, seemed remote to the needs of the impoverished half of the nation's people. The rulers of the land too often seemed to be the very source of misery rather than a means of salvation. During the numerous wars of the period, for instance, the burden of military service fell most heavily upon the poor. Self-mutilation and suicide were not uncommon means of avoiding the call of the press gang, for many an expedition returned from overseas with less than half its original number. In some communities overseers of the poor made a conscientious effort to relieve the more acutely distressed by outright doles or the maintenance of an almshouse. But these measures were stopgap at best, and offered no real hope. Without a voice in the direction of their own affairs, victims in fact of forces beyond the control of any group of men, a generation of "vexed and troubled Englishmen," as historian Carl Bridenbaugh has described them, faced an uncertain future in the first decades of the seventeenth century.

A New World

For more than a half-century after the voyages of John and Sebastian Cabot, the English crown did little to follow up its claims to the New World. One reason was that the Tudors were preoccupied with their position in Europe, especially their relations with France and Spain. The Welsh and Scots posed another problem closer to home, for both peoples resented and resisted the increasing domination by their English neighbors. Furthermore, the conquest and occupation of Ireland required most of the attention that England could spare from more immediate problems. Finally, the nation had not yet accumulated sufficient capital resources to support a major development of its American claims.

The ascension of Elizabeth to the throne in 1558 marked the beginning of England's bid for empire. An age which achieved new heights in literature and drama produced men who took up the challenge of England's drive for overseas expansion as well. First Sir Humphrey Gilbert, then Sir Francis Drake, led expeditions in search of a northwest passage to the Orient. Although by the 1580s John Davis and Sir Martin Frobisher had penetrated deep into the ice-choked waters above the North American mainland, the passage could not be forced. But their voyages generated a fresh interest in the New World for itself, as the attention of Humphrey Gilbert and others turned to the continent that had previously been considered only a barrier to the fabled East.

In 1578 Elizabeth granted Gilbert a charter to settle lands overseas, and when that explorer was lost at sea, his half-brother, Sir Walter Raleigh, fell heir to the patent. After one exploratory expedition, Raleigh dispatched a company of over one hundred men and women in 1587 to establish a colony on Roanoke Island off the coast of North Carolina. Partly because of the distractions caused by the Spanish Armada, Raleigh failed to reinforce the settlement until 1590. But by then it was too late, for the relief force found the colony in ruins and no survivors.

Far more important in the long run than this first futile effort at establishing a permanent English settlement in America was the fact that interest in the New World began to spread throughout the realm from West Country ports like Dartmouth and Plymouth, where the fever of exploration had first appeared. The Richard Hakluyts, father and son, turned out a prodigious amount of literature, compiling what was known of New World geography and urging a policy of colonial expansion for the nation. In 1584 the son wrote a pamphlet entitled *A Discourse of Western Planting,* designed to persuade the

Queen to support overseas ventures out of public funds. However, the only tangible resource she lent to such an undertaking was the name "Virginia," but the tract, unpublished until modern times, remains a useful compilation of the arguments for overseas expansion.

Hakluyt saw that the long-range value of an empire lay in the development of trade between the mother country and planted colonies rather than in reckless exploitation of the New World's natural resources. To be sure, a strong note of national self-interest ran through the essay, as he argued that the most effective way to thwart the growing power of Philip of Spain, the Queen's hated adversary, was by winning the battle for an American empire. New World timber and naval stores would build the fleet needed for control of the seas. Such an appeal suited well the ambitions of Drake, Raleigh, and other activists of the period whose hatred for Roman Catholic Spain seemed almost to match that of their sovereign. But Hakluyt also cited the promise of New World settlements becoming markets for the growing wool cloth industry and for other products of the mother country and as a source of commodities in demand at home, such as salt, wines, and fruit. Furthermore, colonization would give England the opportunity to plant "sincere religion" in the New World, as the Protestant minister-author put it.

In his *Discourse* Hakluyt noted that an overseas empire offered the mother country yet another advantage. "We might settle there such needy people of our countrey," wrote Sir Humphrey Gilbert, "which now trouble the common wealth, and [who] through want here at home are inforced to commit outragious offences, whereby they are dayly consumed with the gallows." Throughout the literature urging colonial expansion at the turn of the seventeenth century ran this concern for what appeared to be a mounting pressure of population at home. Beggars in the streets, criminals at large and in prison, and the poverty-stricken men and women everywhere seemed to cry out for relief. The New World had more to offer these people than did the Old. As matters stood at the close of the sixteenth century, however, the image of the New World was tarnished at best. For one thing, reports of mariners who sailed with Frobisher, Gilbert, and others suggested that the climate was far more hostile than that of the homeland. Nor did news of the failure at

Roanoke inspire confidence in the safety of such an undertaking. Most persons knew, furthermore, of the hazards inherent in any ocean voyage, particularly such a long passage as that to America, with its dangers from pirates and Spaniards as well as from the elements. Other efforts at colonization, such as Bartholomew Gosnold's settlement at Cuttyhunk, off Massachusetts, in 1602, and George Popham's ill-fated outpost at the mouth of the Kennebec River in Maine, gave the pessimists still further reason to doubt the wisdom of such undertakings.

Counter to a negative view of the New World in England ran the gradually emerging ideas of America as a land of opportunity. Numerous elements combined to give shape to this image among many Englishmen who contemplated emigrating from their native land. The idea that America was a paradise gained encouragement from the promoters of colonial schemes whenever an opportunity offered. There is considerable evidence, for instance, that Raleigh carefully edited the journal of a voyage he had sponsored in 1584 to North Carolina and the Chesapeake led by Captain Arthur Barlow. In the version published by Hakluyt, Barlow praised the new land and spoke "of such plenty...that I think in all the world the like abundance is not to be found." One island they visited had "many goodly woods full of deer, conies, hares, and fowls, with high stands of cedar, pines, cyprus," not barren and fruitless like other woods. Yet another landfall revealed soil "the most plentiful, sweet, fruitful, and wholesome of all the world." If the land itself recalled the visions of the Garden of Eden, the inhabitants seemed blessed with the innocence of Paradise, "the most gentle, loving, and faithful void, of all guile and treason, and such as live after the manner of the golden age."

One of the most influential writers was Captain John Smith, whose account of New England published in 1616 waxed eloquent about the local charms. Any healthy man who could not live in that land with ease deserved to starve. Game birds, fish, and beasts of the forest abounded. "Of all the four parts of the world I have yet seen not inhabited," he added by way of personal endorsement, "I would rather live here than anywhere." Through such writings, the idea of American paradise captured the imagination of an expansive generation, many of whose members became in time the victims of their own hyperbole. Thus the poet John Donne, who had never seen the New World, could write of his mistress:

O my America! my new-found-land
My kingdom, safeliest when with one man manned,
My mine of precious stones, my empery,
How blest I am in thus discovering thee![1]

On balance of course, the English view of the New World remained mixed. For every lavish account of America that came from the pen of one who had a selfish stake in promoting colonization could be found a grim tale of disaster at sea or hardships of settlement. Yet, through all the conflicting reports and opinions, many a "vexed and troubled" Englishman at the beginning of the seventeenth century looked hopefully west for a better future.

FURTHER READINGS

For the period of exploration, Samuel E. Morison, *The European Discovery of America: The Northern Voyages* (Boston, 1971) is outstanding. Farley Mowat, *Westviking* (Boston, 1965) is a readable account of the Norse voyages. An excellent natural history of America is Peter Farb, *Face of North America* (New York, 1963), while Betty F. Thomson, *The Changing Face of New England* (New York, 1958) is a well-written study of that region's geology. For a history of America's first inhabitants, see William T. Hagan, *American Indians* (Chicago, 1961) and Willian N. Fenton et al., *American Indian and White Relations to 1830: Needs and Opportunities for Study* (Chapel Hill, 1957). Both Wallace Notestein, *The English People on the Eve of Colonization, 1603-1630* (New York, 1951), and Carl Bridenbaugh *Vexed and Troubled Englishmen, 1500-1642* (New York, 1968) are excellent studies of the setting from which most early American immigrants came. A. L. Rowse, in *The Expansion of Elizabethan England* (New York, 1955) examines the thrust for colonization in its Old World context. One of the principal colonizers is the subject of a study by Philip Barbour, *The Three Worlds of Captain John Smith* (Boston, 1964).

---

[1] John Donne, *Elegies. XIX. To His Mistress Going to Bed.* (1669).

2

First Settlements

What little we know of the first Europeans who made their homes in America tells us that over half of them did not long survive the experience. The Atlantic passage for white immigrants as for black slaves took its deadly toll. Disease, Indians, and childbirth killed off many others. Yet still they came like the proverbial lemmings, carrying on where others had left off in the settlement of a continent. Along the warm shores of Chesapeake Bay and the Carolinas, along the banks of the Hudson and the Delaware, and along the rock-bound coast of New England they settled. By the end of the seventeenth century a quarter-million people from Europe and Africa stood where none had stood a hundred years before, men and women, blacks and whites, elders and children, all of them laborers in the vineyards of the New World.

The Migration

England's long period of preliminary exploration of the New World came to an end with the death of Elizabeth in 1603. When her successor, James I, made peace with Spain the following year, the way cleared for a more concentrated effort at founding settlements. Not that James altered the earlier Tudor policy by offering state assistance to such undertakings, but he did grant royal charters to several companies eager to establish outposts in America.

The joint-stock companies, which King James authorized in the early years of the seventeenth century, were modeled on trading organizations like the East India Company and the Muscovy Company. For only by combining the capital of numerous investors, rich and not so rich, could the joint-stock company amass the funds necessary for so ambitious a venture as overseas settlements. The motive for most shareholders was of course economic, for each anticipated a generous return on his investment, which might be as small as £ 12.10s., the price for one share in the Virginia Company of London. Whether expectations were met depended entirely on the operation of the company during the first critical years. The fact of the matter is that most groups showed little if any financial profit for their activities.

The royal charter outlined in considerable detail the actual scope of operations permitted each company. Typical was the third charter awarded the Virginia Company of London in 1612. First came a description of the territory granted the company, in this case "all those lands...from the point of land called Cape or Point Comfort, all along the sea coasts to the northward two hundred miles and from the said point of Cape Comfort...southward two hundred miles, and all that space and circuit of land...throughout from sea to sea...and all islands lying within three hundred leagues of the aforesaid coast." At four general courts (or meetings) each year, company members were authorized to elect officers like the governor and his assistants, and "to make such laws and ordinances for the good and welfare of the plantation" as thought necessary, so long as such laws were not contrary to the statutes of the realm. The charter authorized the company to transport both subjects and strangers to settle in the plantation, along with weapons, clothing, beasts, and all other merchandise necessary to establish and defend the settlement and to trade with the Indians. All commerce with the new colony was to be exempt from custom duties for seven years, although the king did expect to receive one-fifth of all gold and silver found in company territory.

During the first three decades of the seventeenth century, the Stuarts granted many charters to groups of adventurers eager to invest in the New World. The original Virginia Company charter, issued in 1606, authorized a group based in Plymouth to establish settlements in an area to the north of that controlled by the London group, but it was fourteen years and one reorganization later that the Plymouth adventurers founded a permanent plantation in what Captain John Smith called New England. Other companies founded colonies at Bermuda and in the Caribbean during this period.

No one knew better than the adventurers themselves that they needed more than a concentration of capital and the royal blessing to establish a successful colony. Most of all they needed people. In general, Englishmen had numerous reasons for migrating to the New World. Some sought farm land and a permanent residence; others hoped to discover gold and return home with their newly found wealth. Many came in search of religious freedom; many more were driven to the New World by the poverty of their Old World lives. Despite the immigrants of all descriptions who flooded into the American colonies throughout the seventeenth century, labor remained in desperately short supply. America seemed to have everything in abundance except workers. The fact that people made a valuable cargo is one of the fundamental explanations for the great migration of Englishmen to the New World.

Numerous historians have attempted to find out more about the first colonists in America. The task is difficult because few of these immigrants left any record of their English background or their American experiences. Nevertheless, enough evidence has been assembled from various sources to give us an adequate picture of those who came to America in the seventeenth century. The city of Bristol was a major port of embarkation. Records there indicate that about one-third of those sailing for the New World in the seventeenth century were yeomen and husbandmen, another twenty percent were artisans and tradesmen, and ten percent were laborers. Women comprised one-quarter of the passengers. Those styled gentlemen accounted for only one percent of the immigrants. Other records also show that a large proportion of these Englishmen were surprisingly young, many between the ages of eighteen and twenty-four, and there were some as young as fourteen making the voyage without parents. These and other sources suggest that relatively few hopelessly impoverished Englishmen took the opportunity to come to America, while at the other end of the scale, almost no men of wealth and position did either.

Colonists arrived in all sorts of conditions. In addition to those thousands who came over as individuals, a large number of immigrants arrived as part of a previously cohesive group, a parish led by a Puritan minister perhaps, or a group of artisans hired by the Virginia Company and sent over together. Many others made the voyage with their families or with neighbors, so that the shock of migration for them was somewhat eased. Another distinction between immigrants separated those who could afford to pay for their own passage and those who could not. The latter signed contracts called indentures, by which they agreed to work for a period of four years or more in exchange for their transportation to America. Most of these "colonists in bondage" at least had voluntarily surrendered their freedom in order to reach the New World. Thousands of others came involuntarily, criminals transported as punishment, prisoners of war, or simply unfortunate victims of kidnappers. Within this last category we find the hapless African, captured in his native land by tribal enemies and sold to the European slave trader for transportation to the Caribbean or Continental colonies of North America.

Rich or poor, servant or free, all immigrants found that there was only one way to reach America. Crossing the Atlantic in the age of sail was a traumatic experience. For the weak and ill, it was often their last journey, as many never reached their destination alive. For others, the voyage became a nightmare, frightening at the time and in recollection as well. For most immigrants, the crossing became a symbol that marked an irrevocable commitment to the New World.

That part of the Atlantic Ocean stretching for three thousand miles between Land's End and the New England coast was more a barrier than a highway to America. Prevailing headwinds and the steady flow of the Gulf Stream made the most direct passage across extremely difficult for sailing vessels. Many masters shaped their course to the southwest after leaving England to pick up the northeast trade winds off the Cape Verde Islands, then made a landfall in the West Indies, and finally ran up the coast to their destination. A few others tried the old Viking route south of Iceland and Greenland, making a landfall at Newfoundland and working south along the coast. In either case, the typical passage took at least nine weeks, and those that lasted twice as long were by no means uncommon.

Vessels in the servant trade measured on the average around two hundred tons, ships and brigs of perhaps 100 feet overall length. But many of the early immigrants came in much smaller craft. No matter what the size, overcrowding seemed to be characteristic of all vessels. When Pennsylvania finally enacted regulations in 1750, a space six feet square was required for every four adults, who were expected to sleep in relays. In practice, the typical passenger list numbered around 300 souls. Provisions for ten or twelve weeks were usually carried, although not always in adequate quantities, and rationing of both food and water was a commonplace. Passengers on vessels delayed by storms faced starvation, as in the case of those on board the *Good Intent,* few of whom were left alive after a hideous crossing that lasted twenty-four weeks.

Shipboard disease was another common danger. Crew members often contracted smallpox or other contagion, which spread through the vessel like wildfire. Scurvy and similar illness related to malnutrition broke out on longer passages. Common seasickness could not be taken lightly by its miserable victims whose constitutions were seriously weakened by dehydration and the inability to hold down any nourishment. One eighteenth-century voyager catalogued the following ills: "terrible misery, stench, fumes, horror, vomiting, many kinds of sea-sickness, fever, dysentery, headache, heat, constipation, boils, scurvy, cancer, mouth-rot, and the like." In fifteen vessels arriving at Philadelphia in 1738, altogether 1600 passengers had died en route. One vessel in 1752 brought in only nineteen survivors of an original two hundred passengers. Shipwreck, capture by pirates or privateers, and most of all death by disease combined to make the Atlantic crossing the most hazardous undertaking most of the immigrants had yet faced. No wonder that they would long remember the crossing.

The Chesapeake Colonies

In mid-December 1606 three vessels dropped down the Thames with a little over one hundred men on board, bound for America. They sailed under the auspices of the Virginia Company of London, which held an immense grant of land. Once clear of the Channel, Captain Newport took his fleet southwest to the Canaries before crossing the

Atlantic to the West Indies. After lingering for awhile, the fleet headed north and entered Chesapeake Bay in late April 1607. The colonists had been told to find a site on the banks of a river which reached well into the interior. After a little exploration, the leaders chose the James River. Although instructed to settle as far up the river "as a bark of fifty tons will float...the further up the better," as a defense against attack from the sea, the colonists chose a swampy island close to the northern shore of the river only a few miles in from Chesapeake Bay. In the months and years ahead residents of Jamestown would rue the choice of such an unhealthy location.

Troubles descended upon the settlement from the beginning. Within the first year Indian attacks, disease, and famine claimed nearly half the 105 men who had landed. Late in 1608, the adventurer Captain John Smith took over the leadership of the colony and put everyone to work under threat of being turned out into the wilderness; the next winter was not so disastrous. With the arrival of three hundred new settlers in August 1609, however, those who could not stomach Smith's harsh command turned him out. Smith left behind a settlement of almost 500 persons as he sailed for England in October 1609. Once again Indians and famine took a frightful toll. When still more reinforcements arrived the following spring, they found the survivors only sixty men, embarking to return home. In the words of one who lived through it, this had been Jamestown's "starving time."

It should be remembered that Jamestown was a "company town," owned and operated by the Virginia Company. Settlers were employees, and the investors in London expected a handsome profit from their labors. The directors' solution to the problems of the colony was to institute a "get tough" policy toward the workers. Under Governor Sir Thomas Dale in 1610-11, Jamestown virtually came under martial law. Whippings were meted out to those careless enough to lose or break tools; one year in the galleys awaited those who for the third time showed up late for work; and death was the punishment for colonists who persisted in complaining about company policy. Jamestown was turned into a military outpost.

In the next few years, however, three developments presaged a new era for Virginia. In 1612 John Rolfe experimented with the growth and curing of tobacco, and two years later he sent his first marketable crop to England. In a short time tobacco would become the god of the Chesapeake. At the same time Governor Dale granted each settler a small plot of land for his own use, thus introducing private property and putting an end to the threat of starvation. In 1618 the company offered to every person agreeing to settle in Virginia fifty acres for each member of his household including himself. Thus began the "headright" system, by which thousands of colonists came to Virginia and other colonies in the succeeding decades of the seventeenth century.

In 1619 came additional changes. The company called for a legislative assembly in the colony to repeal the laws enforced by Governor Dale and to draw up new statutes founded on English common law. Because settlement had by this time spread out far beyond Jamestown, the eleven communities of the colony each sent two delegates to sit in the newly created House of Burgesses. Through the hot summer of 1619 they labored, in the choir of a Jamestown church, to hammer out a new code of laws. Although only sharing in the government of Virginia, for the company did not relinquish control of the colony for another five years, the House of Burgesses established an important precedent for future legislatures in the New World.

Also in the year 1619 the first blacks arrived, brought by a Dutch man-of-war. For the next several decades, however, only a handful of Africans reached the Chesapeake country, there being but 300 among Virginia's 15,000 whites in 1649. Historians continue to disagree whether these blacks worked as indentured servants, on the same terms as white laborers, or whether they were from the beginning regarded as slaves for life. At any rate, evidence suggests that by mid-century the blacks' status as slaves rapidly gained re-enforcement in the laws of the Chesapeake colonies. The tensions created by the institution would have devastating effect on the lives of both blacks and whites thereafter.

For the next several years Virginia enjoyed a moderate prosperity. By 1622 there were over 1,200 inhabitants, including the women, who had first arrived three years before to provide wives for some of the colonists. Prospects for economic growth appeared good. But then in the spring of 1622 disaster struck when the Indians launched a major attack against the settlements along the James River. By the end of the year over three hundred whites, mostly able-bodied men, had perished and many more had lost their homes and other possessions. In a long war of attrition that continued for several years the whites wreaked revenge by indiscriminately destroying the natives' crops and villages. During this time Virginia slowly recovered.

In London, company officials were hopelessly discouraged. Since 1609 over 4,000 settlers had emigrated to Virginia, and yet by 1624 only 1,100 inhabitants resided in the colony. The company had sunk nearly £200,000 into the enterprise with very little to show investors by way of return. Made a royal colony in 1624, Virginia was thereafter ruled by a governor and council, appointed by and representing the king, and by the House of Burgesses, representing the landholders of the colony. Except for the period of Cromwell's rule in England, it remained a royal colony until the Revolution.

While Virginians made steady progress in their struggle for security and self-sufficiency during the next decades, a different kind of colony took root at the head of Chesapeake Bay. In 1632 Charles I granted a large tract to a loyal Catholic supporter, George Calvert, whose ambition was greater than his modest fortune. The territory extended from the mouth of the Potomac northward to the fortieth parallel and contained over ten million acres. Although George Calvert died before the charter became official, his son Cecilius, who became the second Lord Baltimore, carried out his father's dream of establishing in the new world those landed estates that the family had failed to acquire in the old. The charter granted the "Absolute Lord and Proprietary of Maryland and Avalon, Lord Baron of Baltimore," as he styled himself, complete authority over the province. He owned all the land, received all the income from its rental, and held absolute control of its government. This proprietary colony, as it was called, became the model for similar grants made by future kings to other favorites.

Baltimore was wise enough to realize that he would collect no rents without settlers. As a Catholic, he hoped his province would serve as a haven for his coreligionists seeking refuge from persecution in England. At the same time, however, he recognized the importance of attracting Protestants as well. The first shipload of colonists, who arrived in 1634, therefore included Protestant artisans and laborers along with seventeen Catholic gentlemen and their families and two Jesuit priests. In the instructions issued to his brother Leonard, the deputy governor, Lord Baltimore required that he "be very careful to preserve unity and peace among all the passengers," for Calvert knew that if word of religious dissension reached England, his project was doomed to failure.

In a few years the two groups tended to settle in different parts of the colony, the Catholics around St. Mary's at the mouth of the Potomac, while the Protestants founded Providence, later renamed Annapolis, farther up the bay. An uneasy truce reigned. Meanwhile Lord Baltimore ruled his personal domain from England through instructions to his officials in America. Affecting a regal style from the beginning, he outdid Charles I himself. One result was the establishment of manorial life and customs in Maryland patterned after these fast-dying institutions of seventeenth-century England. All settlers held their land as tenants of the Calverts, though of course major holders simply leased the land yet again to tenants whose rents supported them in the grand style. The whole system depended upon the rapidly expanding market for tobacco, the staple crop raised throughout the Chesapeake. By the mid-seventeenth century, Maryland was well established, but an undercurrent of discontent suggested that the Calverts would not maintain forever their iron-clad grip on the affairs of the colony.

New England

Since the beginning of the seventeenth century, navigators had been probing the coastline north of the Chesapeake in the region Captain John Smith would ultimately name New England. In 1602 Bartholomew Gosnold attempted to establish a settlement on Cuttyhunk Island in Buzzards Bay, while five years later another band under the leadership of George Popham tried to plant a colony at the mouth of the Kennebec River in Maine. Both efforts failed because the men did not have the will to overcome the stark prospects facing them. Even after the publication in 1616 of John Smith's enthusiastic account of his voyage along the New England coast, several years elapsed before the Europeans next attempted to carve out a toehold there.

Even so, the first group to succeed in settling New England landed there quite by accident. In 1620, a group of extreme Puritans, who had fled England for the more tolerant atmosphere of Holland ten years before, accepted terms offered by the Virginia Company to become the nucleus of its latest effort to increase the population of its holdings in the new world. The Pilgrims had their own motives for migration, i.e., primarily escape from the worldly life of Holland and establishment of their own religious community. About thirty-five joined up with some eighty other prospective colonists in Plymouth, England, from whence they set sail in September 1620 on board the *Mayflower*. Making a late autumn landfall at Cape Cod, several hundred miles north of their intended destination, northern "Virginia," Captain Christopher Jones was unable to weather the treacherous shoals south of the cape, and after explorations landed his passengers in a broad bay they named Plymouth.

Because they had settled beyond the territorial limits of Virginia, the band of 102 settlers thought best to "combine ourselves into a civil body politic, for our better ordering and preservation...and frame such just and equal laws,...as shall be thought most meet and convenient for the general good of the colony, unto which we promise all due submission and obedience." Thus the Mayflower Compact assured, in the absence of Company authority, that the most precious possession of Englishmen, a government of laws not of men, would accompany the settlers in their new-found wilderness home. Like Jamestown before them, the Pilgrims suffered through their own "starving time" during the first hard winter, which claimed the lives of half the settlers. At one point only six or seven men were strong enough to feed and nurse the others. Religious faith provided some of the Pilgrims with the will to survive, while all the settlers taxed their physical resources to the outer limits of human endurance. When the *Mayflower* set sail for home in the spring, the crew sailed alone, for none of the survivors had suffered a change of heart. Plymouth colony eked out a modest existence from fishing and its fur trade with the Indians. The colonists bought out the London Company in 1627, managing their own affairs until merger with Massachusetts Bay in 1691. Of modest significance in itself, perhaps, Plymouth Colony has nonetheless deserved its place in American history as a symbol of spiritual strength in the face of adversity.

While the Pilgrims labored to survive against the hostile environment of the New World during the 1620s, their Puritan cousins waged their own struggle in England. The ascension of Charles I in

1625 brought an attack against nonconformists led by Bishop Laud, who seemed to represent everything the Puritans most despised within the established church — authoritarian bishops, elaborate ritual, and other trappings. Unlike the Pilgrims, most other Puritans believed that under guidance from the Scriptures they could improve the Anglican church from within, although their hopes grew dimmer as the authorities steadfastly opposed all "purifying" efforts. At the same time numerous middle-class farmers and artisans, Puritan and otherwise, faced an equally discouraging economic future, as periodic depressions and the continuing process of enclosures seemed to put severe limitations on their opportunity for improvement.

In the years immediately following the successful establishment of the colony at Plymouth, other settlements took root along the New England coast. One of these, little more than a fishing post, struggled along for several years, first at Gloucester, then after 1626 at Salem, north of present-day Boston. Meanwhile, a group of Puritans, mainly from Lincolnshire, East Anglia, and London, had begun to search for a site in the New World where English Puritans might find freedom from the corrupting influence of Anglican bishops. They took over the Salem enterprise, established a new company, and prepared to send out settlers. Because of conflicting claims, however, they sought and obtained, in the name of Massachusetts Bay Company, a charter from the crown in 1629 that granted a swath of territory embracing Boston Bay, from a point three miles north of the Merrimack River to a point three miles south of the Charles. An aggressive group within the company, led by John Winthrop, Thomas Dudley, and Sir Richard Saltonstall, agreed at Cambridge, England, in August 1629, to migrate to Massachusetts Bay, provided they could transfer the charter and seat of government with them.

The reason Winthrop and his supporters made such a requirement lies in their purpose of establishing a different kind of community from the usual company-sponsored fishing and trading post like Jamestown or Plymouth. These men had in mind establishing a religious community based upon the laws of God as found in the Scriptures. Only by taking the company with them could the Puritan settlers guard against the possibility of investors unsympathetic with their goal buying control of the enterprise, for only members resident in America would be able to vote.

In the spring of 1630, the Puritans gathered together a large fleet of vessels, led by Saltonstall's *Arbella*. More than one thousand immigrants made the crossing to Massachusetts Bay before the end of the summer. Rarely had a colony begun with such strength both of purpose and of numbers. With assistance from the settlers formerly at Salem, as well as from Plymouth colony to the southward, the newcomers quickly established their main settlement on a peninsula deep within the protected heart of Boston harbor. There among the three prominences called Tremont, soon renamed for the Lincolnshire town of Boston, the Puritans established what Winthrop called a "city upon a hill."

For ten years immigrants poured into the new colony. When the outbreak of civil war in England ended the Great Migration in 1640, more than twenty thousand immigrants had crossed to the Puritans' New Canaan in the wilderness. Unlike the settlers in Virginia, many of those coming to Massachusetts arrived in groups, several families together or occasionally whole parishes led by their Puritan ministers from the mother country. This high degree of organization gave the immigrants much-needed reinforcement during and after the difficult passage to America. More significantly, it meant that the social and cultural ways of the old country were more likely to survive the transition to the new, and indeed life in Puritan Massachusetts bore a striking resemblance to that of Lincolnshire for years to come.

There were important differences, too. Winthrop and his fellow leaders believed they had covenanted with God to establish a community based on His holy laws, and that He had responded by extending His protection to the undertaking. "When God gives a special commission," said Winthrop, on board the *Arbella* in his sermon *A Model of Christian Charity*, "He looks to have it strictly observed..." If the Puritans failed to uphold their end of the covenant by permitting immorality or materialism to take root, "the Lord would surely break out in wrath against us, be revenged of such a perjured people, and make us know the price of the breach of such a Covenant." Furthermore, Winthrop was conscious that others watched the experiment with interest. Withdrawal of God's protection would bring disgrace not only upon themselves but would "open the mouths of enemies to speak evil of the ways of God and all professors for God's sake...." It was therefore the duty of the entire population to lead righteous lives and to punish sin; to do otherwise was a breach of the Covenant with God. To strengthen themselves in these tasks, they covenanted together into church polities and hired preachers to help them understand their Bible, the source of God's word.

Not all immigrants to the Bay Colony found Puritan rule fully to their liking, nor in truth did Winthrop and his followers extend to all comers the right hand of fellowship. As the flood of immigration continued, others objected to crowded conditions in the settlements around Boston Bay and longed for solitude (and cheaper lands) found in unsettled parts. In 1636 the Reverend Thomas Hooker led a group of restless spirits through the wilderness to the Connecticut River valley, where they founded the towns of Hartford, Windsor, and Wethersfield, and obtained a charter as the colony of Connecticut. Soon after, a band of Puritans arrived from England under the guidance of the Reverend John Davenport and established a settlement at New Haven in 1638, which remained a distinct colony under that name until its merger with the colony of Connecticut in 1662.

These settlements were in most significant ways carbon copies of Massachusetts Bay, but the colony of Rhode Island and Providence Plantations was decidedly different. Founded in 1643 by Roger Williams, Anne Hutchinson, and Samuel Gorton, refugees from intolerance in Massachusetts, Rhode Island firmly established the principle of religious liberty for all inhabitants. Furthermore Williams offered peace and friendship to the Indians at a time when such an overture was regarded by most orthodox Puritans as literally a pact with the devil himself. North of Boston two other clusters of settlements appeared, the proprietary colonies of New Hampshire, founded near the mouth of the Piscataqua along the shores of Great Bay, and Maine, where a few hardy colonies established themselves along the coast as far as the Kennebec River.

By the middle of the seventeenth century, about 23,000 Europeans lived where thirty years before none had dared remain. Perhaps, as John Winthrop and other Puritans devoutly believed, this was indeed a land favored by the protection of God. At any rate their faith gave them the determination to succeed where others had failed.

It is well to remember that Englishmen were not the only

Europeans to establish colonies in America during the seventeenth century. In addition to the Spanish outposts in Florida and Carolina, both the French and the Dutch settled significant parts of the continent, and groups of Finns and Swedes clung to the shores of the Delaware River in the short-lived colony of New Sweden. Scattered throughout all the English colonies by the end of the seventeenth century were enclaves of other nationalities including Scots, Welsh, Irish, and German. And of course by 1700 some twenty thousand Africans swelled the population of the southern colonies. The heterogeneous nature of America was therefore a principle established early in its history.

North of New England lay the vast regions of Canada with the St. Lawrence River its natural gateway. In this valley began New France, with the founding of Quebec in 1608 by the great explorer Seigneur Samuel de Champlain. From this and other outposts established later, the French commanded the inland waterways of the continent, including the Great Lakes, the Ohio Valley, and ultimately the Mississippi Valley as well. A clever Indian policy gradually funneled the fur trade through this water system to Montreal, founded in 1643, and temporarily gave to the French a dominant leadership in one of America's major resources — the beaver pelt. At the same time, from villages along the coasts of Acadia and Nova Scotia, French fishermen worked the Grand Banks offshore for cod and herring. For over a century the presence of France in Canada dangled as a threatening sword over the heads of New Englanders.

The Proprietary Colonies

Equally dangerous to the safety of the English colonies seemed the Dutch possession of the Hudson Valley. Settled in the wake of Henry Hudson's explorations, New Netherland represented a major bid on the part of the Dutch for control of the fur trade. Their outpost at Albany, established in 1624, commanded the interior Mohawk Valley, while the purchase of Manhattan Island two years later gave protection to the great North River, later named the Hudson. During the first half of the seventeenth century, England's greatest rivals for commercial domination of the world were the ubiquitous Dutch, and indeed Amsterdam served as the world's capital market for many decades before the emergence of London. When the Dutch established trading posts in the Connecticut Valley and on the northern shore of Long Island, and later expanded southward to swallow up New Sweden along the Delaware, the threat seemed real enough.

But New Netherland only appeared to be strong. Under the short-sighted policy of the Dutch West India Company, land was distributed to wealthy patrons, who established estates up the Hudson in duplication of Europe's oppressive manorial system. The prospect of a tenant's miserable existence in the New World failed to entice many Dutchmen to emigrate from the old, and consequently the population of New Netherland lagged behind that of its English neighbors. An aggressive Indian policy embroiled the Dutch in disruptive wars, and the high-handed rule of Governor Willem Kiefft and later Peter Stuyvesant alienated many inhabitants from the company. When Charles II gained the throne of England in 1660 one of his first goals was the capture of New Netherland, which Col. Richard Nicolls accomplished four years later with ease. The king thereupon granted to his royal brother, the Duke of York, not only this prize but all the land between the Delaware and Connecticut rivers as well. Thus began the establishment of a series of proprietary colonies granted by Charles II to favorite members of his Restoration Court.

English possession of the Hudson valley brought little change at first, save for such place names as Albany instead of Fort Orange, and New York for the province itself. Dutch landowners kept their estates along the Hudson, they continued to worship in their Reformed church, and the merchants maintained their interests in both fur trade and overseas commerce. The future pre-eminence of New York among the other colonies in fact owed no small debt to the Dutch families who remained after the English take-over. Meanwhile, the Duke of York restored those lands to the east which had been part of Connecticut and granted most of the land south of New York to his two favorites, Sir George Carteret and John, Lord Berkeley.

Named New Jersey in honor of Carteret's protection of the Channel island during the recent civil war, the province received from its proprietors a most generous guarantee of political liberties in the "Concession and Agreements" of 1665, but unfortunately these were modified seven years later. Disputes over land titles nullified much of new colony's attraction, moreover, and the province was wracked with divisive squabbles for years to come. For a time late in the seventeenth century the province was separated into two parts, West Jersey for Berkeley and East Jersey for the Carterets. Quakers soon purchased Berkeley's interest, and it became a haven for members of that oppressed sect. William Penn served as a trustee over much of the territory and through this experience dreamed of still greater plans for his coreligionists in America. Meanwhile, East Jersey was also put up for sale, and Quakers joined with Presbyterians and Catholics to purchase the grant in 1680. Settlers from New England as well as from the old country flocked into both parts of the province, establishing large farms in the interior and the whaling industry along the coast. Though disputes over land titles continued throughout the colonial period, New Jersey's cosmopolitan population achieved material prosperity and religious freedom.

To the south of Virginia, meanwhile, still another group of proprietors struggled to fulfill dreams of profit first aroused when in 1663 Charles II granted them lands bound as ultimately defined by Currituck Sound on the north and a point midway along the coast of Florida on the south. Among the proprietors of what became the Carolinas were Berkeley and Carteret, of New Jersey fame, along with numerous other favorites of the Restoration Court. Several major problems loomed from the beginning. Much of the territory granted by Charles II was claimed by Spain, and from its stronghold at St. Augustine that nation soon challenged the invaders. Secondly, word from various New England voyagers suggested that the country was unhealthy. Finally, the proprietors had their own ineptitude to overcome. Perhaps their most serious error lay in the form of government they proposed. The Fundamental Constitutions of Carolina, drawn up by John Locke, secretary to one of the proprietors, would have established a landed aristocracy the equal of New France or New Netherland and about as unattractive to settlers. Nobles and gentry, with such titles as barons, "casiques," and landgraves, were to sit in an upper house with veto power over legislation enacted by the lower house.

Fortunately for the future of the colony, Locke's scheme was abandoned before much harm was done. As for the ugly rumors concerning the climate, the proprietors turned out a spate of literature attesting to the healthfulness of the region and the fertility of its soil. A few squatters settled along the edge of Albemarle Sound near the Virginia border, and after several false starts a permanent post named for King Charles was founded in 1670 near the mouth of the Ashley and Cooper Rivers. For several years the colony eked out a mean existence, trading a little with the Indians and with inhabitants of the Caribbean islands. Many of the colony's early immigrants came from the overcrowded British West Indies, in fact, principally Barbados. Then came the first big break. French Huguenots, in search of asylum after Louis XIV revoked the Edict of Nantes in 1685, flocked to the new colony. At the same time rice proved to be most suitable to the region's climate. Carolina planters preserved an interest in commerce along with the production of rice, lumber and naval stores. Charleston (originally "Charles Town") became a major entrepôt for these and other products and for the Indian and African slaves so much in demand as plantation labor in Carolina and the West Indies. By the end of the century, the port played a major role in the slave trade, and numerous families began their climb to the top in this business. Because of the almost unbearable heat and humidity of the inland sections many planters spent the summer months in Charleston, where companionship and ocean breezes combined to make life more comfortable. The settlement was also important as the southernmost outpost of British America, as the Spaniards had overrun Port Royal in 1686 and forced its inhabitants to abandon the outpost.

Without question the most significant colonial enterprise undertaken in the latter half of the seventeenth century was the founding of Pennsylvania. Though familiar, the story remains a dramatic account of how intelligent planning, energetic promotion, and benevolent government contributed to the establishment of a successful proprietary colony. William Penn was the irrepressible son of a royalist admiral much in the favor of Charles II and his brother James, Duke of York. Young William became converted to the Quaker faith while still a youth, and despite his family's high station was twice jailed for expressing his views; naturally he felt great compassion for the sufferings of his fellow Friends. The key to Quaker theology lay in the belief that God spoke directly to man and therefore no ministry, much less an episcopate, was necessary to teach or interpret God's word. To Puritans like John Winthrop, and to Anglicans as well, such doctrine was heresy, and Quakers found no rest within the domains of either establishment. Such habits as refusing to doff their caps and make oaths attracted additional scorn. Like others before and since, however, Quakers seemed only to flourish under persecution, and by the last decades of the seventeenth century thousands of Englishmen and Europeans professed the new faith.

After his father's death in 1676 William Penn traded on the Duke of York's friendship with the Admiral, and in 1681, at the age of 38, he received a large portion of the Duke's American holdings along with a royal charter assuring his proprietorship. Within a year Penn published *Some Account of the Province of Pennsylvania*, describing the country as being "600 miles nearer the sun than England" because of its southerly latitude, with plentiful timber, fowl, fish and other game for provision. He opined that the country was "capable of . . . silk, flax, hemp, wine, sider, . . . tobacco, potashes, and iron" among other commodities, and that it already produced hides, tallow, beef, pork, wool, corn, wheat "and also furs, as your peltree, mincks, racoons, martins, and such like." He pointed out that the Delaware River was navigable for vessels of 200 tons for seventy miles, and he described the commerce carried on by inhabitants already settled along the river. Penn pointed out that the charter provided for a legislature chosen by the people and that the rights and freedoms of England would prevail. In addition he guaranteed religious liberty. Finally, to assure himself of good colonists, Penn suggested that "Providence seems to have most fitted for plantations . . . industrious husbandmen . . . laborious handicrafts, especially carpenters, masons, smiths . . . etc . . . ingenious spirits . . . [and] younger brothers of small inheritances." To them all, Penn issued a guide for the journey ahead, complete with a list of what to bring, when to arrive, and how much the passage should cost.

Immigrants rapidly poured into Pennsylvania during the first three years. Penn himself served as governor during this period. The plan of Philadelphia was largely the product of his own orderly mind; it was his fairness in dealing with the Indians that assured Pennsylvania of many peaceful decades; and it was Penn who called the first popular assembly in 1682, which guaranteed the right of religious liberty to all Christian inhabitants. By 1685 Penn could report in *A Further Account of the Province of Pennsylvania* that in addition to some one thousand people already settled along the Delaware, the colony could now boast some seven thousand newcomers. French, Dutch, Germans, Swedes, Danes, Finns, Scotch, and Irish joined the dominant English, for Penn's publications had been translated into several languages and were widely read throughout the continent. Not only did Quakers and other harried sectarians find religious liberty in Pennsylvania, but immigrants of all nationalities discovered that they were under no obligation to forsake their native language, place names, or other familiar customs of the old country. Pennsylvania was indeed one of the world's most cosmopolitan communities.

Philadelphia, the city of brotherly love, reached westward from the banks of the Delaware to the edge of the Schuylkill. Along its streets, some of which Penn named for "the things that grow in the country," stood over 350 houses. Beyond the city ranged rolling farmland, where settlers cultivated the rich soil in holdings averaging around five hundred acres each. Penn reserved for himself a lovely tract overlooking the Delaware about twenty miles north of the city, where he built "Pennsbury," a large residence surrounded by stables, gardens, and orchards. The proprietor could truly state in 1684 that he had achieved a major accomplishment by his colonizing Pennsylvania without recourse to outside credit. Penn's Holy Experiment made a promising beginning, as indeed had all the English colonies in America.

FURTHER READINGS

The most authoritative account of the seventeenth-century English settlement in America remains Charles M. Andrews, *The Colonial Period of American History* (4 vols., New Haven, 1934-38). John E. Pomfret, *Founding the American Colonies, 1583-1660* (New York, 1970) is a valuable new survey with a fine bibliography. Wesley Frank Craven, *The Colonies in Transition, 1660-1713* (New York, 1968) continues the story into the eighteenth century. James M. Smith, ed., *Seventeenth-Century America: Essays in Colonial History* (Chapel Hill, 1959) contains several excellent essays including Mildred Campbell, "Social Origins of Some Early Americans," pp. 63-89. Important essays on individual colonies are found in Charles M. Andrews, *Our Earliest Colonial Settlements* (New York, 1933). More specialized studies of early settlements include Richard L. Morton, *Colonial Virginia* (2 vols., Chapel Hill, 1960); Newton D. Mereness, *Maryland as a Proprietary Province* (New York, 1901); George D. Langdon, Jr., *Pilgrim Colony: A History of New Plymouth: 1620-1691* (New Haven, 1966); Douglas Leach, *The Northern Colonial Frontier, 1607-1763* (New York, 1966); Edmund S. Morgan, *The Puritan Dilemma: The Story of John Winthrop* (Boston, 1958); Darrett B. Rutman, *Winthrop's Boston* (Chapel Hill, 1965); Perry Miller, *Roger Williams: His Contribution to the American Tradition* (Indianapolis, 1953); Albert E. Van Deusen, *Connecticut* (New Haven, 1961); and Isabel M. Calder, *New Haven Colony* (New Haven, 1934). For the proprietary colonies, see Samuel G. Nissenson, *The Patroon's Domain* (New York, 1937); John H. Wuorinin, *The Finns on the Delaware, 1638-1655* (New York, 1938); John E. Pomfret, *The Province of West New Jersey, 1609-1702* (Princeton, 1954) and *The Province of East New Jersey, 1609-1702* (Princeton, 1962); M. Eugene Sirmans, *Colonial South Carolina: A Political History, 1663-1763* (Chapel Hill, 1966); Hugh T. Lefler and Albert R. Newsome, *The History of a Southern State: North Carolina* (Chapel Hill, 1954); and Edwin B. Bronner, *William Penn's "Holy Experiment": The Founding of Pennsylvania, 1681-1701* (New York, 1962).

3

Seventeenth-Century America

Once settled in America, colonists faced the problem of establishing the sound institutions needed to manage these societies so distant from England. Everyone recognized that for mere survival increasing numbers of workers were essential. At the same time, leaders were confronted with the task of governing the ever-changing settlements that resulted from encouraging immigration. Threats from Indians, Canadians, and even the English government at home complicated matters. By 1700, English settlements would spread from their tidewater beachheads well into the interior Piedmont in the southern colonies and far up the river valleys of New York and New England. Population would reach nearly 300,000, of whom about ten percent were blacks. Midst all the turmoil of a changing social structure emerged a degree of stability by the end of the century discernible in various life styles of the colonists themselves. At the beginning of the eighteenth century, colonial America stood prepared for the period of phenomenal growth ahead.

Land and Labor

For most immigrants coming to America in the seventeenth century, the New World meant land. In many parts of England, Ireland,

Scotland, and in most European countries, land was virtually unavailable for those who did not already have any. Yet in that preindustrial age the possession of real property was the principal distinction between the "haves" and the "have-nots." Land not only meant economic security and opportunity but political power as well. No wonder then that the availability of land in America was one of the New World's greatest attractions.

Most immigrants arriving in New England came as members of a group rather than as individuals. Unless there was ample space in an existing community that would welcome them, the leaders applied to the General Court for a grant of land. If the group's members met with approval, which meant they had to be good Puritans, the court awarded a township, usually about six miles square, and contiguous to a settled area for security against the Indians. Further distribution of the land, "ordering the town," it was called, became the responsibility of the leaders.

Two methods were in common use in the seventeenth century, depending upon local practices in the region from which the group had come. Most of the selectmen of early Watertown, Massachusetts, for instance, hailed from East Anglian counties in England, and they naturally adopted for their new town the familiar principle of "enclosed" fields. Each family head received a house lot on the central village green, along with perhaps fifty acres of arable land. He could expect to share in subsequent distributions of town land as well. These holdings he farmed as an individual, although there was also some common use of undivided pasturage. In contrast, the founders of Sudbury, preferred the "open-field" system of their native Hampshire, Wiltshire, and Dorset. Under this system, each householder received strips in the several common fields cultivated in cooperation with all the settlers. In addition to his house lot, he was also granted other pieces scattered all over the divided part of the town, usually in five- to ten-acre lots, some meadow, some upland, much of it heavily wooded. Finally, he had the right to graze his livestock on the town common.

The open-field system of course required close cooperation among the settlers. In medieval England, generations of inhabitants had long since achieved sufficient stability to make the system work well. But the passage to the New World, the jumbling together of people from different villages, and the constant flow of fresh arrivals tended to break down group cohesiveness. Within twenty years of the founding of Sudbury, for instance, a major dispute arose among the townspeople over land policy. The dissident minority broke off, applied to the General Court for its own grant, and established the town of Marlborough northwest of the mother settlement. When they distributed the land, they abandoned the open-field system of Sudbury for the individualistic closed policy of Watertown and other communities, a system more suited to the growing independence of the new town's settlers. Before the end of the seventeenth century, most New England settlements had adopted the enclosed method of land tenure, and the independent family farm became the cornerstone of New England society. Uneven terrain, hostile Indians, and the scarcity of labor limited the size of most holdings commonly to two or three hundred acres, as much as most men could use in the subsistence economy prevalent at the time.

In Virginia, several different methods of land distribution operated during the course of the seventeenth century. In the earliest years, the Company made small grants to its Jamestown settlers and as stock dividends to shareholders in England. Some stockholders pooled their shares and established "particular plantations," sending out workers but rarely taking up occupancy themselves. Most of these operations suffered from absentee ownership and were split up and sold to individual purchasers.

By far the most common way in which land was distributed in Virginia, and later in Maryland as well, was by the "headright" system. Under this plan, each arriving colonist received rights to a fifty-acre plot for himself and for every other person he brought over at his own expense. Paying for the passage of subsequent settlers entitled him to additional fifty-acre plots. After choosing a suitable place for his plantation (from among lands not previously granted), he had his claim surveyed and recorded, but not until he had actually "seated his property" — begun to farm it — could his deed be validated. An annual quitrent of two shillings per 100 acres was due the crown, but faulty means of collection made evasion easy. Headrights were in fact negotiable, and shipmasters among others who underwrote the passage of immigrants to the Chesapeake colony could accumulate rights to thousands of acres if they wished. Once surveyed and recorded, however, the lands had to be occupied, although sometimes "seating" was only perfunctory in practice.

Despite efforts to curb it, land speculation became a serious abuse and contributed to the virtual abandonment of the headright system by the end of the seventeenth century.

In addition to settlers brought over by planters, thousands of other immigrants made the crossing at the expense of someone else. In fact during the course of the seventeenth century one of the most important cargoes in trans-Atlantic commerce was people. Unable to pay for their passage, "colonists in bondage" signed an indenture, a legal contract binding them to servitude for a term of about five years on the average. The shipper then sold this document for 15 to 20 pounds to a planter in need of labor for his tobacco plantation. In purchasing the agreement, the planter undertook to house, clothe, and feed the worker during his service, and in both Maryland and Virginia laws protected both parties against serious breaches of contract. Upon expiration of his term, the servant received his "freedom dues," occasionally a grant of land but more often a sum of money or tools and clothing, according to the "custom of the country."

Altogether at least half of the immigrants arriving to the colonies south of New York in the colonial period came as indentured servants. In addition to those coming voluntarily, many others were transported as the result of court sentences, as prisoners of war, or because they were paupers without employment. Those who survived the passage to America faced a strange climate, harsh working conditions, and in many cases, premature death. Those who could not wait for freedom ran away, and because the wilderness was not far, most of them were never apprehended. As cruel as the system of indentured servitude was, it nevertheless fulfilled its primary purpose of providing cheap labor for the plantation colonies. The steady arrival of nearly two thousand new immigrants as indentured servants each year led to rapid expansion throughout the Chesapeake region, as tobacco planters occupied new lands and hired additional servants.

So great was the demand for labor in the southern colonies that planters welcomed new workers from whatever source. And one of these sources was Africa. Captured by coastal tribes and sold to Dutch and English traders, blacks had for many years been marketed throughout the West Indies and the Spanish Main. The first blacks in the English colonies came via a Dutch warship to

Jamestown in 1619. For the next several decades small numbers of Africans continued to arrive. The status of these first blacks has been the subject of considerable debate among historians. Some maintain that they held the position of indentured servants. Only when white servants won exclusive new rights and protection under the law, the argument goes, did the status of the black begin to deteriorate by comparison. The first statutes defining blacks as slaves appeared in the 1660s. Other authorities, however, point out numerous instances as early as the 1640s of Africans serving for life. They suggest that whatever the statutes said (or did not say) about blacks, in practice slavery was established before the middle of the seventeenth century. By 1680 some 6,000 Africans were bound to perpetual servitude with no hope of freedom for themselves or their progeny. And slavery would become the basis of the southern labor system for the next two centuries.

A number of factors combined to fasten the institution of slavery upon the English colonies. Central of course was the continuing shortage of labor, particularly in the southern colonies. But the colonists relied on numerous peoples as workers, English, Scots, Irish, Germans, as well as Indians and blacks, yet only the latter two groups were enslaved. It is not simply because these two peoples were different that they were singled out for special abuse, it was the nature and extent of their difference. For one thing, they were heathens, considered uncivilized savages, without the claim for freedom that their Christianity gave other servants. Still more important, they were not white. The African's color, his language, his manners and customs combined to emphasize how different he was from Europeans. By comparison the black was judged the white man's inferior. African servants became slaves less as the result of a positive act than by the withholding of freedom ordinarily accorded white servants after a term of years. Once perpetual servitude became legally possible, economics and racism condemned the black to slavery, "proving" his alleged inferiority to still more whites.

In the proprietary colonies, prospective landowners acquired their estates from the proprietary family or group. Land was often granted free of charge in exchange for annual quitrents vigorously collected. In Pennsylvania, land was available in 500-acre pieces, including a house site in the town center, for a modest quitrent. In New York, most of the Dutch patroons remained on their Hudson estates after the English took over the colony, and in fact a pattern of large landholding continued throughout the seventeenth century. In Carolina, as in the other proprietary colonies, the headright system attracted numerous settlers and distributed the land in pieces that ranged up to 1,000 acres or more. In short, the leaders of every colony, whether charter, proprietary, or royal, recognized the need for settlers and geared their system of distributing the land in ways that would encourage immigrants to settle there. By the end of the seventeenth century, well over 200,000 colonists lived in the continental colonies of America.

Colonial Government

It is a commonplace to note that because of the distance separating the English settlements in America from the mother country, self-government developed early and with little interference from London. Not until the Restoration in 1660 did the English government take much interest in American political affairs, and in fact with the exception of the five-year period 1685-90, the colonies continued to enjoy almost complete freedom from interfering English officialdom. Left to themselves, the settlers in most colonies established practical forms of local and provincial government that gave property holders representation in public affairs and guaranteed the basic rights of citizenship that they had come to expect as Englishmen.

The road to representative government had modest beginnings in most of the colonies. We have already seen that Jamestown started as a fortified outpost under the arbitrary rule of the Virginia Company, and that its first legislative assembly did not meet until 1619, twelve years after settlement. In 1624, Virginia became a royal colony with governor and council appointed by the crown. The royal governor held considerable power. He was commander in chief of the militia; with the consent of his council, he appointed sheriffs and justices of the peace on the county level; and he could veto acts of the assembly. The council served both as an upper branch of the legislature and as a superior court of appeals as well. Councilors were prominent men in their home counties, and since they held virtually life appointments, they wielded considerable political power throughout the colony. But the House of Burgesses, meeting annually after 1628, maintained the principle of self-government by its power of enacting legislation. Its representative nature was confirmed in 1661 by the provision that each county was entitled to send two representatives, elected by the freemen, although in the period from 1670 to 1675 the franchise was restricted to property owners. The towns of Jamestown, Williamsburg, and Norfolk, along with the College of William and Mary, sent one burgess each.

Local government in Virginia was focused in the county. Here the justices of the peace met in monthly courts to hear minor legal cases brought before them and to make decisions in such civic affairs as the maintenance of highways, the regulation of public houses, and the apportionment of taxes. County sheriffs, assisted by constables in each precinct, carried out court orders, collected taxes, and maintained public order. The lowest level of government in Virginia was the parish, generally a subdivision of the county. Vestrymen, elected by the property holders, administered such local activities as poor relief and looked after the religious health of the parish. Settlements in seventeenth-century Virginia were scattered over wide areas, and it is uncertain how directly any of these levels of government bore upon the people as a whole.

A fall in the price of tobacco after 1660 and the threat of Indian warfare on the frontier in 1675, as well as grievances against the royal government of Virginia, were responsible for bringing a rebellion and reform. Governor Berkeley had steadily concentrated political authority into his own hands by appointing friendly members of the House of Burgesses to remunerative offices and by refusing to authorize the election of a new House for fourteen years. His political influence reached down to the local level by the favors he extended to county officers and judges. Meanwhile, the burden of taxation fell more heavily than ever on the small landowner, since many of the colony's wealthiest inhabitants enjoyed tax exemption through their status as councilors.

Matters might have gone on in this fashion for many more years had not an Indian war broken out in 1675. Berkeley's defensive policy was too conservative for backwoods Virginians, who soon rallied around a tempestuous young patrician, Nathaniel Bacon, lately arrived from London. What had begun as a war between English settlers and Indians quickly became a rebellion against the royal government. Bacon marched the militiamen who had rallied around him against Jamestown and forced Governor Berkeley to flee. But as the governor retained support of the eastern shore, he counterattacked and defeated Bacon's forces in several skirmishes. In control once more, Berkeley hanged twenty-three of the rebels just before word of royal pardons reached the colonies. Bacon himself had died of dysentery on the eve of the final battle, thus escaping the gallows. He and his fallen supporters had not died in vain, however, for even before their march on Jamestown, Berkeley had called for a new assembly, which met and redressed many of the former abuses. Never again would a royal governor succeed in dominating the affairs of Virginia quite as Berkeley had done.

Government in Massachusetts Bay also rose from the foundations of a company charter. When the Puritan migrants brought with them in 1630 not only the charter itself but company headquarters as well, the way was opened for several changes. The charter provided that the "freemen," or shareholders, of the company should meet in a Great and General Court four times a year to enact laws for the company and once a year to elect the governor, deputy, and assistants. Perhaps as few as a dozen stockholders had in fact immigrated to Massachusetts, however, and all but one of them currently served the company in some official capacity. To this small group, therefore, fell complete authority for governing a settlement of some two thousand inhabitants.

In the fall of 1630, a petition from more than one hundred colonists requested that they also be admitted to the rights of freemen even though they held no company stock. Realizing the necessity of responding to their demands lest the malcontents move elsewhere, John Winthrop and the other officers worked out a compromise. Adult males who were church members were thereafter to be recognized as freemen but with power only to choose the assistants, who in turn would elect the governor and deputy. The assistants also assumed exclusive authority to enact legislation. Under this arrangement, 116 new freemen gained recognition in the spring of 1631. The compromise worked for a short time only, and in 1632 the freemen were granted the power to elect the governor and deputy directly by attending the election meeting of the General Court. At the same time the court headed off another dispute by authorizing each town to choose two men to consult with the governor and assistants concerning matters of taxation.

Dissatisfaction broke out again in 1634, however, when this elected group discovered that the charter gave the freemen power to enact laws, a function the assistants, sitting as the General Court, had reserved for themselves. When Governor Winthrop replied that the freemen were too numerous a body to fulfill such a function, he merely invited the obvious proposal that the freemen from each town choose representatives to sit with the assistants at legislative sessions of the General Court. Reluctantly Winthrop acceded to this next step toward popular government. The assistants, however, claimed a veto power over the decisions of the deputies even though they sat together in one body. Several years of bickering culminated in 1644 in a famous lawsuit involving a wandering sow. Thereafter the General Court divided into a bicameral legislature, the assistants sitting separately as an upper house, with the assent of each house being necessary for the enactment of laws.

The adoption of *The Body of Liberties* in 1644 guaranteed citizens basic rights such as freedom of speech and assembly and protection against self-incrimination, excessive bail, or double jeopardy. Still more rights were assured with publication of *Laws and Liberties* in 1648. By mid-century, Massachusetts Bay had become a government of laws rather than of men. Its inhabitants, along with those in the other New England colonies, where similar developments had taken place, enjoyed a greater degree of self-government than settlers elsewhere in America.

For most inhabitants of the New England colonies, local town government played a far more direct role in their lives than did the provincial authorities. The town meeting, the powers of which derived from the General Court, elected a myriad of local officials each year — from selectmen, who administered the town's affairs on a day-to-day basis to overseers of the poor, measurers of wood, and fence-viewers, whose titles explained their duties. Although the requirements for participation varied from time to time, town meeting was generally restricted to property owners after the first heads of households had completed the important task of distributing the land. With only a thin line drawn between the church and state, early town meetings also called ministers, settled terms of their compensation, and eased them out when found unsatisfactory. The town was also the electoral district for representatives to General Court, inhabitants qualified to vote sending two deputies each year, sometimes with implicit instructions concerning issues pending before the legislature.

Generally speaking, popular government developed at different rates in the various proprietary colonies. In Maryland, for instance, the Calverts were required by the charter to consult with the freemen concerning legislation. Though retaining the power of appointing the governor and council, Lord Baltimore did call for an elected House of Burgesses, which formed with the council a bicameral assembly. But the burgesses could not initiate legislation; they could only give or withhold assent to laws proposed by the governor. In New York the proprietor ruled through his appointed governor without benefit of an assembly at all until 1683, but the delegates who met then had little effect, and truly representative government did not come to New York until the turn of the century. In both North and South Carolina the proprietors appointed governors and members of the councils, with the freeholders electing representatives to a lower house (called in South Carolina, the House of Commons). But, as in Maryland, the proprietors claimed the sole right to initiate legislation and did not surrender to the demands of the lower houses until 1693.

Under his royal charter William Penn was empowered to legislate for his colony as well as to appoint a governor and all other officials. As in other proprietary colonies, his laws required the approval of the freemen. The Second Frame of Government, adopted in 1683, provided for an assembly of representatives from each of the six counties, elected by all taxpayers, as the term *freemen* was defined. Freemen also chose the members of the council. The governor was somewhat weaker in Pennsylvania than in other proprietary colonies, and in fact the executive branch was occasionally administered by the whole council. If the power to initiate legislation is important, self-government came slowly to the proprietary colonies.

Threats from Within and Without

Seventeenth-century America did not develop in a sort of New World cocoon sealing off the tidewater settlements from outside interference. On the contrary, challenges to the growth and expansion of the English colonies came from the French, the Spaniards and Dutch (as we have seen), the Indians, and from the home government itself. Nor did these threats end (except from the Dutch) with 1700; they continued to be major sources of difficulty throughout the eighteenth century as well. War was a fact of life to American colonists, but English settlers were not well prepared to wage military campaigns, for very few of them had had any experience in the art of war.

That the early settlements survived at all in the face of Indian hostility resulted in part from a series of epidemics that had reduced the number of natives in the early seventeenth century and also from the fact that the tribes were unable to form permanent alliances among themselves. The first colonists generally strove to establish friendly relations with the natives. But in Jamestown a fierce Indian attack in 1622 wiped out nearly a third of the settlers. Warfare continued intermittently until 1644, when the natives struck once again, this time killing nearly five hundred whites. Thereafter, the tidewater settlements were safe, although on the Piedmont and mountain valley frontiers trouble broke out on several more occasions, most notably in 1675, with the Indian scuffle that contributed to the explosion of Bacon's Rebellion.

For the first few years, the settlements in New England also enjoyed peaceful relations with the neighboring Indians, partly because a devastating smallpox plague had reduced the native population in 1617, and rendered them less of a threat than they might have been. The attitude of the typical Puritan toward the Indian was hardly conducive to peace, however. Many New Englanders believed the natives to be agents of Satan. John Eliot and Roger Williams, on the other hand, took a genuine interest in the natives by defending their rights and establishing peaceful communities among them. But more than one such reservation was put to the suspicious white man's torch.

Peace did not last long in New England. The first serious outbreak came in 1637, when the Pequots, a tribe that had recently moved into the area from the Hudson Valley, launched an attack on the newly established settlements along the Connecticut River. The whites struck back and slaughtered over five hundred men, women, and children huddled in the Pequot encampment. As one Puritan minister summed up the massacre: "On this day we have sent six hundred heathen souls to hell." Partly because of the victory, an uneasy peace settled over the steadily advancing frontiers of New England for almost forty years. Another factor was the establishment in 1643 of the New England Confederation uniting the colonies of Massachusetts Bay, Plymouth, Connecticut, and New Haven, a defensive league against French and Dutch aggression as well as that of the Indians. By 1675, however, the natives had suffered through a generation of grievances. For years the New Englanders had ignored Indian land claims, and the white man's widening influence through trade led to a gradual breakdown of tribal ways of life. Powerful Iroquois to the west made withdrawal from New England impossible, and therefore several tribes united under "King Philip," the leader of the Wampanoags, in a "now or never" campaign against the English.

During the summer and autumn of 1675, village after village went up in flames — Providence, Groton, Andover, and Springfield among them. Wholesale evacuation of exposed communities was the only recourse in some areas; in others the settlers holed up in garrison houses watching the attackers destroy their homes and crops. Barbarism broke out on both sides. The Indians scalped and tortured their victims, while the English slaughtered the inhabitants of native villages en masse, including 300 neutral Narragansett women and children. In the spring of 1676, the tide turned in favor of the colonists. With the death of Philip, the fighting petered out except along the coast of Maine, where the Abnakis continued to struggle for two more years.

No other Indian war matched this one for death and devastation. Over 1,000 whites (one in every fifty men, women, and children) were killed outright, while countless others died of starvation and disease. Not for nearly forty more years would the New England frontier advance beyond the prewar line of settlement. For the Indians, the outcome was disastrous. The few survivors took to the wilderness in disorder; captives were executed or sold into slavery in the West Indies. Peaceful Indians came under more suspicion than ever. The degradation of the native, begun earlier in the century, continued apace after Philip's last stand.

Only in Pennsylvania did the settlers make more than a cursory effort to establish peaceful relationships with the Indians. There William Penn and his followers posted a better than average record for living up to the terms of treaties and land purchases. But even the Quakers were not above taking advantage of the natives. Perhaps the most famous case was that of the "walking Treaty," in which the whites had purchased a piece of land "as far as a man could go in a day and a half." By hiring three runners and clearing a trail Thomas Penn managed to acquire a half million acres of prime hunting and planting fields. Despite such treatment, Pennsylvania Indians remained at peace until well into the eighteenth century, when tough Scots-Irish formed the spearhead of the advancing frontier.

One of the great failures of the seventeenth-century settlers was their unwillingness to work out a just policy toward the Indians. The only consistent policy was the progressive acquisition of the native's lands, by purchase or subterfuge if possible, by force if necessary. Consigning the Indians to an inferior status because they were heathens and savages, the Puritans, the Anglicans, and later the Scots-Irish showed little interest in an accommodation with the native. For his part, the Indian showed almost no capacity to deal with the newcomer in other than violent terms. The result was over two centuries of interracial warfare leading to the virtual genocide of the native Indians.

North of New England, the French went quietly about the business of expanding their fur trade from Quebec and Montreal, but the population of the province grew very slowly, and by 1672 it had reached only about 7,500. Its narrow society was dominated by seigneurs along the St. Lawrence and by Jesuit priests. With the arrival in 1672 of Louis de Buade, Count Frontenac, as governor of Quebec, the fortunes of New France took a new turn. French influence reached far into the interior, with the explorations of René Robert Cavelier, Siéur de la Salle, who successively led expeditions to Green Bay on Lake Michigan, along the Illinois River, and finally in 1682 down the Mississippi to the Gulf of Mexico.

As the power of French Canada expanded, so too did the pressure it put upon the English settlements to the south. Furthermore, England and Louis XIV were maneuvering for a showdown in Europe. In 1689, along with their allies the Abnakis, the French began a series of raids against villages in Maine and New Hampshire. Thus began what the Americans called King William's War. New Englanders countered in the spring of 1690 with a successful attack led by Sir William Phips on Port Royal, the French outpost on Acadia, now Nova Scotia. A more ambitious assault against Quebec late in the autumn was beaten off by Louis de Buade, Count Frontenac. The Abnakis thereupon counterattacked along the frontier once more, sacking Haverhill, Wells, and York, and the French recaptured Port Royal. Throughout the decade the raids continued, the New Englanders just barely holding their own without aid from the mother country. Not until 1699 did hostilities peter out. No one in New England doubted that the peace that followed would have a short life.

As if these external threats from the French and Indians were not enough, New England suffered through the sordid witchcraft hysteria during the 1690s as well. A mania, begun in 1692 by a bevy of young Salem girls looking for excitement, ended in the hanging of nineteen citizens and the pressing to death of yet another victim. By the end of the seventeenth century most people did not really believe in witches, but on the other hand not many were sure enough of themselves to step in and stop the nonsense. Those who did intervene during the height of the hysteria were themselves accused of being witches. The only certain means of escaping execution was then to implicate others by false accusations. Those who refused to do so died a martyr's death. Not until so prominent a figure as Increase Mather pulled himself together and denounced the proceedings did the mania come to an end.

Relations with England

During the course of the Puritan Revolution, the mother country had lost what little touch it had had with the American colonies. With the Restoration of Charles II in 1660, however, the King and his Parliament turned their attention to problems of the empire. The most significant development came in the regulation of imperial commerce formulated in a series of Acts of Trade and Navigation. By the end of the century, this mercantile system created a closed empire.

The first principle restricted commerce between the colonies and the mother country to vessels built and manned in England or America. One result was a boom in colonial shipbuilding, for

American vessels were noted for their low-cost construction if not always for their durability. The second principle required colonists to export certain produce only to the mother country or to other English colonies. Among these so-called enumerated commodities were tobacco, sugar, cotton and, later, masts and naval stores. Other goods like fish, rum, and most lumber products could go anywhere. Americans were also required to import whatever foreign produce they needed through England, except for wine, salt, and fruit from the Mediterranean and the Atlantic islands, and molasses, rum, and sugar from the West Indies. Even when other statutes later organized customs commissioners and set up vice-admiralty courts in America, enforcement was a continuing problem, for the colonists, like their English cousins, were inveterate smugglers, given the opportunity.

It was in fact a dispute between England and Massachusetts Bay over the assignment of Edward Randolph to Boston in 1676 as customs collector that led to a major crisis. The General Court denied that acts of Parliament had any force in America, on the grounds that the colonists were not represented in that body. When the New Englanders persisted in their opposition, authorities in London dissolved the charter of Massachusetts Bay and made it a royal colony in 1684.

In the year following, the Duke of York became James II. To tighten his grip on the refractory colonies of New England, and also to provide more effective defense against the French and Indians, James II established a new government under which he eventually brought all the colonies from Massachusetts Bay to New Jersey, including his own proprietary colony of New York. In 1686 Sir Edmund Andros became the governor of the new reorganized territories and he ruled with the assistance of a royal council but without the representative assemblies. Not only were the cherished institutions of self-government thrown aside, but to make matters worse to the Puritans, Andros and his cohorts were Anglicans. Under his government Puritan leaders were certain they detected an upsurge of public immorality.

Boston remained in turmoil through the winter of 1688-89 as rumors circulated that James II would soon be overthrown by William of Orange. Irrational fears that somehow New England would come under Catholic control heightened the tension. A strange combination of events led to an outbreak of violence and the capture of Governor Andros and his supporters in mid-April 1689. Although not yet sure that William had actually succeeded to the throne in England, Puritan leaders proclaimed the overthrow of Andros' government and announced an interim regime directed by a Council of Safety and an assembly of representatives. Stability was difficult to achieve because of the Abnakis' attacks along the northern frontier and the necessity of high taxation. In England, affairs remained in flux for two years before authorities could turn to the problem of the colonies. Then in 1691, by a new charter Massachusetts Bay became a royal colony, with the governor appointed by the king but with the guarantee of a representative legislature and elected council. Massachusetts had at least partially regained its cherished self-government.

The establishment of the Dominion of New England made still more remote the possibility of self-government in New York. Wealthy landholders and ambitious merchants supported Andros, but opposition to their high-handed rule made the colony ripe for rebellion. News of Andros' overthrow in Boston set off a spontaneous uprising against Lieutenant Governor Francis Nicholson. A provisional government was established under a group of colonial militia captains, one of whom, Jacob Leisler, was appointed commander in chief by a representative Council of Safety. But Leisler himself soon turned to arbitrary rule and met with violent opposition from Nicholson's supporters, particularly around Albany and other interior towns. An unsuccessful invasion of Canada further weakened his position. With the arrival early in 1691 of the advance forces belonging to Henry Sloughter, the new governor appointed by King William, Leisler made the mistake of ordering the fort at the Battery to open fire on the royal troops. After a brief struggle, Leisler gave in, and two days later was arrested on charges of treason. The old aristocratic supporters of Andros and Nicholson quickly rallied around Sloughter's banner and demanded full punishment for Leisler. His conviction and barbaric execution plunged the colony into bitter factionalism that lasted for a generation.

The revolution of 1688 set off rumblings in other colonies too, particularly Maryland, where a Protestant Association seized control of the proprietary government and declared its loyalty to William and Mary. One result was that Lord Baltimore was deprived of his charter, and Maryland became a royal colony. The Calvert family remained the largest landholder in the province and ultimately regained its proprietorship when a subsequent heir became a Protestant. In Maryland, as in New York and Massachusetts, the cause of representative government was ultimately advanced by the Revolutionary Settlement.

Life Styles

Until the end of the seventeenth century, the settled areas of the Chesapeake colonies stopped at the fall line, the boundary between tidewater and the Piedmont. Tobacco plantations lined the banks of the major rivers that reached into the interior for one hundred miles or more. English and Scots merchant vessels called at the wharf of each plantation in the early autumn to pick up the hard-packed hogsheads and to leave off goods ordered by the planter and brought out from London. Major seaports had no place in such an economy. Only by access to tidewater could the planter hope to get his product to market at a reasonable cost. The planter also needed land, plenty of it, for tobacco exhausted the soil at an appalling rate. Because of these requirements, plantations could not be very close together.

By 1660, so much tobacco was being cultivated that when the Restoration Parliament re-enacted the Navigation Acts limiting the market to England, tobacco fell to a half cent a pound and less. One lesson learned by increasing numbers of planters was the need for diversifying crops, and as the eighteenth century neared, landholders began turning to wheat as one marketable alternative. Others moved west toward the Piedmont for fresh soil. The Chesapeake world nonetheless remained dominated by the tidewater tobacco planter throughout the seventeenth century, and it was his life style that set the pattern others strove to emulate.

One could hardly do better than to follow in the footsteps of William Fitzhugh, a young Englishman from a substantial Bedfordshire background, who immigrated to Virginia around 1670. By purchase and an advantageous marriage he acquired extensive holdings on the Northern Neck, between the Rappahannock and Potomac rivers. By 1686 he possessed a thousand-acre tract on the Potomac, two-thirds of which was wooded, the rest cleared for cultivation. A thirteen-room residence dominated the plantation, furnished and hung after the style of English country homes. Among the outbuildings stood a stable, a barn, a henhouse, and a dairy, while an orchard, kitchen garden, and a pasture for the livestock were near at hand. Twenty-nine black slaves and a half-dozen indentured servants provided the labor force necessary to produce an annual crop of about 60,000 pounds of tobacco, worth about £300 at market. Fitzhugh also owned several parcels upriver totaling nearly 25,000 acres more.

From London, he ordered draperies, leaded windows, and furniture for his house, and fashionable clothing for his family. As did others of his class, Fitzhugh purchased as much silver as he could for an investment as well as for use while entertaining friends. He maintained a good wine cellar, imported cheeses, sugar, and spices for his table, and bought numerous books ranging from legal volumes to the classics. He was able to entertain overnight a company of twenty, providing in addition to good wine, "three fiddlers, a jester, a tight-rope dancer, [and] an acrobat. . . ." Before his death at the age of 50 in 1700 (he had written of "declining age" thirteen years before), Fitzhugh had been a planter, a lawyer, a land speculator, a justice of the peace, a militia officer, and a member of the House of Burgesses.

Down the ladder of wealth and position from Fitzhugh and his fellow "aristocrats" stood the yeoman farmers, the indentured servants, and the blacks. Generally the yeoman held lands in the interior regions between the rivers, cut off from a direct access to tidewater. Smaller holdings and higher production costs per hogshead curtailed his margin of profit, but by frugal living and hard work many a yeoman acquired extensive holdings, along with the servants and slaves needed to operate a large plantation. Still, a wharf of his own saved transportation costs, and the rising yeoman purchased tidewater property when possible.

Life for the indentured servant had only a glimmer of promise at the end of a four- to seven-year term of labor. During that period the quality of his life was at the mercy of his master, within the broad range of protective legislation. Typically, the indentured servant worked in the fields for twelve hours each day, breaking new land (the hardest job), or planting, hoeing, and harvesting tobacco, depending on the season. Those with skills learned in the old world often worked their trades as blacksmiths, millers, or coopers. The planter provided food, shelter, and clothing, and the servant's freedom dues according to the "custom of the country," land, cash, or perhaps only clothing and tools necessary to give the new freeman a start in life. When conditions became too unbearable, the servant simply fled. Virginia was so large and its population so mobile that white runaways rarely suffered recapture. For the black slaves, still relatively few in number, such escape was far more difficult, because they served for life, as did their progeny. The owner's investment in the slave was far larger than that in the indentured servant. His native language and customs made it difficult for him to make his way in freedom and, wherever he went, his black skin called attention to his probable status as a runaway.

In New England the role of religion and the pattern of settlement combined to shape an entirely different life style for seventeenth-century Yankees. A sense of community pervaded most of the earlier settlements, encouraged by the belief that as Puritans they had been sent by God on "an errand into the wilderness." In town meetings, as well as through the congregational form of their church, New Englanders strove together to govern their community according to the laws of God. Sin, like Indians, was regarded as a common enemy, and everyone had to pitch in to fight the insidious influence of the Devil. One image often used was that of the soldier. "In the spiritual warfare in which every Christian is engaged," warned one New England pastor, "everyone must be continually on the watch and keep on him the livery of a Christian soldier." Puritans recognized that temptation to do wrong was a part of human nature. Instead of hopelessly struggling to prohibit the source of temptation (such as alcohol, for instance), they tried to limit its abuse. Not surprisingly, they did not always succeed.

For most New Englanders, home was the family farm. In towns originally laid out as open-field, the dwellings tended to remain around a central green. But by the mid-seventeenth century many of these towns changed the basis of land tenure to the closed method, and families built homes on their principal holding often at some distance from the village, as was the pattern in some closed towns from the beginning. A farmer might own perhaps 200 acres altogether; those holding more were considered wealthy.

But few men could cultivate more than a small fraction of this land. Not only was the process of clearing arable land difficult and time-consuming, but there was also the problem of planting, hoeing, and harvesting. Furthermore, the family farmer, at least in the seventeenth century, had no reason to raise more crops than met his own needs. Since most other inhabitants were also farmers, the market for surplus produce was limited. Indian corn, and to a lesser extent wheat, barley, and oats, were the staple crops of most farms, along with the inevitable kitchen garden, which provided potatoes, turnips, peas, and other vegetables. Cattle grazed on open pasture land, and survived on salt or upland hay during the winter. Pigs rooted about the woods, feeding on acorns and ground plants throughout the summer and on fodder in wintertime. An apple orchard, a hen house, and a wood lot provided other produce necessary to make the family farm a nearly self-sufficient operation.

The New England farmer could not entirely support himself without the help of others. The blacksmith, the miller, and the local storekeeper provided services that the average family farmer could not fulfill himself. The storekeeper in turn depended on the merchant for much of his stock, since items like crockery, ironware, tools, sugar, and cloth goods came from overseas. And when, toward the end of the seventeenth century, New Englanders began producing some commodities in surplus such as pork and beef, onions, and peas, the farmers looked to the storekeeper as an outlet, often exchanging his produce for the manufactured goods needed by his farm and family.

Even before 1700 the seaport merchant became a fixture on the New England scene. Samuel Sewall of Boston carried on an extensive trade, shipping tar, fish, pork, and lumber to the West Indies in exchange for molasses and sugar. From England came cargoes of silks, lead, and iron, cotton and wool, spades and shovels, nails, shot, and frying pans. Sewall ordered stone, timber, and lead for his own house under construction in Boston. Also for his own use were orders for pewter and brass pieces, silver tableware, and large quantities of fancy silks and damasks to be made into clothing for the family. The New England merchants were still but a small group at the end of the seventeenth century, but they had already laid the foundations for commercial expansion in the decades to come. After 1700 the seaport became a community in New England, the inhabitants of which led a style of life markedly different from their country cousins.

By the end of the seventeenth century the middle colonies had become "middle" in more than the geographical sense. The farms were smaller than those of the Chesapeake region but larger than a typical New England farm. With help from indentured servants, Pennsylvania farmers had already begun marketing surplus grain crops, although not on so large a scale as Virginia's tobacco exports. Mercantile activities centered in New York and Philadelphia, although neither port could yet match Boston. In their general style of living, inhabitants of the middle colonies were more southern, but in the eighteenth century they would emerge with a style of their own.

FURTHER READINGS

In addition to the volumes cited at the end of Chapter 2 are numerous other works concerning seventeenth-century America. The following are extremely useful: Sumner C. Powell, *Puritan Village: The Formation of a New England Town* [Sudbury, Mass.] (Middletown, 1963); Kenneth A. Lockridge, *A New England Town The First Hundred Years: Dedham, Massachusetts, 1636-1736* (New York, 1970); Philip J. Greven, *Four Generations: Population, Land, and Family in Colonial Andover, Massachusetts* (Ithaca, 1970); and John Demos, *A Little Commonwealth: Family Life in Plymouth Colony* (New York, 1970). Abbot E. Smith, *Colonists in Bondage: White Servitude and Convict Labor in America, 1607-1776* (Chapel Hill, 1947) is an excellent study. Winthrop Jordan, *White Over Black: American Attitudes Toward the Negro, 1550-1812* (Chapel Hill, 1968) discusses the establishment of slavery in America as well as later developments. For Bacon's Rebellion, see Wilcomb E. Washburn, *The Governor and the Rebel: The Story of Bacon's Rebellion and Its Leader* (Chapel Hill, 1957). Michael Kammen, *Deputyes and Libertyes: The Origins of Representative Government in America* (New York, 1969) is an excellent analysis. Governmental developments in Massachusetts are well documented in Edmund S. Morgan, ed., *Puritan Political Ideas, 1558-1794* (Indianapolis, 1965). Indian-white relations and problems of expansion in New England are discussed in Alden Vaughan, *New England Frontier: Indians and Puritans, 1620-1675* (Boston, 1965) and in Douglas Leach, *The*

Northern Colonial Frontier, 1607-1763 (New York 1966) and his *Flintlock and Tomahawk: New England in King Philip's War* (New York, 1958). For other regions, see Wilcomb E. Washburn, ed., *The Indian and the White Man* (New York, 1964); Allen W. Trelease, *Indian Affairs in Colonial New York: The Seventeenth Century* (Ithaca, 1960); and Verner W. Crane, *The Southern Frontier, 1670-1732* (Ann Arbor, 1929). The most readable of many books on the Salem witch trials is Marion L. Starkey, *The Devil in Massachusetts* (New York,1949), while Chadwick Hansen, *Witchcraft at Salem* (New York, 1969) is the most recent. Michael G. Hall, Lawrence H. Leder, and Michael G. Kammen, eds., in *The Glorious Revolution in America* (Chapel Hill, 1964), have put together an excellent volume on the crisis of 1688-1691. For the beginnings of mercantilism, see Lawrence A. Harper, *The English Navigation Laws: A Seventeenth Century Experiment in Social Engineering* (New York, 1939). A good general survey of life in seventeenth-century America is John C. Miller, *The First Frontier: Life in Colonial America* (New York, 1966). Other valuable studies include Carl Bridenbaugh, *Cities in the Wilderness: The First Century of Urban Life in America, 1625-1742* (New York, 1938), and *Myths and Realities: Societies of the Colonial South* (New York, 1963); Bernard Bailyn, *The New England Merchants in the Seventeenth Century* (Cambridge, 1955); Daniel J. Boorstin, *The Americans: The Colonial Experience* (New York, 1958); Louis B. Wright, *The Cultural Life of the American Colonies, 1607-1763* (New York, 1957) and *The Atlantic Frontier: Colonial American Civilization* (New York, 1947); Perry Miller, *Errand into the Wilderness* (Cambridge, 1956); and Edmund S. Morgan, *Visible Saints: The History of a Puritan Idea* (New York, 1963).

Part II

The Eighteenth Century

4

Government and Politics

From the beginning of the eighteenth century, the tempo of political life in the colonies steadily increased. Tension between royal governors and representative assemblies grew in almost every colony. Executive power, far stronger in theory than in practice, seemingly threatened the concept of self-government embraced by many colonists. And yet the significant political battles of the century were not essentially ideological. Factions composed of wealthy landholders or merchants vied with each other for control of government, not to preserve liberty but to gain the favors such power would bring them. Another paradox of the era saw the electorate, which included the vast majority of adult white males, accept the principle that the "better sort" of inhabitants should rule. Out of the strife, the assemblies emerged rather unexpectedly in several colonies as defenders of the American idea of government by consent. By mid-century many colonists had become deeply suspicious of executive rule, and their faith in the established forms of colonial government was seriously weakened.

Royal Government

The charter issued for Massachusetts in 1691 heralded a new phase in the history not only of that colony but, symbolically, in many other colonies as well. Thereafter, except for three proprietary and two charter provinces, the royal governor became the central figure in the administration in each of eight colonies. Even the proprietary governor enjoyed a similar position to his royal counterpart, because after 1696 his appointment also required royal approval. The governors became in fact the principal link between English crown and the king's American provinces. Their commission as governor, as well as the colony's charter, served as the basis for colonial government. And the royal prerogative also reached America through the king's instructions to his governors, usually issued by the Board of Trade, after 1675 the body responsible for administering the provinces.

The governor enjoyed considerable influence as direct representative of the crown, holding the same position relative to the legislature as the king did to Parliament, though actually wielding more power. He summoned, prorogued, and dissolved the assembly, generally with the advice of his council. He could veto absolutely all acts of the legislature, and in theory appropriations could only be expended through his offices. With the council, he sat as the highest court of appeal and, with its advice, he appointed many minor officials, including justices of the peace and other judges of the lower courts. The governor also nominated members of the council itself and could make interim appointments to that body. Such patronage provided an important basis of influence for colonial governors, for as one pointed out, "men look up to their superiors and obey their directions according to the emoluments received from them." When London insisted on control of such an appointment as that of the naval officer, the governors were sorely distressed.

As captain general and commander in chief, the governor controlled the militia of his colony but had little authority over any British troops stationed in his province. He could, however, commission privateers and enforce the Navigation Acts, and he pocketed the fees charged for passing papers under the great seal. Before the middle of the eighteenth century, he could grant land to worthy supporters. Also, as the king's representative, he stood at the head of the Anglican church in his colony.

In the exercise of these powers, the royal governor faced very few restraints. Although after 1700 he was technically bound by the laws of his colony, only one governor was ever convicted of such improprieties as bribery, embezzlement, or theft. Although generally appointed "during the King's pleasure," the average governor was in office for only five years. Nearly a third of them died in office, and others left to accept more remunerative positions. Only in the charter colonies, Connecticut and Rhode Island, did the inhabitants in fact enjoy the power of voting bad executives out of office. In the proprietary provinces as well as in the crown colonies, the electorate had no practical means of ridding itself of an unpopular governor.

Next to the governor stood the provincial council. Its members were chosen from among prominent residents, numbering as a rule about twelve and normally serving for life. These men were in theory appointed by the crown, though actually by the Board of Trade, which acted on the recommendations of the royal governor of the colony. Those suggested were to be "of good life, well-affected to the [royal] government, of good estates and abilities, not...much in debt." In fact anyone else familiar with the colonies, like British merchants and army officers serving in America, also proposed likely names to the Board of Trade. And occasionally individuals unabashedly offered themselves for the honor.

The duties of the council fell into three areas — executive, judicial, and legislative. Its executive powers came from the fact that the governor was required to gain the consent of the council in making certain major decisions. Among these were the calling of assemblies, appointment of officials, and expenditure of funds. In less important matters, the governor was free to accept or reject the council's "advice." With the governor presiding, the council also sat as the highest court of law within the colony. As a legislative body, the council acted as an upper house, somewhat analogous to the House of Lords, although its seats were not hereditary. It could not initiate revenue bills, but its assent to all legislative measures was necessary for enactment. Occasionally the governor sat with the council when it acted as an upper house, sometimes even voting. But such conduct provoked serious opposition, and few governors persisted in the practice.

Governor and council exercised considerable power over the system of justice. In some colonies they were authorized to establish the courts themselves, although in most provinces the legislature enjoyed this power. But in all the royal colonies the governor and council appointed justices to the various tribunals and, as has been noted, themselves constituted the highest court of appeals. Early governors in the colonies bitterly complained about the lack of trained lawyers who qualified for appointments to the bench. According to the governor of New York, Richard Coote, second earl of Bellomont, the so-called lawyers in that colony around 1700 included a dancing master, a glover, and one who "was condemned to be hanged in Scotland for burning the Bible." As the eighteenth century progressed, governors had less difficulty finding competent men to serve as justices, although most candidates still had no formal training at law. When governors tried to remove some of their appointees, they often ran into fierce opposition from the legislatures, which resented the continuing control this practice gave the governor over the justices.

The colonial courts were expected to make rulings according to English law. The problem was what English law to follow, for there were a baffling dozen or more systems in seventeenth-century England. In Massachusetts, for instance, the colonists focused particularly on those aspects of English common law concerned with public order, rejecting as irrelevant to America those segments dealing with private matters. Common law was thus seen as a limitation on the authority of government. Beyond this, virtually every colony had, within a few years of its founding, adopted a code of laws governing personal conduct, proscribing numerous misdeeds, and establishing punishments therefor. Provisions in these codes were by most colonial charters to conform to the English practice. Still another body of law, the Acts of Navigation, were enforced in the vice-admiralty courts, established by English authority and totally independent of the colonial legislatures. Worse still, the admiralty judge sat without a jury. Englishmen and Americans both bitterly protested the procedures of these tribunals in their respective lands. Restrictions adopted in England were not extended to the colonies, however. And so for worse as well as for better, the American colonists recognized that English practice lay at the foundation of much of their law.

The Colonial Assembly

Despite governors and councils appointed in England, Americans had already gained a measure of self-government by the close of the seventeenth century. The key institution in this development was the lower house of assembly. One of the most significant themes through the next sixty years in most colonies was the rise of the legislature's powers at the expense of the governor. Notable battles in the struggle included fights over the executive's salary, the appointment of officials, the powers of the upper house, and the granting of land. In almost every case, the legislatures came off the victors in the competition. Not surprisingly, the most notable gains were made during the administrations of popular governors, for these officials were often more interested in preserving harmony than in defending the principles of royal prerogative.

In general, the Americans had reached the point by 1700 of asserting that their lower houses of assembly existed by right, much as the House of Commons claimed for itself, especially after 1688. English authorities countered with the contention that the colonial legislatures were the creations of the crown, through the charter and the commissions and instructions issued to royal governors. The American idea, only vaguely expressed until the 1760s, of government by consent of the governed clashed head-on with the English concept of government by royal grace and favor. The conflict would only be resolved in the outcome of the American Revolution.

In Connecticut and Rhode Island, the legislature dominated the government almost from their founding, since no appointed governor stood in the way. In Massachusetts, the Charter of 1691 gave the General Court the unusual right of choosing the Governor's Council, thus weakening its bicameral function as a check on the lower house and depriving the governor of allies. In 1700, the Pennsylvania assembly succeeded in depriving the upper branch of any meaningful voice in the legislative process. A series of inept governors in New York during the early decades of the eighteenth century deferred to the advancing power of the lower house, but in the other colonies change came more slowly. Despite its reputation for independence in the Revolutionary Era, for instance, Virginia's House of Burgesses added very little to its powers during the first half of the century. In both Maryland and Virginia, strong governors succeeded in fending off legislative advances until the 1760s.

The rise of the colonial legislatures was not the result of a plan for power, nor was it a conscious struggle in anticipation of the national independence that came later in the century, as some historians felt. Rather, it was an issue-oriented movement; for example, when in

1745 the New Hampshire legislature demanded the right to bar five delegates summoned by royal writ from new towns, it was more concerned with the practical "right" to control its own membership than any theoretical "right" to thumb its nose at the governor. Once a "right" had been gained (this one was not), it became part of the "traditional" powers of the legislature, to be sure. But as Virginia's Governor Francis Fauquier said of the Burgesses in 1760, "whoever charges them with acting upon a premeditated concerted plan, don't know them, for they mean honestly, but are Expedient Mongers in the highest Degree."

Without question, the assembly's greatest power was its ability to initiate legislation. By the early eighteenth century, the lower houses in all the royal and most of the proprietary colonies had gained this right. The governor could suggest legislation; he could veto undesirable measures; and he could prorogue sessions that failed to enact what he wanted. But in the end he could not force the legislation upon the assembly. The Board of Trade, however, not only could but often did use its powers to withhold the royal assent from acts that colonial governors found it expedient to approve. Worse still, any act designed to amend or repeal a previous law could not take effect until specifically approved by the Board of Trade. Still, the power to initiate legislation gave the American assemblies a major role in their own government.

One of the most important kinds of legislative action controlled by the houses of assembly was the power to raise a revenue for the support of government and its officials. The home authorities made continuing but largely futile efforts to establish a permanent system of revenue in each colony, especially to provide a dependable salary for the governor. Most provinces went no farther than to enact measures effective for five or six years at a time. Another tactic was to appropriate salaries for officials by name rather than by office, thus restricting the governor's power of appointment. Such measures were sometimes attached to defense appropriations to forestall a veto. The assemblies also insisted that the upper houses could neither initiate nor amend money bills. Still another means by which legislatures retained a hold on appropriations was by the appointment of a provincial treasurer empowered to make expenditures. This provision openly defied the Board of Trade's efforts to place authority for disbursements in the hands of the governor. By the middle of the eighteenth century, most colonial legislatures had gained as much power over provincial finances as the House of Commons enjoyed in England. When challenged, they defended with tenacity their hard-won control of the pursestrings.

The struggle for power between the assembly and the governor resulted in dynamic rather than static politics in almost every colony during the first half of the eighteenth century. The wide disparity between theoretical powers of the executive on the one hand and his real strength on the other increased this tension. The governors were at more than one disadvantage in their battles with the assembly. In the first place, they were hemmed in by their instructions, deprived of the flexibility essential to politicians. Nor did they have a widespread system of patronage at their disposal by the 1750s, for both the authorities in London and the colonial assemblies had usurped control of many offices formerly at the disposal of the governor. We have already seen how the appointment by the legislature of a colonial treasurer worked to the disadvantage of the executive. Still another problem for the governor was his comparatively short tenure of office, averaging about five years. It was not unusual, on the other hand, for prominent leaders of the assembly to remain in office for a decade or more. Worse still, the governor was, during his service in America, far removed from the locus of influence for his political world — London — while the colonists had the advantage, as it were, of playing on the "home field." By mid-century, many assemblies had established their own direct lines to the London authorities through agents, thus bypassing the governor altogether as the constitutional link between colony and crown.

The Franchise

One of the most significant differences between politics in America and politics in England was the widespread enjoyment of the franchise in the colonies. A broad basis for political power was never the intention of seventeenth-century founders. But the adoption of English property qualifications in land-rich America resulted by the early eighteenth century in a far different electorate from that found in England. Because the colonial legislatures were comprised of representatives from towns and counties, these bodies gained an important source of strength from their local foundations. The assemblies were soon regarded as legitimate, because they were representative. Well before the 1750s, government by consent of the governed had become a cardinal principle of American political doctrine. In order to understand the significance of this principle, we must know something of the franchise in the various colonies.

Every American colony required potential voters to hold property as evidence of their "stake in society." Historians are generally agreed that by the middle of the eighteenth century, however, more than two out of three adult white males could participate in the election of representatives to their colonial assembly. Among the adult groups excluded in most colonies — aside from women and free blacks — with some exceptions, were slaves, indentured servants and apprentices, recent immigrants, as well as all others who did not possess sufficient property. In addition, at one time or another various colonies excluded Quakers, Catholics, or Jews from exercising the ballot.

In about half the colonies, voters were required to possess freehold estates, of varying size or value, from 50 acres in North Carolina and Georgia to 100 acres in Virginia, although 25 acres of improved land was held sufficient in the last-named province. New Hampshire, Rhode Island, and New York required a freehold worth forty to fifty pounds. New Jersey also restricted the vote to freeholders. In the other colonies, possession of a similar freehold estate entitled one to vote, but there were two additional ways an inhabitant might qualify, ownership of other property or the payment of taxes. Personal property like livestock, tools, clothing, or furniture, alone or in combination with a small real estate holding, could be used to meet the required amount. In Massachusetts, Connecticut, Delaware, and Maryland, property valued at 40 pounds sterling was sufficient, while Pennsylvania required 50 pounds sterling. South Carolina was unique in permitting two-year residents who paid a tax of at least 20 shillings to vote. Residents of some cities, like Albany, New York, Philadelphia, Annapolis, and Norfolk, faced somewhat lower requirements than rural inhabitants. An even more important exception, found in New York and Virginia, permitted tenants with lifetime leaseholds to vote in provincial elections.

While considering the fact that on the average about sixty or seventy percent of all free, adult white males could vote in colonial America, we must realize that probably less than half of those qualified actually did vote in any one election. Travel difficulties, indifference toward candidates and issues, and the habit of deferring in political matters to the community's social and economic leaders all had the effect of keeping many colonists from the polls. Balloting was often done by a show of hands, or registering one's preference in some other public manner, and undoubtedly some inhabitants were reticent to participate under those conditions. It was perhaps not coincidental that the first secret ballot in Salem, Massachusetts (after the Revolution) resulted in a complete turning out of the incumbent selectmen. In the mildly hierarchical society of the eighteenth century, tenants, artisans, and general workers might understandably be reluctant to vote against their landlord or employer.

We must also consider the candidates for whom the voter might cast his ballot. While the franchise itself was broadly held, the requirements for officeholding, both specified by law and in practice, resulted in candidates whose economic and social position was well above the average. In the first place, relatively few artisans or small farmers aspired to officeholding, some because they could not spare the time and others because they did not feel qualified to sit in the legislature. Secondly, many colonists looked to men of wealth, position, and education for leadership in civic affairs. Evidence abounds to show that certain individuals and families played dominant roles in the public service of their colony. Even so, in Virginia, for instance, two out of three delegates to the House of Burgesses sat for three terms or less.

In addition to frequent elections (usually annual) and the resultant turnover of officeholders, there was another important means by which the electorate could make certain their views were well represented in the assembly. New England towns often instructed their delegates how to vote on important issues scheduled for the next session of the General Court. In Virginia, constituents had the right to petition their burgesses for the same purpose. Of course such action prevented the delegate from benefiting by debate in the legislative chamber; indeed the very purpose of instructions was to offset the persuasive arguments of those with opposite views.

Historians have recently expended much time, energy, and occasionally vituperation in their efforts to determine the nature and degree of "democracy" in colonial American politics. Not surprisingly, much of the debate depends upon one's definitions. If we mean by "democracy" government *by* the people, then eighteenth-century America fell far short of the mark. Not only was the governor in most colonies appointed by the king, but the upper house of the legislature was too. Furthermore, significant numbers of inhabitants — women, servants, blacks, as well as adult males without property — could not vote for representatives in the assembly, and only men of above-average wealth and position felt free to hold office. To say that politics in colonial America was relatively undemocratic, on the other hand, is not to suggest that the inhabitants were discontented with their lot. On the contrary, one of the most difficult propositions for modern Americans to accept is that their colonial forebears did not *believe* in the value of democracy as we define it today. The eighteenth century was one of stratified society in which deference to one's "betters" was the accepted norm. The key to understanding this fact is to realize that in 1780 the adult white males of Massachusetts, in a vote unrestricted by property qualifications, accepted a state constitution which prohibited propertyless inhabitants from electing representatives under the new government. That some of those voting thus chose to exclude themselves from a role in their government can only be explained by the widespread "habit of deference" among the middle and lower classes.

Political Life of the Colonies

The patterns of political life in America varied considerably from one colony to another. Despite wide differences, however, a few common characteristics stand out. In the first place, only a small elite actively involved themselves in politics. By their habit of deference, as we have seen, the ordinary colonists, enfranchised or not, left the squabbles of the political area to the upper classes. Secondly, the normal state of political affairs was, as one historian put it, "chaotic factionalism." In most colonies for much of the eighteenth century, various factions among the elite struggled among themselves for ascendancy. Finally, the object of all this political infighting seemed to be the attainment of power for self-serving purposes, land grants, military contracts, or simply prestige, rather than the triumph of "democracy" over "tyranny" or any other such ideological goal.

The degree of factional strife varied from colony to colony and from time to time within each province as well. The politics of New Hampshire remained more stable during the eighteenth century than that of any other province to the southward. From 1741 to 1767 Governor Benning Wentworth used his extensive London connections to dominate the political, social, and economic affairs of the colony and to prevent any opposition faction from gaining strength. The judicious exercise of power (and patronage) assured the Wentworths of support from a broad sector of the populace and even gave them virtual control of the legislature. Sharing this power with other mercantile families in the province sharply reduced the possibility of opposition from these potential rivals.

Following the Glorious Revolution and establishment of the Charter of 1691, politics in Massachusetts took a new turn from seventeenth-century directions. Merchants on the make dominated the Governor's Council and worked hand in hand with the lower house, representing the smaller property owners of the colony, in reducing the power of the royal governor, until by the 1740s they were largely successful. But then the unusually clever Governor William Shirley managed to gather around him a strong coterie of followers who shared political power and economic favors like war contracts until Shirley's departure in 1756. Shortly thereafter, newly wealthy merchants, under the leadership of James Bowdoin, seized control of the Governor's Council from Shirley's political heirs, who included Thomas Hutchinson and Peter Oliver. Like factional squabbles in other colonies, the one in Massachusetts had significant overtones as the colonial quarrel with Great Britain took shape in the 1760s.

While Massachusetts witnessed a political struggle between two mercantile factions — one entrenched, the other on the rise — the situation in Connecticut was quite different. There the contenders for political domination in the mid-eighteenth century represented two religious groups — the Old Light and Anglican conservatives on the one hand, and, on the other, the New Light sects brought to life by the Great Awakening controversy of the 1740s. But the situation was made still more complicated by the fact that most of the New

Lights hailed from eastern Connecticut and were involved in Pennsylvania land speculation through the Susquehanna Company, while their conservative opponents were from the western part of the colony. As in Massachusetts, this quarrel too became intertwined with the struggle with the mother country after the Stamp Act crisis.

In the proprietary colonies, the line distinguishing contending factions was often that between "court" party (the proprietors' administration) and the "country" party (independent property holders whose strength lay in the lower house of assembly). Rarely was the alignment that simple, however. In Pennsylvania, for instance, the proprietors, led by James Logan, drew most of their support from the Philadelphia merchants, while the opposition party under the lawyer David Lloyd depended upon wealthy landholders from outside the city. At first both factions were predominantly Quaker, but by mid-century the Proprietary party gathered Anglicans and Presbyterians around it while most Friends joined in a new "Quaker party" to contest the authority of the proprietors. In 1756, in the midst of the French and Indian War, several Quakers followed their leader, James Pemberton, in resigning from the Assembly in order to preserve their pacifist principles and, not so incidentally, to avoid a weakening division within party ranks. Under largely non-Quaker leadership, including that of Benjamin Franklin, the "Quaker party" continued to oppose the proprietors until events of the quarrel with Great Britain altered the nature of the battle.

Virginia almost alone among the American colonies achieved political stability early in the eighteenth century. Beginning with the decision of Governor Alexander Spotswood in 1722 to work with rather than against the ruling oligarchy of planters until well past mid-century, disputes between distinct factions within Virginia rarely occurred. One historian has estimated that of more than 600 men who sat in the House of Burgesses between 1720 and 1776 only about one hundred played influential roles in provincial politics. At any one time this group numbered about a dozen and generally followed the leadership of an even smaller clique. In 1736, for instance, twelve burgesses held more than half the committee seats, assignments being made by the speaker. These are the men who gave Virginia its large measure of political stability throughout the middle decades of the eighteenth century.

Most of these 100 leading political figures were wealthy planters, three-fourths of them holding more than 10,000 acres and well over half of those for whom records have been found owned at least fifty slaves. Many of the planters were also active as lawyers, land speculators, and merchants. Most of the ruling group were of families who had come to Virginia after 1635, a significant proportion in fact with ancestors who had arrived after 1690. More than half the elite came from less than a dozen families, with the Randolphs, Carters, Beverleys, and Lees dominating the group. Intermarriage made these connections still stronger. Although originally based in the tidewater region, the geographical roots of the ruling class spread steadily northward and westward along with the cultivation of the tobacco.

Yet even this powerful elite, with its broad support among the electorate, could not maintain political tranquility indefinitely. Two mid-century controversies sent ripples through the colony with long-lasting effects. In 1753 the Assembly learned that newly arrived Governor Robert Dinwiddie had raised the fee for land patents by a pistole. Speaking for the conservative ruling clique, Richard Bland charged the governor with illegal taxation. Within a few years, yet another crisis broke. In 1755 there was a serious shortage, because of drought, which drove up the price of tobacco. This effected a considerable raise in income for Anglican clergymen throughout the colony, as these were customarily paid a salary of 16,000 pounds of tobacco. The planters objected and passed an emergency measure through the legislature fixing the parsons' payment at the rate of twopence per pound. In order to make the law effective immediately, the house omitted the suspending clause that was required on innovative measures. The purpose of this requirement was to permit the British authorities to review new measures. Three years later the Burgesses enacted the Two Penny Act, but in 1759 both measures were nullified by the Privy Council. Both the Pistole Fee controversy and the Parson's Cause, so-called, stirred the political waters rather more than the ruling clique would have liked, for some of the younger men among them no longer had so much confidence in the leadership of Speaker John Robinson and his supporters. One of the consequences was a loosening of control by the older group and the rise of new leaders like Richard Henry Lee and Patrick Henry.

One of the most significant political struggles in eighteenth-century America tore the colony of New York into irreconcilable factions and incidentally gave the printer John Peter Zenger an unintentional and largely unearned reputation as a hero in the struggle for a free press. New York's political turmoil was born in the aftermath of the Glorious Revolution, with the battle between Jacob Leisler's supporters and opponents lasting well into the eighteenth century. After a decade of peace under Governor Robert Hunter, new factions emerged in the 1720s. One group was led by Governor Hunter's henchman, Lewis Morris, chief justice of the colony's Supreme Court, the other by the mercantile de Lancey family, whose scion, James de Lancey, also sat on the Supreme Court bench. Soon after the arrival of the greedy and unpleasant Governor William Cosby, in 1732, came a lawsuit between the governor and his temporary predecessor. When the governor dismissed Morris as chief justice and appointed instead his rival de Lancey, the offended leader declared political war. Other malcontents, including Philip Livingston and the lawyers William Smith and James Alexander, flocked to the banner.

For the next two years the Morrisites waged unremitting warfare against Cosby and the de Lanceys. To publicize each and every indiscretion of the arrogant governor, they founded an opposition newspaper, The *New York Weekly Journal,* edited by James Alexander and printed by John Peter Zenger. In almost every article and item, the editor managed to attack Cosby, now in satirical verse, now in a terse political essay. In the process, Morris's *Journal* adopted many of the arguments levied at Robert Walpole's leadership by English essayists like Trenchard, Gordon, and others, thus bringing the language and arguments of the English opposition to America.

The Cosby-de Lancey faction had a few tricks of its own, however. In November 1734, the governor had Zenger jailed on charges of publishing seditious libels against the government. Chief Justice de Lancey promptly set an abnormally high bail and disbarred the printer's lawyers, Alexander and Smith. A clumsy effort at enpaneling a packed jury failed. Fortunately for Zenger, his supporters retained the services of the celebrated Pennsylvania lawyer, Andrew Hamilton. When the court finally convened in August 1735, Hamilton presented an appealing argument. He ignored the accepted law of the day that required the judge to decide whether the alleged statements were libelous and that allowed the jury to determine only whether the defendant in fact published the material in question. Instead, the brilliant barrister invited the jurors to accompany him in a new departure, that truth was a valid defense against libel and that a jury of the people, not an appointed judge, had the right to decide such matters. In making the argument, Hamilton took advantage of a growing popular sympathy for the fact that Zenger had already languished eight months in jail under excessive bail merely for exercising his citizen's right to criticize the governor. Particularly in America, he argued, was freedom of speech important, for inhabitants had no other way of bringing irresponsible royal officials to heel than to rouse public opinion against their excesses. Public opinion sided with Zenger, even if contemporary English law did not, for upon Hamilton's conclusion, the jury quickly acquitted the printer.

The fact that the Zenger trial failed to become a legal precedent for future trials concerning free speech in America serves to emphasize the immediate significance of the case as a triumph of the Morrisite faction over the Cosby-de Lancey forces. But even here Morris failed to regain his position as chief justice, and the victory was short-lived. By the death of Cosby in 1736 the Morris faction had all but disappeared. For the next two decades former Morrisites, like the Livingstons, changed sides as one of them put it, "as serves our interest best." Meanwhile the de Lanceys tightened their grip on New York politics by consolidating their alliances with influential interests in England. But in the 1750s a new opposition faction emerged, the "Presbyterian party" under William Livingston, William Smith, Jr., and others. Livingston's *Independent Reflector* became the worthy successor to Zenger's *Journal* as a voice of outraged opposition. This rivalry lasted until it too, like so many other in the colonies, was absorbed into the greater struggle between America and England after the Stamp Act crisis. Politics in New York, as throughout eighteenth-century America, involved constantly shifting factions of elites contending for power, prestige, and material gain. The colonists' respect for governmental authority, never so strong as that of their English cousins, sank lower as they witnessed these disputes.

Political Ideas of Colonial America

The battling politicians of colonial America rarely spoke from deep-seated commitment to a set of ideological principles. The differences separating the various factions of upper-class colonists were not matters of philosophical conviction. And yet as the eighteenth century proceeded, would-be statesmen began appealing more and more to principle in their effort to unseat their rivals and gain a larger share of power for themselves. For the most part, these arguments were matters of rhetoric rather than conviction. But one kind of battle, that between the lower houses of assembly and the governors, cut across much of the factional strife, and out of it gradually emerged a set of ideas which became an important foundation for the development of American political thought later in the century.

One principle firmly established by the 1750s was that of government by consent of the governed. In America this meant that the representative assembly had powers in its own colony modeled on those of Parliament within England. Among these was the right to alter and develop their own colonial constitution free from imperial interference. In short, as one historian has pointed out, "the American colonists saw their constitutions as living, growing, and constantly changing organisms." This theory directly clashed with the imperial view, maintained by most royal and proprietary governors, that colonial constitutions were determined by the royal charters, commissions, and instructions issued by the London authorities, and that the houses of assembly were merely subordinate institutions with limited governmental powers.

It would be a distortion to assert that the colonists championed representative government as an expression of political democracy. We have already seen that a relatively small elite controlled the affairs of colonial assemblies by tacit consent of the many lesser property holders who enjoyed the franchise. In this context, the main purpose of representative assemblies was more to protect the people from the threat of tyrannical executive government than to express "popular will" in the wholesale enactment of specific legislation.

In their defense of American political freedom, the colonial leaders relied heavily upon the ideas of British writers, particularly those of the radical whigs in opposition to the rule of Robert Walpole.

We have already noted that in their struggle against the Cosby-de Lancey forces the Morrisites of New York borrowed from Gordon, Trenchard, and, other English essayists of the time. The reasons that the ideas of these English dissenters proved so appealing to Americans were several. For one thing, many colonists, as members of various dissenting sects, harbored grave suspicions toward the intentions of the Anglican church in America, viewing the institution as an instrument of the English Establishment, more corrupt now in the eighteenth century than when their Calvinist forebears had fled the homeland one hundred years earlier. Puritan ministers therefore showed no reluctance to join in the defense of American freedom.

What really made the works of the radical whigs germane to the colonial situation was that in their struggles against the royal governors the Americans saw themselves as political dissenters involved in a fight similar to that being waged by Walpole's opponents in England. They shared with Trenchard, Gordon, and others the central concept that liberty was everywhere at the mercy of power, and that too much power in the hands of the executive, whether he be the king, the first minister, or the royal governor, posed a serious threat to the liberties of the ruled. Of course John Locke's contract theory offered a solution to the problem of tyranny from above, but rebellion was a last resort, and like other recourses to "overkill," often resulted in anarchy and confusion more damaging to liberty than the original threat.

Indeed most Englishmen, both in the colonies and in the mother country, shared the general belief that power in the hands of all men, whether kings or commoners, was so corrupting that a balance of power was the only safeguard. Thus the traditional English defense against tyranny was founded in the principle of a mixed constitution — the three-legged stool whose sources of power came partly from the monarchy, partly from the aristocracy, and partly from the commoners. Only when the three legs were of equal length "would the stool provide a firm and level seat of government," as one historian has put it. But in the American colonies, the absence of a true aristocracy meant to some observers that the stool had only two legs, the royal prerogative as expressed by the governor and the commons represented in the lower houses of Assembly.

In this context, recent historians have pointed out that some colonists began to rely heavily on their legislative delegates as the main line of defense against what they termed the encroaching powers of royal governors. Bitter experience told these colonists, or so they thought, that "a quest for power," to use Professor Jack P. Greene's phrase, on the part of the lower houses of assembly was the best means they had to defend the frail liberties of the people from the devouring tyranny of the executive. To many Americans, it seemed that their own imperfect observations were enforced by the warnings of Opposition writers in England. Many by the 1760s began to see the governors and the authority they represented as part of a dark conspiracy dedicated to their enslavement. Leading men of the colony, chosen by the electorate to represent its interests in deliberative assembly, kept a sharp lookout, occasionally guided by the advice of their constituents and subject to the possibility of recall at each annual election if they failed in their trust. When British policy toward the American colonies took a new turn at the close of the Seven Years' War in 1763, the deepest suspicions of many Americans had seemingly come to pass. Not surprisingly, they turned as before to their assemblies to lead the defensive battle against this new threat.

FURTHER READINGS

The definitive study of British political rule in the colonies remains Leonard W. Labaree, *Royal Government in America: A Study of the British Colonial System before 1783* (New Haven, 1930). See also John F. Burns, *Controversies Between Royal Governors and Their Assemblies in the Northern American Colonies* (Boston, 1923). For the assemblies, Jack P. Greene, *The Quest for Power: The Lower Houses of Assembly in the Southern Royal Colonies, 1689-1763* (Chapel Hill, 1963) is indispensable. Mary P. Clarke, *Parliamentary Privileges in the American Colonies* (New Haven, 1943) is also useful. For local affairs, see Michael Zuckerman, *Peaceable Kingdoms: New England Towns in the Eighteenth Century* (New York, 1970); John F. Sly, *Town Government in Massachusetts (1620-1930)* (Cambridge, 1930); Albert O. Porter, *County Government in Virginia* (New York, 1947); and Ernest S. Griffith, *History of American City Government: The Colonial Period* (New York, 1938). Important studies of the franchise include Robert E. Brown,

Middle-Class Democracy and the Revolution in Massachusetts, 1691-1780 (Ithaca, 1955), and with B. Katherine Brown, *Virginia, 1705-1786: Democracy or Aristocracy?* (East Lansing, 1964); J. R. Pole, *Political Representation in England and the Origins of the American Republic* (New York, 1966); and Chilton Williamson, *American Suffrage from Property to Democracy, 1760-1860* (Princeton, 1960). Other aspects of colonial political life are discussed in George A. Billias, *Law and Authority in Colonial America: Selected Essays* (Barre, Mass., 1965) and Leonard W. Levy, *Legacy of Suppression: Freedom of Speech and Press in Early American History* (Cambridge, 1960). The structure of colonial politics has been the subject of several excellent recent studies including Bernard Bailyn, *The Origins of American Politics* (New York, 1968); Richard L. Bushman, *From Puritan to Yankee: Character and the Social Order in Connecticut, 1690-1765* (Cambridge, 1967); and Stanley N. Katz, *Newcastle's New York: Anglo-American Politics, 1732-1753* (Cambridge, 1968), as well as several older works including Charles S. Sydnor, *Gentlemen Freeholders: Political Practices in Washington's Virginia* (Chapel Hill, 1952) and Theodore G. Thayer, *Pennsylvania Politics and the Growth of Democracy, 1740-1776* (Harrisburg, 1953). The intellectual background of colonial American politics is best illuminated by Caroline Robbins, *The Eighteenth-Century Commonwealthman* (Cambridge, 1959); Bernard Bailyn, *The Ideological Origins of the American Revolution* (Cambridge, 1967); Lawrence H. Leder, *Liberty and Authority: Early American Political Ideology, 1689-1763* (Chicago, 1968); and Leonard W. Labaree, *Conservatism in Early American History* (New York, 1948).

5

Economic Development

As the colonies matured politically during the eighteenth century, at the same time their economy grew more complex. New supplies of labor and capital became available. New lands and resources were developed. Rice and indigo, in addition to tobacco, became staple exports from the southern colonies, while wheat became an important product of the middle provinces. Craftsmen in towns and villages supplied many articles needed by their fellow inhabitants, and larger manufactory operations, such as shipbuilding, iron-making, and flour milling were in full swing. Merchants and shipmasters made possible the exchange of goods between the various provinces and with the mother country too. By mid-century, the American colonies had established dependable economic relationships with each other, along with their roles as suppliers and consumers in the self-sufficient empire of Great Britain.

Agricultural Developments

In the one hundred years between Bacon's Rebellion in 1675 and the outbreak of the American Revolution, the annual shipments of tobacco from the Chesapeake colonies increased from an average of nearly 18,000,000 pounds to over 100 million pounds, worth about

£ 1,000,000. By mid-eighteenth century, arable tidewater lands were becoming exhausted from the intensive cultivation, and much of the tobacco now came from newer Piedmont plantations. Packed in large hogsheads weighing nearly 1,500 pounds, the crop was sent down the rivers to warehouses for inspection and sale to factors representing the English and Scots merchants who dominated the trade. Planters used their sales receipts as currency for the purchase of British cloths and other manufactures that the factors offered for sale.

The cultivation of tobacco varied little from one plantation to the next. Fields were prepared by ox-drawn plows and harrows, and the seed was planted in March if possible. If the land was old, it had first to be well manured, but the fresh soil of recently cleared woodland produced a good crop without dressing. Because of the moist climate, the field hands waged a constant battle with the weeds, hoeing the long rows of tobacco through the hot summer months. By September, the crop was ready for harvesting and the laborious task of curing, stripping, and packing the leaves for shipment to the factors' warehouses. Transportation from Piedmont plantations presented a major problem. Often the hogsheads were rolled along behind a team of oxen, through potholes and streams where necessary, to reach the tidewater.

It was not unusual for a prosperous tobacco planter to own five or ten thousand acres of land, and a handful of very wealthy men could claim four or five times that much in parcels scattered throughout the colony. Resident overseers assisted the planter in managing the operation of his more distant possessions, while the owner himself often took charge of the home plantation. Tobacco was by no means the only crop cultivated, although Chesapeake planters in general did not fully appreciate the need for rotation until well after mid-century. George Washington turned to wheat at Mt. Vernon. Others experimented with hemp, flax, and corn. The larger plantations often cut timber for market and produced pitch, tar, and other "naval stores" from the extensive pine forests. Each plantation had a cooperage, where hogsheads for the tobacco were constructed. An abundance of shellfish, shad, herring, and sturgeon was harvested from the rivers to provide nourishment for master and slave alike, and of course vegetable gardens and orchards were planted nearby as well. Chickens, hogs, cattle, and other livestock helped make the plantation self-sufficient, along with attendant dairies, smokehouses, and root cellars. Smithies, carpenters' shops, tanneries, and other outbuildings were also commonly found on the larger plantations.

For the majority of Virginians, a 5,000-acre plantation with its one hundred or more slaves was simply a dream. Yet even the smaller landholders could generally produce a tobacco crop for market, sometimes laboring alone but often with the help of three or four slaves who worked and lived almost as a part of the family. Poorer soil, transportation difficulties, and the reduced scale of operation limited the small landowner's margin of profit; nevertheless, mere subsistence farmers were few in number in the Piedmont and tidewater areas of the Chesapeake.

Several hundred miles to the south an entirely different agricultural world came into being toward the end of the seventeenth century as settlers began moving into the Carolina low country. Wide rivers wound their way through the swampy lands to the sea, flooding the rich soil bordering their courses at every heavy rainfall. The Ashley and Cooper "joined to form the Atlantic Ocean" at Charleston, it was commonly said, while the Edisto, Ashepoo, and Broad Rivers reached the ocean further south. Along the coast from Charleston to Florida stretched the remarkable sea-islands, low-lying, fertile lands separated from the mainland by tidal creeks and marshes. Here was the scene of an agricultural revolution that gave birth to the distinctive ruling class of South Carolina.

Long-staple cotton and other semitropical crops including sugar were successfully cultivated in small quantities here, along with the more common North American corn and wheat. But the region's fame and wealth came from two specialized crops — rice and indigo. The planting of rice had begun at the end of the seventeenth century, but not until 1709 was as much as one million pounds exported. Thereafter production doubled and sometimes even tripled every decade until the eve of the American Revolution, when the planters were exporting a rice crop of 80 million pounds, worth £340,000. To cultivate rice, the planter had first to build dykes along the edge of a river and drain the adjacent bottom lands. Planting even amongst the rotting cyprus stumps, the work force immediately flooded the field through carefully prepared canals to protect the seeds from hovering birds, and then alternately flooded and drained the fields until the crop was ready for harvesting by the end of August. As in the case of indigo, preparing rice for market was at least as troublesome as the cultivation. One author[...] plantation required thirty slaves. With a lit[...] crops could be cultivated by the same work[...] seasons overlapped only slightly. As a combined[...] digo ranked third in value among the exports of the[...] colonies.

To the north, Pennsylvania, New Jersey, and Ne[...] become centers for the production of wheat and other gr[...] these so-called "bread" colonies was shipped each yea[...] £ 500,000 of flour and bread with wheat, barley, and other grai[...] sent to market. The soil and climate were so favorable that even[...] farming practices netted twenty or thirty bushels per acre, a [...] higher yield than that produced in England. Flax for linen, barley fo[...] malt beer, and hay and corn for cattle fodder were other important cash crops. Potatoes and other vegetables, especially apples for cidermaking, and of course beef and dairy provisions, came to ready markets along the seacoast.

When the Scandinavian traveler, Peter Kalm, described the agriculture of Pennsylvania, he showed astonishment at the habits of the American farmers. "The grain fields, the meadows, the forests, and the cattle, are treated with equal carelessness," he reported. "Their [the farmers'] eyes are fixed upon the present gain, and they are blind to the future." Undoubtedly most American farmers were guilty of such an indictment. Almost alone, among them all, the Germans of Pennsylvania stood out as practitioners of conservation. Approximately half the typical farm of about 200 acres was cleared for "cultivation and pasturage," the rest remaining in woods. With the help of several good "Conestoga" horses, a German and his family could handle the work without resorting to outside labor, although the more prosperous landowners occasionally took on a few redemptioners from the home country, especially as household servants. Enlightened farmers supplemented their crude methods of crop rotation with the more general practice of letting fields lie fallow or turning them into pasturage once every three years or so. Because they kept their livestock in barns during the winter months, the German farmers made greater use of manure for fertilizing than those who let their cattle run loose all year. Some Germans also used lime, but gypsum did not come into use until after the Revolution.

In the autumn, the German farmer brought his crop to market in

ith sailcloth stretched over
s, and drawn by at least
in the wagon en route to
erman farmer exercised
cultivation of his fields,
ad.

, the New England farmer
s and seaports, to find a
ght though it was in most
deserved the name "Hard-
cularly good, the ground was
ven under these difficult con-
managed to scratch out a living
subsistence, and in some favored regions, such
necticut River Valley, outright prosperity was not uncommon.

Around Wethersfield, Connecticut, farmers specialized in onions, peas, and corn, and other vegetables abounded throughout the southern New England colonies. Efforts to grow marketable wheat crops were less successful, and the region soon came to depend on the middle colonies for much of its flour. By the mid-eighteenth century, many rural New Englanders had already turned to raising livestock as a more profitable source of income. Yankee hillsides swarmed with sheep, goats, and cattle, while through the woods ranged the lowly pig. In Rhode Island a particularly fine breed of horse was developed, the Narragansett pacer, much sought after in the plantation and island colonies to the south. On the eve of the Revolution, New England was exporting nearly 2,000 horses a year to the West Indies alone, along with 1,200 oxen and over 3,000 sheep and hogs.

For the New England farmer, as for his counterparts in other colonies, innovation came with difficulty, for the man of the soil was more tradition-bound than most. But just as the Virginia planter began to turn to wheat as his tobacco lands gave out, and the Pennsylvanian searched for new ways to sweeten his soil, so, too, the New Englander discovered that he could profitably "grow" four-legged crops.

Patterns of Commerce

By mid-eighteenth century, the American economy had, as we have
seen, grown far beyond the subsistence level which characterized
most of the previous period. Several factors of course brought this
about. In addition to the steadily expanding population, which
provided both a labor pool and a domestic market for surpluses,
there was the steady acquisition of capital, which made possible
further purchases of land and labor to increase production of salable
commodities like tobacco and rice. Of equal importance was the
development of commerce, which made possible the exportation of
these and other products of the continental colonies and the importation of goods needed in America.

Commerce is much like a seamless web; it is almost impossible to
determine where to begin a description of its patterns. For colonial
American commerce, one might well start with New England, for
this was the region that dominated the trade of eighteenth-century
America. Deprived by nature of an agricultural product marketable
in the mother country (and contemptuously dismissed as the "most
prejudicial" of the colonies because of this failing), New England
turned to its forests and seas for exports. Lumber, shingles, staves,
and even house frames were sent to the West Indies along with vast
quantities of fish, in exchange for molasses and sugar. Fish and
timber thus became the cornerstones of New England commerce, and
to this day the "sacred cod" hangs in its place of honor in Boston's
State House.

Since well before the first English settlements of North America,
Europeans had come each summer to the banks off Newfoundland in
pursuit of the cod. As early as 1635 the Reverend Hugh Peter of
Salem reminded the colonists that a rich bounty awaited under the
offshore seas, and soon thereafter the coastal communities of
Massachusetts Bay and Plymouth were swept with the fishing fever.
Before the end of the seventeenth century, Yankee fishermen vied
with the French Canadians for domination of the Grand Banks. Not
until after the Treaty of Utrecht in 1713, however, when France was
forced to surrender Newfoundland, were the New Englanders able to
compete on equal terms. Even so, from the settlements they were
allowed to retain on Cape Breton, the French continued to work the
Banks with extraordinary success. But the eighteenth century

belonged, primarily to the Yankee fishermen pushing out from Marblehead, Gloucester, and Plymouth in their sturdy schooners to fish Georges Bank off Cape Cod and Jeffries Ledge in the Gulf of Maine, as well as the larger Banks off Newfoundland. By the beginning of the Revolution, about 5,000 fishermen brought in annually a catch worth over £300,000. The best quality fish found markets at home or in Catholic Europe, while the less desirable kinds went to the plantation colonies to the south and to the West Indies.

Related to cod fishery but rather more specialized was whaling. In the seventeenth century, residents along the shores of Cape Cod and Nantucket succeeded in capturing these mammals from shore stations, but before long determined fishermen had to take to their boats to catch the whale, valuable for the oil extracted from the thick blanket of blubber surrounding its warm-blooded body. By mid-eighteenth century, the whaling industry had become the special preserve of Nantucket and New Bedford, those two ports accounting for about eighty percent of the oil shipped to market, worth with other whale products well over £100,000. Cod fishing and whaling gave New Englanders valuable commodities to help make up for the paucity of agricultural production.

The forests of New England, like its waters, also yielded valuable products. Stately white pines grew in profusion from the Piscataqua River Valley on the Maine-New Hampshire border well beyond the Penobscot River Valley to the eastward. Far into the wilderness, gangs of woodcutters worked their way through the bountiful stands, sending the fallen trees down the rivers to awaiting sawmills. Most of the pine was sawn into boards and planks, or split into shingles and clapboards, but the largest specimens were reserved for the royal mastyards. From oak the workers shaped barrel staves, hoops, and heads, in great demand by distillers for shipping rum. Much of the timber, of course, stayed right in New England, for the construction of houses, and more especially of vessels for the fishing, coastal, and overseas trade.

But timber and fish were the principal commodities of New England's rapidly expanding maritime commerce. Deprived of a product in demand among London merchants, the New Englanders had to search elsewhere for the "returns" necessary to balance their accounts with London. "Elsewhere" quickly became the West Indies. There the planters needed New England fish, meats, and vegetables as foodstuff at the same time that they required house frames, lumber, and the makings of sturdy casks. In addition, New England horses were needed to work the sugar mills and pull the wagons. In exchange, the Yankee shippers purchased quantities of molasses, from both English and French colonies, as well as some rum and sugar. The molasses was converted into dark New England rum and it enabled the merchants to trade with other colonies of the North American continent, and with overseas areas like Africa. Yankees also imported salt for the fisheries, and sugar, rum, cocoa, and cotton, for domestic consumption and for re-export as well.

The West Indies were by no means the private preserve of New England traders. Vessels from New York and Philadelphia carried bread and flour to the islands, along with the more general cargoes of provisions, soap and tallow, bricks, furniture, and other manufactured articles. The middle colonies also imported molasses from the West Indies, New York and Philadelphia rum finding a good market in the Indian trade as well as in other continental colonies, where it was deemed of slightly better quality than the New England variety. The southern colonies also traded with the British and foreign West Indies. Virginia exported over 200,000 bushels of corn, along with cargoes of oats, peas, and beans, and stood second only to New England as an exporter of timber products. Both North and South Carolina also had shares in trade to the Caribbean, especially by the exportation of rice, corn, naval stores, and other commodities.

The middle colonies emulated New England by bringing cocoa and molasses from the West Indian islands. In addition they imported rather more sugar and rum than did the Yankees, and they also sought mahogany from the Bay of Honduras for the cabinet-makers of New York and Philadelphia. In contrast, the southern colonies received relatively few cargoes from the West Indies, suggesting that their exportations thither were carried in vessels from the northern colonies, which then returned directly to their home ports. South Carolina was an exception, for it had established commercial ties with the Caribbean in the previous century and in fact imported many slaves from the West Indies throughout the eighteenth century.

Whatever the ultimate destination of the commodities brought back from the West Indies, profits from this business largely depended on still further commercial transactions, particularly involving coastal trade with other colonies. In an era when roads were simply too crude for the portage of bulky goods, coastal and inland waterways served as America's highways. About half the entrances and clearances at Boston, for instance, involved commerce with the other continental colonies. New England needed wheat and flour from Philadelphia and Baltimore, iron, tobacco, and even corn from Virginia. Rice, indigo, and naval stores played prominent roles in the exchanges between the middle colonies and those to the south.

Dominant in the West Indies and coastal commerce, American merchants had to settle for a secondary role in the trans-Atlantic trade with the mother country. The tobacco trade, for instance, was virtually monopolized by Scots and English merchants, whose factors residing in Norfolk and other Chesapeake ports channeled the crop to their employers' vessels and took orders for British goods in great demand among the planters. Even tighter was the mainline run between England and the sugar islands of the Caribbean, and few Americans succeeded in breaking into that trade. Although no figures are available, most historians agree that over half of all English goods imported into the continental colonies came in British bottoms.

Yet there was still room in the trans-Atlantic trade for American merchants willing to use a little ingenuity. New Englanders, for instance, carried their cargoes of fish to the Spanish ports, obtaining salt, wines, and fruits in return. The same commodities were brought back from the Azores, Cape Verde, and other Atlantic islands in exchange for staves and headings for wine casks. More often, the American trader would take his profit in bills of exchange instead of goods and then purchase a cargo of English woolens and other manufactures in Bristol or Plymouth before heading home across the Atlantic. Wheat and flour from Pennsylvania and Maryland also found a good market in southern European ports. In 1770, for instance, the master of the Marblehead ship *Venture* exchanged molasses, fish oil, and shoes at Annapolis for a cargo of grain and flour, which he then took to Lisbon. Other products that the northern colonies marketed in the United Kingdom were flax for the Irish linen industry, potash and pearlash used in the manufacture of soap, masts for the Royal Navy, some iron, and a few furs.

English goods comprising homeward cargoes ran to a regular pattern, whether purchased by Virginia tobacco, Carolina rice, or the bills of exchange that Yankee skippers picked up after tramping their miscellaneous wares through the West Indies and Mediterranean markets. The English commodities most in demand throughout America were woolen and linen cloths and other clothing materials like silk and occasionally cotton goods. Also popular were various hardware items difficult to make in the colonies, such as pots and pans, knives, tools, and firearms. But Americans also sought tea, damask and paper hangings, books, and other marks of gracious living. The demand for English goods knew no limits. During the first decade of the eighteenth century, the continental colonies imported from the mother country at an annual average of £250,000; by the 1730s the average had reached £645,000, and thirty years later imports were averaging £1,800,000. By the last period, exports from America had fallen far behind, yet still the colonists bought and still the English sold. Yankees strove hard to find bills of exchange and other means to restore the balance of trade with the mother country.

Servants, Slaves, and Smuggling

The flow of indentured servants into the colonies, already considerable during the latter half of the seventeenth century, reached new heights after 1700. Unlike the earlier migrants, who were predominantly English, a large proportion of those who came in the eighteenth century were Scots-Irish, Rhineland Germans, or French Huguenots. Another change in the earlier pattern brought increasing numbers of servants to the middle colonies rather than to the Chesapeake, where Negro slavery had by then become the basic labor system. New York and New England, on the other hand, did not seem as hospitable as Pennsylvania and Delaware. Joining the servants and redemptioners were the usual English convicts and vagabonds, and after each of the unsuccessful Scots uprisings between 1690 and 1745, hundreds of captured Highlanders were shipped off to the colonies. The Jewish communities in New York and Newport gained numerous coreligionists, particularly Sephardic Jews from the Iberian peninsula.

While many immigrants continued to come as indentured servants, most of the Rhinelanders and many others arrived under a slightly different status. The redemptioner, so-called, was one who was able to pay for a part of his passage. Upon arrival he was given two weeks to find, from friends and relations already in America, the balance due the shipmaster. Failure to find it resulted in the sale of his service for a period sufficiently long to cover the sum still owed. Redemptioners generally came in family groups and had a somewhat more stable European background than the indentured servant, who almost always emigrated alone, more as cargo than as passenger.

At the beginning of the eighteenth century, there were perhaps no more than 25,000 Africans in North America, almost all living as slaves on the plantations of the Chesapeake and Carolina colonies. Seventy-five years later, nearly 500,000 blacks inhabited the mainland colonies. This extraordinary increase, at an even greater rate than that of the white population, was a result primarily of the vastly stepped-up importation of slaves rather than the natural increase of the blacks already here. The slave trade, dominated by Dutch and English companies through most of the seventeenth century, was thrown open to individual merchants in 1697, and numerous Americans thereafter became involved in the business. By the eve of the Revolution, sometimes as many as 100,000 blacks were carried away from Africa in a single year, most of them destined for the Caribbean islands, but several thousand would be landed in various ports of the American mainland, especially in Charleston, South Carolina.

One of the most thoroughly documented operations involved the firm of William Johnston and Company of Newport, Rhode Island. In March 1752, for instance, Johnston's brigantine *Sanderson* cleared for the Caribbean under the command of Captain David Lindsay, with a cargo of boards, staves, and horses, among other items. These commodities he exchanged for cocoa and molasses for the passage home. Perhaps Lindsay made another such voyage in the summer or fall. In February 1753, the *Sanderson* was at Anamaboe on the coast of Africa, selling rum for slaves. During this period a hogshead of rum, worth about £11, would purchase one black, who would bring on the average £30 in slave markets of the West Indies or North America.

After a "middle passage" of 10 weeks, Lindsay reached Barbados in June, having lost only one of his fifty-seven slaves. He sold all but ten of his blacks there, realizing net proceeds of £1,324, most of which he laid out in a cargo of good West Indies rum and sugar, while taking the balance in Liverpool bills of exchange. Allowing for costs, the voyage probably netted profits equal to about £10 per slave, or £570.

The route of Lindsay's brigantine was indeed "triangular," but so were voyages involving most other commercial transactions, and it is misleading to refer to the slave trade as "the triangular trade." In this case New Englanders needed molasses to make the rum by which they purchased Africans. South Carolinians in the trade, on the other hand, carried pitch, indigo, and rice to various British ports, where they were exchanged for such commodities as cloth, hardware, and gin with which to purchase slaves in Africa. Whatever the pattern of trade, the demand for blacks in the southern plantations seemed insatiable. "There never was a better opening for a cargo of Callabar Slaves than in the months of October and November last," wrote Henry Laurens in May 1755, "a number of small Indigo planters finding a ready sale for their crops...which brought them in such large sums they were all mad for more Negroes...." Laurens believed that many landowners had planted much more indigo than they could harvest without purchasing more slaves during the coming summer.

Man's inhumanity to man has never reached lower depths than by the notorious "middle passage" of slaving voyages from the coast of Africa to American ports. Packed into the 'tween decks spaces rarely more than four feet high, the men were shackled two by two and made to lie on the rough plank floor, each chained into a space less than two feet wide and six feet long. More commonly, the women and children remained unshackled. Economics if nothing else made it worth the shipmaster's while to provide sufficient food, water, and ventilation for his human cargo, to minimize losses en route, but miscalculations were frequent. Many deaths among the blacks resulted from disease and starvation and from the inhuman methods used to suppress uprisings among them. There are numerous instances also of blacks committing suicide to avoid the fate that awaited them in America. Overcrowding was probably even more serious on the large slaving vessels hailing from Liverpool and Bristol, which carried the bulk of blacks to America, than on the smaller colonial-owned slavers of the eighteenth century, but the differences were hardly significant.

Another kind of trade that netted profits almost as lucrative as slaving was the illicit importation of goods from Europe or the West Indies. Smuggling has always been a problem for any nation that limits or taxes the importation of certain goods for whatever purposes. England, for instance, depended on the revenue collected by an impost of duties on a multitude of commodities. Not surprisingly, bands of smugglers made a handsome living along the English Channel by running in goods from France and Holland. For them, smuggling was a profession, and they did not hesitate to kill revenue officers if intercepted. Few Americans made a profession of smuggling, however, and none went quite so far as murder. Most illicit goods came in the holds owned by men who were also legal traders, respected merchants like the Whartons of Philadelphia and the Hancocks of Boston.

Among the most common goods illegally brought into America were molasses from the French West Indies and tea from Holland. Under the terms of the Molasses Act of 1733, foreign molasses was subject to a six-pence-per-gallon duty, in order to favor the molasses produced in the British West Indies. If collected, such a duty would in fact have been prohibitory, because it would have priced American-made rum out of the market altogether. And the British islands simply did not produce enough molasses to meet the demand. Fortunately for New Englanders, however, the customs officials made only perfunctory efforts to enforce the law, and French molasses continued to enter the colonies with little difficulty. Tea was another matter, for under the law only tea sold by the English East India Company in London could legally enter the colonies. Because Parliament laid heavier taxes upon the importation of tea into its own country than did the Dutch, the commodity was always cheaper to obtain in Amsterdam than in London. The result was that some Americans joined many Englishmen in the profitable business of smuggling Dutch tea into their respective homelands. By the time of the Revolution, perhaps as much as one million pounds of tea was annually smuggled into the American colonies, and merchants frequently realized net profits of £10 per chest, with cargoes ranging in size from ten or fifteen up to seventy-five chests or more. Because capture meant confiscation, tea smugglers usually committed relatively small amounts of Dutch tea to each vessel. Dutch gin, French cloths, and wines from the Atlantic islands were other popular items in the illicit trader's hold as his vessel slipped quietly into a small cove to unload.

Colonial Industry and Crafts

We think of agriculture as the basis of the colonial American economy, supplemented by the marketing of farm surpluses, but such a view overlooks the importance of other kinds of productive enterprise. One of the most complex manufacturing processes in colonial America was the shipbuilding industry. Throughout the New England and middle colonies, almost every little harbor had a shipyard or two. With the ready availability of oak, pine, and other woods, local craftsmen constructed the sloops, schooners, and square-rigged brigs and ships that became the mainstays of the American merchant fleet. The Navigation Acts gave vessels built in the colonies free run of the empire (except India) as though they were of English construction. This fact, indeed, proved a boon to American shipbuilders, who found a ready market for their vessels in England, where they could undersell British shipyards. At the Revolution, fully one-third of the vessels sailing under the English flag had been built in the colonies.

The shipyard was in a real sense America's first factory. Concentrated at the building site were not only the materials necessary but the various workmen and their special tools as well. As the vessel passed through each stage of its construction, shipwrights, carpenters, caulkers, and painters all contributed their skills to the project. The products of still other specialists were needed before the vessel was ready for sea. Masts, rigging, blocks, pumps, and sails were manufactured in artisans' shops throughout the seaport. Shipsmiths made anchors and other ironware, while carvers executed fancy trail boards and figureheads for the larger ships and brigs. Most vessels were built on order, with the prospective purchaser putting up capital as the project moved ahead, but some shipyard owners built on speculation, providing the necessary financing themselves. In many respects the shipbuilding industry represented colonial industry at its most complex.

Another highly developed colonial industry involved the manufacture of iron. From the modest beginnings of such seventeenth-century operations as the Saugus Iron Works north of Boston, ironmongers in various colonies had by the mid-eighteenth century established more blast furnaces and forges than England had itself. A successful operation, like Alexander Spotswood's works at Massaponax near Fredericksburg, in Virginia represented a capital investment of about £12,000, including 15,000 acres of ore-field and two square miles of woodland to provide fuel. Great numbers of workers, many of them slaves, were needed to haul the ore out of the bogs and mines and to chop cord upon cord of wood to feed the fires and make the charcoal mounds used in the smelting process. Water-powered bellows brought the blast furnace to a high temperature, which burned out the impurities, with the help of heaps of limestone to absorb the sulphur. The Spotswood furnace turned out about twenty tons of iron a week. Some of the pig and bar iron smelted in the colonies was exported to England, £60,000 worth in 1770, but most of it went to slitting and plating mills, which rolled it into more useful sizes and shapes to be worked by blacksmiths into axe heads, nails, horseshoes, and scores of other products much demanded by the inhabitants.

Yet another heavy industry was the merchant mill that ground wheat and other grains into flour for market. The largest con-centration of these mills was in the Philadelphia area, though by the outbreak of the Revolution Wilmington and Baltimore had become important centers. Unlike the local grist mill, where the miller ground the farmers' wheat for a small percentage of their grain, the merchant mill operated on a much larger scale. The owner purchased wheat outright, milled and bolted it into flour, which was then packed into barrels for shipment to markets near and far. Often the miller operated ovens on the premises, in which he baked bread and biscuits for quantity sale. Waterpower drove the big grinding stones and auxiliary machinery like bolting mills and hoists. By 1770, the four middle colonies were exporting 45,000 tons of bread and flour, mostly to the West Indies and southern Europe. Thousands of barrels also reached local markets by wagons and coastal vessels.

Other mills included of course the ubiquitous sawmill found at the falls of innumerable rivers throughout colonial America. There the water-powered blades sawed into planks and boards timber from the hinterland that had been floated downstream to the mill site. Almost single-handedly Benjamin Franklin helped to establish nearly a score of paper mills that converted old rags into reams of fine paper. This paper was sold by the enterprising Philadelphian to printers throughout the colonies. Another entrepreneur, Christopher Leffingwell, founded a number of industries at Norwich, Connecticut, including a paper mill, a chocolate factory, a fulling mill, and a hosiery manufactory, all operated by water from the Yantic river. Nail factories, potteries, and dyeworks could also be found in numerous towns of the northern colonies. Nor should the busy rum distilleries of Newburyport, Medford, Providence, Philadelphia, and other seaports be omitted, or such other specialized activities as glassmaking, and spermaceti candleworks. By the outbreak of the Revolution, the American colonies teemed with industries, large and small, which employed thousands of skilled workers under a single roof to turn out, with the aid of machinery, the necessaries and luxuries of eighteenth-century life.

The line between the entrepreneur's "factory" and the craftsman's shop has never been easy to draw, especially for colonial America. The master craftsman was a small businessman who, with the help perhaps of a few journeymen and apprentices, turned out handcrafted products usually of his own design. Generally he had the assistance of his wife and children. The special skills of his trade he passed on to his apprentices, if any, who generally lived in his household. The craftsman required only his tools, materials, and a place to work, usually the ground floor of his dwelling house. Among the artisans doing business in a typical New England town in the mid-eighteenth century were bakers, cabinetmakers, clock makers, goldsmiths and silversmiths, hatters, tailors, and cordwainers (shoemakers). Other workers, like housewrights, painters, and bricklayers had no need for a shop.

In the rural villages, craftsmen usually confined themselves to making goods on order only. In the larger towns, however, the artisan was a shopkeeper as well, often facing stiff competition from others. The quality of his work was of course his best advertisement, along with the sign that hung over his shop door. A small box in the weekly newspaper called attention to his wares, and occasionally he would sell goods at auction. The most successful craftsmen, especially cabinetmakers and silversmiths, enjoyed a market far beyond the limits of their own communities. The Townshends and Goddards of Newport, for instance, sold chairs and other furniture from Portsmouth to Charleston, giving keen competition to local artisans.

Eighteenth-century America was far from the free-enterprise paradise modern businessmen dream of. Colonial craftsmen faced two sets of regulations — those from the British government and those from local authorities. As American artisans turned out increasing quantities of finished goods, old-line mercantilists in England grew concerned, for they believed that colonies were especially valuable as markets for the manufactures of the mother country. Under no circumstances should they be allowed to produce for export goods that the parent herself manufactured. From time to time, Parliament enacted legislation designed to limit the sale of specific colonial manufactures. Thus the Woolen Act (1699) prohibited the export of cloth from Ireland and the colonies but with little effect, since commercial weaving was virtually nonexistent in America. To be sure, many families wove their own woolen or linen cloth (or the combination known as linsey-woolsey), but Parliament wisely made no attempt to halt this practice. To protect another influential industry, the Hat Act (1732) did prevent the export of colonial-made hats from one province to another as well as to England, but the local market remained open to American hatters. Again in 1750, Parliament passed the Iron Act, both to encourage the export of raw iron to England and to prohibit the establishment or operation of slitting mills in America. The first provision did in fact increase the shipment of bar and pig iron to the mother country, but the second part proved hopelessly unenforceable, as mills continued to operate throughout America.

The purpose of local regulations was rather different. Because the quality of hand-wrought products varied greatly, efforts were made to maintain reasonable standards. The most successful regulations were those that assured fair weights and measures. The selectmen of many New England towns, for instance, decreed the weight of one-penny and two-penny loaves of bread, depending on the fluctuating price of flour. Almost every community had its sealers of weights and measures, surveyors of lumber, and inspectors of various other kinds of goods. *Caveat emptor* remained the basic principle of the colonial marketplace, to be sure, but at least the buyer had some protection from the more unscrupulous shopkeepers. These regulations mirrored similar provisions for the inspection of exports from the middle and southern colonies. The high quality of Philadelphia's superfine flour was rigidly enforced, for instance, as was the tobacco sent out from Virginia and the rice and indigo exported from South Carolina. Those who claim "free enterprise" to be the American way will not find its roots in the colonial period.

Currency, Credit, and Capital

One of the most serious problems of the colonial economy was the chronic shortage of currency. Virtually no coinage was minted in the colonies, and because of the unfavorable balance of trade with the mother country that continued throughout the eighteenth century, very little English metallic money remained in America for long. The most common coin was the Spanish piece of eight (a quarter of which was worth two *reals*, or "two-bits") and its later equivalent, the Spanish milled dollar. Gold coins in circulation were the Portuguese *johannes*, or "joe" and the Spanish *pistole*. Because monetary transactions were expressed in terms of British pounds, shillings, and pence, those using foreign coinage constantly had to translate into English equivalents, which varied somewhat from colony to colony.

The lack of metallic currency forced the colonists to find other media of exchange. Commodities like tobacco, rice, and wheat, commonly known as "country pay," became legal tender in numerous colonies for wages, taxes, and other debts. Commodity prices fluctuated widely, of course, adding to the confusion. In the late 1750s, for instance, the price of tobacco sharply increased because drought cut down production. To avoid having to pay the salaries of clergymen and others at the higher rate, the House of Burgesses "pegged" the price of tobacco at two-pence per pound for such payments. When the Privy Council disallowed the measure, one of several clergymen sued for his rightful compensation in what became known as the "Parson's Cause." By stirring up resentment against the Privy Council's action, however, the young lawyer, Patrick Henry, succeeded in limiting the award to one penny.

Merchants had for years enjoyed the use of bills of exchange, which circulated among them. A West Indian planter, for instance, might purchase a cargo of New England fish in part with a bill of exchange for £100 sterling, drawn on a Bristol merchant with whom he had a favorable balance from the previous sale of sugar. The New England merchant could then use this bill toward the purchase of goods from the same Bristol merchant or from anyone else who would honor it. The face value of the bill might be subject to discount if there was doubt that the Bristol merchant would ultimately honor it. The colonial merchant constantly searched for good bills of exchange that would not be subject to "protest" — refused acceptance. However useful to merchants, bills of exchange were never intended to circulate in public, and the shortage of currency continued.

Not surprisingly, most colonies resorted to issuing paper currency as a solution to the problem. Massachusetts Bay was the first to do so, as a means of financing the unsuccessful attack on Quebec in 1690 during King William's War. Other colonies issued similar currency during the various wars of the eighteenth century. In all but Pennsylvania, paper money rapidly depreciated as legislatures printed new issues and recirculated earlier bills in an effort to meet the mounting costs of war. Debtors, of course, welcomed the resulting inflation, for they could pay back their debts with "cheaper" pounds, to the dismay of their creditors. Many creditors were themselves debtors to English merchants, however, and they recognized that business prosperity depended upon an ample circulating medium. Colonial opposition to paper money was therefore ambivalent at least, and one royal governor, William Burnet of New York, even defended the practice as a means of expanding credit to generate more trade and business.

Credit was itself still another problem in the colonies. Merchants customarily extended credit to each other and to shopkeepers, who in turn sold goods on credit when necessary. Merchants and planters also lent money at interest, whenever the risks seemed reasonable, to small manufacturers and artisans setting up in business. But farmers found it extremely difficult to obtain credit for the purchase of land, livestock, or other necessities. The idea of emitting currency secured by land originated in England. Massachusetts first issued such paper money in 1715, but in 1739 Governor Jonathan Belcher announced a policy of contraction. With the anticipated recall of some £250,000 in public notes by 1741, private capitalists in Massachusetts grew alarmed. Nearly four hundred men from over sixty towns thereupon pooled resources to establish a private bank.

Many of the subscribers were substantial property owners who recognized the need for easier credit and more currency. The land bank was prepared to issue £150,000 in notes as loans secured by land or in some cases by personal property. In addition to a three percent interest, borrowers were to repay the principal in twenty annual installments, in land bank bills, or in certain commodities like hemp and iron, which were acceptable. But the Massachusetts Land Bank never succeeded, because of fierce opposition first from a rival group of bankers, then from Governor Belcher, and finally from Parliament, which applied an ex post facto law to close it down.

The Land Bank controversy caused major divisions within the colony and embittered many inhabitants of Massachusetts Bay toward the mother country for its peremptory act of nullification. But worse was to come. In 1751 Parliament severely limited the issuance of paper money by the New England governments, and in 1764 all the colonies were prohibited from issuing paper money as legal tender. The latter legislation came as a particular blow to colonies like Pennsylvania, which had managed its currency in such conservative fashion that depreciation was minimal. Currency and credit remained major financial problems in colonial America right up to the outbreak of the Revolution.

FURTHER READINGS

An excellent general approach to colonial economic development is Stuart Bruchey, *The Roots of American Economic Growth, 1607-1861* (New York, 1965). For the development of agriculture, see Percy W. Bidwell and John I. Falconer, *History of Agriculture in the Northern United States, 1620-1860* (Washington, D.C., 1925) and Lewis C. Gray, *History of Agriculture in the Southern United States to 1860* (2 vols., Washington, D.C., 1933). Significant regional studies include Avery O. Craven, *Soil Exhaustion as a Factor in the Agricultural History of Virginia and Maryland, 1606-1860* (Urbana, 1926); David Doar, *Rice and Rice Planting in the South Carolina Low Country* (Charleston, 1936); and Stevenson W. Fletcher, *Pennsylvania Agriculture and Country Life, 1640-1840* (Harrisburg, 1950). The background for a study of colonial commerce is provided by Charles M. Andrews, *The Colonial Period in American History,* vol. IV (4 vols., New Haven, 1938). Special aspects are covered by Robert G. Albion, *Forests and Seapower: The Timber Problem of the Royal Navy, 1652-1862* (Cambridge, 1926); Joseph J. Malone, *Pine Trees and Politics: The Naval Stores and Forest Policy in Colonial New England, 1691-1775* (Seattle, 1964); Bernard and Lotte Bailyn, *Massachusetts Shipping, 1697-1714: A Statistical Study* (Cambridge, 1959); Charles C. Crittenden, *The Commerce of North Carolina, 1763-1789* (New Haven, 1936); Roland M. Hooker, *The Colonial Trade of Connecticut* (New Haven, 1936); Arthur L. Jensen, *The Maritime Commerce of Colonial Philadelphia* (Madison, 1963); Arthur P. Middleton, *Tobacco Coast: A Maritime History of Chesapeake Bay in the Colonial Era* (Newport News, 1953); Daniel Mannix and Malcolm Cowley, *Black Cargoes* (New York, 1962); Richard Pares, *Yankees and Creoles: The Trade Between North America and the West Indies before the American Revolution* (London, 1956); and Stuart Bruchey, ed., *The Colonial Merchant: Sources and Readings* (New York, 1966). For artisans, Carl Bridenbaugh, *The Colonial Craftsman* (New York, 1950) and Lawrence C. Wroth, *The Colonial Printer* (New York, 1931) are excellent studies. Colonial labor in general is discussed by Marcus W. Jernegan, *Laboring and Dependent Classes in Colonial America*...(Chicago, 1931); Richard B. Morris, *Government and Labor in Early America* (New York, 1946); and Abbot E. Smith, *Colonists in Bondage: White Servitude and Convict Labor in America, 1607-1776* (Chapel Hill, 1947), while John Hope Franklin, *From Slavery to Freedom: A History of American Negroes* (2d ed., New York, 1956); David Brion Davis, *The Problem of Slavery in Western Culture* (Ithaca, 1966); Lorenzo J. Greene, *The Negro in Colonial New England, 1620-1776* (New York, 1942); and Winthrop D. Jordan, *White Over Black*...(Chapel Hill, 1968), contain useful sections on the role of the blacks in colonial America. For piracy, see John F. Jameson, ed., *Privateering and Piracy in the Colonial Period: Illustrative Documents* (New York, 1923). For currency questions, see Curtis P. Nettels, *The Money Supply of the American Colonies before 1720* (Madison, 1934) and George A. Billias, *The Massachusetts Land Bankers of 1740* (Orono, 1959).

6

Colonial Society

The society of colonial America as seen by the settlers themselves was comprised of several ranks or classes of men. In making distinctions, the colonists generally recognized occupation, style of living, but most of all property. At the top were the very wealthy, at the bottom the dependent poor, and in between the "respectable" men of the middle class. Though colonists took for granted that their society should be divided into these general classes, they did not assume that any individual family's place was forever fixed within one rank or another. What one did, and how well he did it, rather than his family name, was what ideally determined a man's proper place on society's ladder. The colonists realized how much mobility there was between the classes, and social change was a familiar fact of their lives.

Another fact they accepted, "with resignation" as they would have said, was that life with its dangers, disease, and sudden death, was a struggle. Hardships were a commonplace; the mere acquisition of food, shelter, and clothing absorbed the everyday energies of a majority of colonial Americans. Travel was difficult, and communication no more swift than a man could move on horseback over wretched roads. Most colonists lived perforce in relative isolation, unaware of much that went on more than fifteen or twenty miles away. America in the eighteenth century was indeed a provincial society.

The Structure of Colonial Society

The problem of dividing any society into classes centers on the problem of definition. Economic lines of distinction that would set apart a planter worth £ 600, for example, from a neighbor worth only £450 seem so arbitrary today as to be meaningless. To differentiate between men solely by their occupations, on the other hand, would ignore the fact that one farmer might own a thousand acres from which he harvested a marketable wheat crop each year, while another might only scratch out a bare existence from his twenty-five acres of rocky hillside. Clearly a combination of these two variables, property and occupation, must be recognized in determining the structure of society in colonial America. Even so, any delineation is bound to be somewhat arbitrary.

At the bottom of the ladder stood the blacks, whether slave or free, representing about twenty percent of the population throughout the English settlements in 1760, and nearly forty percent of the southern colonies alone. Also at the bottom were white indentured servants and other landless whites, including urban laborers, farm workers, and the foot-loose who lived on the fringe of organized society. Perhaps one-third of all Americans, black and white, comprised this lowest stratum of colonial society. At the other extreme was the upper class — the wealthy planters, merchants, and professional men whose property and personal prestige commanded respect from those of lower stations. Not more than one in fifteen settlers, about seven percent of the total population, merited such distinction, although here the line of demarcation is more difficult to draw.

The majority of colonists, around sixty percent, fell into the large, amorphous middle class — the farmers, the artisans, the storekeepers. The historian might if he wished divide this class in turn into lower, middle, and upper strata. Subsistence farmers, artisans who owned half a house and a few tools only, and the struggling rural storekeeper were at the bottom. At the top, of course, were the market farmers whose estates fell somewhat short of being plantations or manors. The wealthy artisan, such as a Philadelphia miller or a skillful New England shipwright, and the successful shopkeepers of the larger seaports, were likely to be found among the upper middle class. The majority of the middle class, constituting perhaps a third of the total population of the colonies, formed the heart of American society.

The gulf between these ranks varied considerably from place to place. In rural areas of the northern colonies, particularly in frontier regions, distinctions were least pronounced. To the limited extent that wealth alone is a guide, the fact that the top ten percent of New England's population controlled only twenty-five percent of the property suggests the relatively egalitarian nature of society. In the seaports, however, the distribution of wealth was less well balanced. In Portsmouth, New Hampshire, for instance, the wealthiest ten percent accounted for nearly half the taxable property of the town, while in Salem and Boston the ratio was even higher. New York, Philadelphia, and river towns like New Castle, Delaware, reflected a similar pattern in the concentration of wealth.

Social distinctions were also somewhat sharper in the plantation colonies of Maryland, Virginia, and South Carolina than in most northern provinces. For here the possession of a plantation and a large slave-labor force not only suggested greater wealth but a somewhat distinctive life style as well. The wealthiest ten percent of southerners owned forty percent of the property, significantly higher than the twenty-five percent controlled by wealthy northerners. At the other end of the scale, a larger proportion of white southerners owned no land at all, perhaps more than a third, while another third possessed modest holdings of less than 500 acres. The southern middle class, while smaller than its northern counterparts, nevertheless formed an important segment of society, especially where it engaged in commercial farming, as in the Chesapeake region. Subsistence agriculture was largely confined to the frontier regions of the Carolinas, where transportation to the seacoast was difficult.

Eighteenth-century commentators on the American scene frequently noted how egalitarian American society was by European standards. While the condition of the slave was far worse than that of Europe's most impoverished classes, among the ranks of freemen property was distributed far more evenly. Observers particularly commented upon the absence of a landed aristocracy in the European sense, cloaked in privilege by both law and custom, and controlling vast reserves of wealth and power. What struck most commentators about America, however, was the high degree of social and economic mobility. The structure of society itself remained relatively unchanged; that is, the proportions of the population distributed among the lower, middle, and upper ranks remained more or less stable throughout the eighteenth century. But a family's place on that ladder might vary considerably through the course of two or three generations.

Two factors stand out as producing much of this vertical mobility in colonial America — the availability of cheap land on the frontier and the rapid growth of population, particularly in the eighteenth century. Throughout most of the colonial period, many people, discontented with life in established communities, moved to virgin parts of the continent in search of new opportunity. Thus settlement spread into the Piedmont of Virginia, into the Connecticut Valley of New England, into the interior regions of New York and Pennsylvania, and down the Great Valley of Virginia into the back country of North and South Carolina. By the outbreak of the Revolution, this tide of internal migration — horizontal mobility, the social scientists have labeled it — reached full flood, as newcomers to America joined the sons and daughters of eastern settlers in search of cheap land "further on."

The movement into the interior, however, failed to absorb more than a fraction of the steadily increasing population, which doubled every twenty to twenty-five years. As families swelled at geometric rates, parental farms were divided among the several sons, until the holdings became too small for further division. But this increased density of population in the established areas of settlement brought new demands for the services of blacksmiths, millers, and other artisans. Furthermore, villages became towns, and towns expanded into small cities. One result was the revolution of agriculture brought on by the rising demand for foodstuffs in the urban centers. Farmers who formerly struggled along at subsistence level found markets for surplus production, and a more complex commercial economy came into being.

Another result of urbanization was the creation of new opportunities in the cities and towns for those youngsters who were crowded off the family farm but who had no desire to head west for cheaper land. This urban frontier, as it would be called at a later stage in American history, offered the best chance of all for advancement in the eighteenth century. Many a young man learned a trade as an apprentice to a master craftsman and then opened business for himself. Others worked their way up in the mercantile field from the humble beginnings in the fo'c'sle of a small coasting sloop. A few learned a profession like law or medicine and took their places in the forefront of colonial society.

One need not look far to find impressive examples of inhabitants who "made it big" in eighteenth-century America. The most famous without doubt was Benjamin Franklin. His own life exemplified the "rags to riches" theme throughout, from his humble arrival in Philadelphia in 1723, and his establishment of a printing business so successful that he could retire on £1,000 a year by 1748, to his recognition during the Revolution as America's senior statesman. Beyond all that, however, Franklin's writings on the subject of personal advancement established him as an authority in his own lifetime. His immensely popular *Poor Richard's Almanac* was salted throughout with aphorisms, many of them borrowed from other sources, which served as handy guideposts for those seeking to improve their lot. "Experience keeps a dear school, yet fools will learn in no other." "If you will have it done, go; if not, send." "He who riseth late, must trot all day, and shall scarce overtake his business at night." In 1758 Franklin published his last *Poor Richard's*, with an introductory essay best known now as "The Way to Wealth," which obviously struck a responsive chord among tens of thousands of Franklin's fellow Americans, although it greatly oversimplified the sage's own personal values. By the eve of the American Revolution the dream and the reality of opportunity had become the anthem for a continent of people.

The New Americans

The population of the English colonies in America, which stood at about 250,000 in 1700, increased tenfold in the next seventy-five years, to reach two and one half million at the Declaration of Independence. Advancing even more rapidly than the overall average was the number of blacks, which, by 1775, had risen from less than 30,000 to about 500,000. In addition to the natural increase of blacks already here, continued importation of slaves from Africa averaged about 5,000 a year during the middle decades of the century. A handful of blacks did gain their freedom in the New World.

For some of them, particularly those in northern seaports, ingenuity and hard work brought a degree of security despite the enormous odds of race prejudice, which in most colonies denied them the right to hold property, to vote, and to find protection under the laws. For the hundreds of thousands of blacks in slavery, however, America represented little more than the prolonged agony of a life spent in perpetual bondage.

The white population of the American colonies was also swelled by a flood of immigrants from Europe. We have already seen that many arrived as indentured servants and redemptioners during the eighteenth century. Still others came as freemen, particularly from England. A closer look at this immigration will reveal what a diverse ethnic group comprised the population of colonial America on the eve of the Revolution. Were all these people, as Michel Guillaume Jean de Crèvecoeur observed in 1782, truly "melted into a new race of men"?

One of the largest groups emigrating to America in the eighteenth century were the Germans. Devastation during the War of the Spanish Succession from 1701 to 1713, and particularly the harsh winter of 1708-09, brought grinding poverty to central Europeans. In the years immediately following, thousands of Germans fled their homeland, first to England and then to America. In 1710 several hundred settled at New Bern, North Carolina, under the leadership of Baron de Graffenried, a Swiss nobleman. But the colony was virtually wiped out by Indians two years later, and the survivors scattered to other settlements. Somewhat more successful was a group of Palatines headed by Conrad Weiser, whom the British sent to the Hudson Valley the same year to produce naval stores. They were unused to the work, however, and the government failed to provide promised support. An attempt to re-establish themselves in the Schoharie Valley met with resistance from scheming landlords, and the group was once again forced to scatter. Some settled in the Mohawk Valley, where many of their compatriots subsequently joined them.

A more significant movement, however, was the one led by Weiser from the Schoharie into Pennsylvania's Susquehanna Valley in 1723, where the group settled on the fertile lands around Lancaster and York. Religious freedom, clear titles to good soil, and a benevolent colonial government thereafter attracted the main flow of

German immigrants to the Quaker colony, where many of them have managed to retain their old-world culture intact well into the present century. The Pennsylvania Dutch, or *Deutsch,* proved themselves skilled farmers, wagon-makers, and ironmongers, adding greatly to the prosperity of their adopted homeland.

The next largest group of Europeans immigrating to America in the eighteenth century were the Scots. About 50,000 came directly from Scotland, but three times that number emigrated from their new homes in Northern Ireland, where a number of Scotsmen had been settled since early in the seventeenth century on lands the English had confiscated from the Irish. Naturally their Irish neighbors resented the incursion, and border fighting became a way of life for the Ulster Scots. Soon other difficulties befell them. In 1699 the English Woolens Act prohibited the export of their principal product, woolen cloth, to England. As their original leases began to expire after 1715, the Scots found their absentee English landlords doubling and tripling their rents. Religious squabbles with the Church of England and a succession of crop failures added to their woes.

Beginning in 1718, groups of Scots-Irish, often led by their Presbyterian ministers, began to immigrate to the English colonies in America. Because they were Calvinists, they sought homes in New England, where at first they were accorded a friendly reception. Cotton Mather, for instance, though suspicious of the newcomers, recognized that a string of Scots-Irish settlements along the frontiers of Massachusetts Bay would make a fine barrier against the Indians. One group settled at the mouth of the Kennebec; others in Worcester, Pelham, and Colrain; and still others founded settlements like Londonderry in New Hampshire. Many Yankees feared the Ulstermen would strain the region's food resources; many were alarmed at the large numbers of "foreigners" invading their country. The Scots were somewhat short-tempered themselves, and it was not long before serious trouble broke out. Even before the burning of a Presbyterian church in Worcester, Scots-Irish began steering away from New England in favor of New York, New Jersey, and particularly Pennsylvania.

The Scots-Irish joined the Germans in the interior of the Quaker colony, and when conditions became more crowded in the 1730s, many settlers of both nationalities migrated southwestward down the Great Valley of Virginia as far as the Carolinas. Rich land was plentiful in the broad mountain valleys, and the Scots often took up occupation without too much regard to the legalities. These settlements, like those in the interior of New England and the middle colonies, protected other settlements to the east against Indian attacks. Moravians founded a community at Wachovia, later Winston-Salem, North Carolina, and Palatine Germans coming overland from Charleston settled in the Piedmont of South Carolina. For the most part, these regions remained cut off from direct contact with the coast by the mountains and pine barrens, and these western settlers were left to develop a life style of their own.

Among other newcomers to the colonies in the eighteenth century were the Scots Highlanders. After the Battle of Culloden in 1746, many of Bonnie Prince Charlie's defeated supporters preferred emigrating to continued life under English domination at home. They were joined by a number of Scots soldiers, discharged in America after the French and Indian Wars, who elected to remain in the New World. Continuing poverty in Scotland, climaxed by a serious depression in 1772, brought yet another wave of Scotsmen to America, many of them with valuable training as weavers and mechanics. Here they found work alongside the English, Welsh, and French Protestant artisans who had come over earlier and whose ranks continued to grow by steady numbers throughout the eighteenth century.

With the smaller enclaves of Dutch, Jews, and Scandinavians, who had come to America during the seventeenth century, these new immigrants from Germany, Scotland, and Ireland further diluted the dominant English strain within the American population. Despite Crèvecoeur's suggestion that the American environment somehow melted these people into a new race, recent historians have found strong evidence that most of these national groups retained strong ties with their European past for several generations. Cultural pluralism, rather than amalgamation, seems a better description of the American social fabric by mid-eighteenth century.

Total domination by the English majority was challenged in numerous regions by one or more of the various minorities among the settlers. Certainly the influence of a half-million blacks had a profound effect in the southern colonies, where they amounted to about forty percent of the total. In Pennsylvania, where one out of three settlers was German and another third came from other non-English stock, language, customs, and religion reflected a broad cultural background. In New York and New Jersey, the Dutch continued to leave a distinctive mark on the pattern of life. Even on the frontier, ethnic groups tended to remain together rather than to mix with those of other backgrounds. It was in the seaports that Americans of different national origins lost most of their cultural identification. There Apollos De Revoire became the father of Paul Revere, and the pure-bred Irishman Patrick Tracy could become an Anglican with no questions asked.

Domestic Life

Generalizations concerning the daily lives of American colonists in the eighteenth century must be modified by the realization that conditions varied between northern and southern planters, between villagers and rural farmers. But the simple yeoman who worked his land with assistance only from members of his family was representative of most colonists. Furthermore, certain basic conditions and customs affected almost all colonial Americans. First was the fact, more meaningful in the seventeenth century than later, that mere existence in the New World was a struggle. The stark reality of survival in a hostile environment continued to influence the pattern of life for Americans living on the fringe of civilization. While few colonists actually starved after the first generation had passed, disease, Indian attacks, and accidents in the woods or at sea were among the most common perils throughout the colonial period. Writing in 1790, from years of medical practice, Dr. Benjamin Rush found that of one hundred persons born in a given year, less than half reached the age of sixteen and barely one-fourth the age of twenty-six. Medical knowledge was no worse in the New World than in the Old, but physicians were scarce, particularly in the rural areas, where most Americans lived. Death was a frequent visitor to colonial households.

A second common characteristic of American life was the idea of the extended family, a practice brought from Europe. In addition to his parents and numerous sisters and brothers, a colonial child often shared his home with at least one grandparent, an unmarried uncle or aunt, and perhaps a cousin whose mother had died. As the years advanced, his brother might bring a wife into the household, and soon thereafter nephews and nieces would join the family group. It was not uncommon to find households numbering twelve or fifteen, as generations succeeded generation in working the family acres. Large families served an important economic function, for in an era before mechanized methods of farming or labor-saving devices in the home, many hands were needed to provide the necessities of life. Furthermore, in a period when the church offered almost the only organized social activities, the companionship of a large family fulfilled an important social function as well.

Still another characteristic of life in colonial America was the value that society placed on labor. For most Americans, hard work was a virtue — for almost all of them, it was a necessity. The most opulent merchant and the wealthiest planter regularly worked a full six-day week, devoting little time to leisure activities. Even as prominent a planter as George Washington found it desirable to deal with the most minute details of his operations directly, and only the Carolina rice barons made a habit of absenting themselves from their plantations during the growing season. Furthermore, employers placed a high premium on the labor of other men, paying good wages for free laborers and often working alongside their slaves to assure efficiency.

These values were reflected in the institution of marriage. Only rarely did love guide the choosing of a life partner. More often, the parents arranged the match, although the young people could usually refuse to cooperate if unwilling. Dowries were common among the upper classes, particularly among northern merchants and southern planters, but matrimony for most Americans was far less formal. Indeed, along the western frontier itinerant preachers often found themselves marrying couples and baptizing their first-born all in the same visit. The practice of "bundling" was widespread and often more productive than folklore has suggested. Woman's fertility (male sterility was rarely discussed) was important, and besides, contrary to current belief among today's youth, our ancestors enjoyed sex too. Add to that the vulnerability of servant girls to the attentions of male servants, and the custom of early marriages becomes more understandable. One informal survey of a mid-eighteenth century community in New England suggests that the first-born of one out of four marriages arrived less than seven months after the ceremony.

Once married, the young couple either moved in with the in-laws for awhile, or built a house on their own land. In the northern colonies the structure was invariably of wood post-and-beam construction, solidly built around a center chimney, which served as stove and oven for cooking as well as "furnace" for heating. Simpler houses had but two ground floor rooms, perhaps with a sleeping loft above, but wealthier families added a couple of back rooms, thus giving the "saltbox" house its characteristic shape, or built a house with a full second story. In the middle and southern colonies one found many brick and stone houses, along with conventional frame construction. Southerners preferred end chimneys, both because they depended less on fireplaces for heat and because a hallway through the center opened the house to cooling breezes. Overhanging front porches — or verandas — offered southerners a shady place to relax. On the frontier, both in the north and south, pioneers often built log cabins as their first homes, while directing their main energies into the clearing of the land. Some villagers lived in row houses, often substantially built of brick, more frequently of wood. Still others owned or rented half of a house, usually divided sectionally so that each family had a part of the ground floor.

A high rate of infant mortality partially compensated for the absence of birth-control knowledge. While many wives bore a dozen or more children, on the average only half survived to adulthood. Childbirth itself took a grim toll of young mothers, matching the pace at which accidents carried off their husbands. Thrice-married persons were no rarity, and the frequency of this "natural" change of partners helps to explain the relatively low divorce rate in colonial America. The other reason was that in the Anglican colonies such legal separation was extremely difficult to attain, although New England Puritans were more understanding. Divorce was in fact about the only legal recourse a woman had because under the law she had little standing apart from her husband. In most colonies statutes even authorized husbands to beat their wives "when necessary." Women, like slaves and livestock, were expected to be grateful for such kindly attentions.

After the first generation or two, American families rarely faced the possibility of starvation, except perhaps during a particularly hard winter along the frontier or during an Indian war. Plenty of meat was close at hand from both wild and domesticated animals. Pork ranked high in popularity. Pigs were easy to raise, and their meat could be smoked, salted, or dried for preservation in an age without refrigeration. Most Americans lived near streams, ponds, or the ocean, and fish became an important part of their diet. Shellfish like clams and oysters were also popular, though more difficult to preserve by salting or pickling. Indian corn played a central role, not only as a vegetable but as the basis for bread and puddings as well. Colonists also acquired the pumpkin and squashes from the Indian, but the potato that became common in the eighteenth century was an import from Ireland. Most farms had a cold cellar, which kept foodstuffs over the winter, and more affluent households had their own smokehouses.

Despite their best agricultural efforts, however, almost all Americans remained dependent upon the outside world for several necessities. Salt, sugar, and spices all came from overseas, and those who would drink tea (increasingly popular in the eighteenth century), coffee, or chocolate had to trade with the local storekeeper. Whiskey, beer, and cider, on the other hand, could be manufactured at home, along with fruit brandy and a crude wine, but the cellars of wealthier colonists were stocked with the best Madieras, ports, and brandies from Spain and the Wine Islands. Those who could not afford sugar for sweetening settled for molasses, and many householders, especially in New England, purchased a barrel of Philadelphia superfine flour rather than try to raise wheat and have it milled themselves.

The combination of an abundance of wood and the skill of the American colonists provided a wide range of necessary utensils for home and farm. With the help of the local blacksmith for iron fittings, the clever yeoman made his own hand tools, wagons and pungs, buckets, boxes, and barrels. In the kitchen his wife often worked with bowls and plates laboriously turned out from hard wood. In more substantial households ironware, pewter, and occasional pieces of china could be found by the mid-eighteenth century, and of course most of the cutlery had also to be imported from the mother country. The enterprising farmer's wife made many of her family's clothes herself, partly from cloth purchased at the local store and partly from homespun, especially the popular "linsey-woolsey," a blend of linen and wool. On the frontier, deerskin jackets and leather breeches were common items of apparel. At the other extreme, wealthy planters and city dwellers were already aping the fashions of Georgian London, with brocade breeches, silk stockings, and gowns copied from the latest English fads. The sumptuary laws of the previous century, which had restricted the wearing of lace, buckles, and jewelry to "the better sort" had passed from the scene by the early eighteenth century. Even youths and artisans sometimes sported powdered wigs by the eve of the Revolution. The daily lives of most colonists, however, reflected a far simpler style, one determined by utilitarian values rather than by high fashion.

Urban Life

Europeans visiting America in the middle of the eighteenth century stood in amazement before the sprawling urban centers they found along the Atlantic seaboard. While far smaller than the major capitals of Europe, to be sure, they were nevertheless large by the standards of the day, and Philadelphia, with a population of about 25,000 on the eve of the Revolution, in size ranked with every English city but London. While most colonists still lived in the country, the rise of urban centers was a notable development of the eighteenth century. By 1760, the dynamic elements in American life — culturally, socially, as well as economically — were found not in rural hamlets but in cities like Philadelphia, New York, Boston, Savannah, Baltimore, and Newport. Here began the long process, not yet ended, of urban domination of America.

Not by accident, all but one of the twenty largest urban centers in colonial America were located on tidewater, most of them on the banks of rivers that reached far into the interior. For the eighteenth-century city was a seaport, an entrepôt into which goods from all over the British empire flowed, both for local consumption and for distribution throughout the neighboring countryside, in exchange for marketable crops. Even the one exception, Lancaster, Pennsylvania, commanded the northern entrance of the Great Valley of Virginia in much the same manner that New York City controlled the Hudson Valley. Throughout the period, merchants and shopkeepers improved their methods of retailing goods. Each man tended to specialize in particular commodities — dry goods, hardware, or foodstuffs, for instance. Many merchants sold at retail in addition to supplying storekeepers throughout the interior region dominated by that port. Farmers usually sold their produce at a central market, such as Boston's Faneuil Hall, built in 1742. Here the proceedings fell under strict regulations to curtail abuses such as the sale of low-quality produce at exorbitant prices. Even so, the market place did not eliminate those mutual suspicions and recriminations that have long divided country folk from the city dwellers.

Their role as seaports brought several special problems to these rising cities. In the first place, most were bound on two or even three sides by water. Newport and New York were in fact on islands, while Boston could be reached from the mainland only over a narrow peninsula. Philadelphia, Charleston, and Norwich were wedged at the confluence of two rivers, and other seaports were similarly confined. As these communities expanded through the mid-century decades, space became a premium, real estate prices soared, and congestion set in. By 1760, Philadelphia was a city of nearly 3,000 buildings, many of them new but many more in substandard condition. New construction soared in cost as nearby timber grew scarce. Row houses, tenements, and combination shops and homes became the order of the day. Ports were also exposed to attack by sea. Forts, batteries, and facilities for British troops and naval squadrons had also to be provided for as well as customhouses. Roving bands of visiting sailors, bringing the diseases of a score of foreign ports, caused serious problems. Still more people flocked in from the countryside to sell their produce and purchase needed manufactures and other wares. The city of eighteenth-century America paid a high price for the privilege of being at the hub of the action.

Mere size converted what were minor headaches for all communities into major problems for urban centers. For instance, the task of obtaining sufficient firewood taxed the city-dweller. Cordwood and coal brought premium prices during a midwinter cold spell in the New England seaports. Other towns suffered from a scarcity of good drinking water; not only did nearby salt water often seep into the wells, but the proximity of outhouses and other sources of urban pollution were equally hazardous. Food was less of a problem, for the neighboring farmers were of course eager to bring their surpluses to market, and fish remained plentiful throughout most of the year.

For most village and rural communities in America, a simple form of town or parish meeting set policy guidelines for the volunteer selectmen or vestrymen who carried out day-to-day governmental responsibilities. Public affairs in the larger urban centers, however, demanded a more sophisticated structure, although this fact was not always recognized. Boston did not become a municipality until well into the nineteenth century. Upward of two hundred officials were chosen each year to struggle with the task of running the city. Much of what was gained from the sense of participation inherent in this system was lost in such inefficiency as the casual approach to his duties exhibited by Samuel Adams while tax collector from 1756 to 1764. In contrast to the New England communities, New York was by mid-century an incorporated city, with aldermen, and councilors elected by freemen voting in wards, and presided over by a mayor. Philadelphia's corporation was self-perpetuating, on the other hand, creating major friction as the population grew.

Among the problems that public officials had to face, probably care for the poor ranked first both in importance and in cost. A constant flow of immigrants into the cities swelled the lists of indigents who became public charges. Urban areas probably harbored a larger number of unemployables — the drunks, the feeble-minded, and the physically handicapped — than did rural communities. As seaports, these cities included a large proportion of widows and orphans, because of the high mortality rate among mariners and fishermen. In Boston, for instance, very nearly one out of every three adult women was a widow. Orphans were generally bound out until the age of twenty-one as apprentices to local craftsmen, thus learning a trade while relieving the overseers of the poor of additional responsibilities. Another reason the public burden did not mount still higher was the rise of numerous charitable societies. Some of these organizations, such as the Boston Marine Society, for instance, were in reality small mutual life insurance concerns, whose members contributed annually to a fund made ultimately available to their widows. Other groups directed their interests to the society around them, like the "Female Charitable Society" that could be found in almost any seaport. Despite help from such voluntary organizations, cost to the public for care of the poor mounted steadily. In Charleston it had reached £6,000 by 1760 and would climb still higher in the next few years.

The city had also to bear the cost of building and maintaining streets and walks and to provide for the carrying off of sewage. In these regards American communities earned higher marks than most of their European counterparts. Boston and New York paved most of the major streets with stone and managed to keep them fairly clean, though Philadelphia's record in these respects was less laudable. Most of the cities had some sort of underground sewer system by mid-century, its effectiveness somewhat reduced by the fact that it usually emptied into nearby waters. Many households still used the familiar necessary house, and night soil was frequently dumped into the open gutter despite regulations to the contrary. The high number of horses and oxen on the streets simply complicated the task of public cleanliness.

Closely related to the problem of sanitation stood matters of public health. By the middle of the eighteenth century, considerable knowledge had been gained in the fight against many kinds of epidemics. Bounties on rats and strict quarantine of incoming vessels successfully guarded against bubonic plague in America. The two contagious diseases most dreaded were yellow fever and smallpox. Little was known about the causes of either threat, but most cities maintained a hospital often on an island in the harbor, where those willing could be inoculated against smallpox and thus increase the chance of survival tenfold. Much remained to be done in these areas, however, and not until the nineteenth century did Americans in general come to appreciate the significance of sanitation to public health.

Fire ranked next to epidemics as the greatest hazard faced by urban dwellers, though through the years remarkably few individuals lost their lives in the conflagrations that periodically swept through almost every city. Wooden frame buildings packed closely together, numerous barns and stables stored with hay for horses, and of course the universal reliance on fireplaces for heat and cooking all made fire an everyday threat. In addition, each town seemed to have its plague of arsonists, disaffected servants and slaves perhaps, or unruly youngsters. Sooty chimneys overheated, ignited shingled roofs, and quickly set the structure ablaze. Surprisingly often the fire-watch quickly reported the fire, and the volunteer companies turned out on the run with their pumps and buckets to subdue the flames. But occasionally the blaze gained too great a start on a windy night, and by morning acres of buildings lay in ashes with property losses reaching £100,000 or more. In response to such disasters, the residents of communities throughout the colonies passed the hat to raise relief funds, the victims of Boston's fire of 1760 receiving over £13,000 from sympathizers in all parts of the empire.

The eighteenth-century city had more than its share of the hurly-burly disorder that man has come to associate with urban life. Carters, coaches, and men on horseback seemingly vied with each other in an effort to ride down pedestrians and little children along the narrow and busy streets. Pickpockets wandered through the crowded market place in daylight, while nightfall brought out the ubiquitous footpads who waylaid their victims along the dark passages of the town. Drunks, prostitutes, counterfeiters, and common thieves wandered through the streets with virtual impunity. Many of those who were incarcerated experienced little difficulty escaping from the rickety structures that served as jails. But capture was unlikely, for most cities could provide fewer than a dozen constables to keep order. On extraordinary occasions like Pope Day, the small force of officers had no hope of preventing the riots that annually marked November 5 throughout British America. Little wonder that the authorities stood by helplessly as mobs took to the streets to protest British policies in the years preceding the Revolution.

For some, the city did provide a more genteel way of life in addition to the amenities that one might encounter in the homes of wealthy citizens. Public parks like the Boston Common, New York's Bowling Green, and the Philadelphia Commons provided some open ground under shade trees, where citizens could escape the frenetic pace of life. Taverns and coffeehouses offered good food, a quaff of beer, or tote of rum, and most of all good conversation with one's friends. Here the local news went the rounds and out-of-town journals kept readers abreast of the times. Wealthier residents joined social clubs of various types, the Masonic Order gaining many lodges during this period. But for most urban dwellers the city remained a noisy, dirty, but exciting opportunity to escape the particular demands that rural life expected of the individual. Only for a few could the reward of success have been worth the price.

FURTHER READINGS

The most valuable study of American society in the late eighteenth century is Jackson T. Main, *The Social Structure of Revolutionary America* (Princeton, 1965). For the southern colonies, Carl Bridenbaugh, *Myths and Realities: Societies of the Colonial South* (Baton Rouge, 1952) and for an urban area, Carl and Jessica Bridenbaugh, *Rebels and Gentlemen: Philadelphia in the Age of Franklin* (Philadelphia, 1942) are especially useful. For immigration in general, see Marcus L. Hansen, *The Atlantic Migration, 1607-1860: A History of the Continuing Settlement of the United States* (Cambridge, 1940), and for various non-English groups, the following books are recommended: Donald Douglas, *The Huguenot: The Story of the Huguenot Emigrations, Particularly to New England* (New York, 1954); R. J. Dickson, *Ulster Emigration to Colonial America, 1718-1775* (London, 1966); Ian C.C. Graham, *Colonists from Scotland: Emigration to North America, 1707-1783* (Ithaca, 1956); Wayland F. Dunaway, *The Scotch-Irish of Colonial Pennsylvania* (Chapel Hill, 1944); A. B. Faust, *The German Element in the United States* (2 vols., New York, 1909); Lee M. Friedman, *Early American Jews* (Cambridge, 1934); and George F. Donovan, *The Pre-Revolutionary Irish in Massachusetts, 1620-1775* (Menasha, 1932). Two indispensable studies of family life are Edmund S. Morgan, *The Puritan Family: Religion and Domestic Relations in Seventeenth Century New England* (rev. ed., New York, 1966) and *Virginians at Home: Family Life in the Eighteenth Century* (Williamsburg, 1952). Mary S. Benson, *Women in Eighteenth-Century America: A Study of Opinion and Social Usage* (New York, 1935) remains the only such survey. Among the useful studies of population are Evarts B. Greene and Virginia D. Harrington, *American Population before the Federal Census of 1790* (New York, 1932) and Stella H. Sutherland, *Population Distribution in Colonial America* (New York, 1936). For life in urban areas, see Carl Bridenbaugh, *Cities in the Wilderness, The First Century of Urban Life in America, 1625-1742* (New York, 1938) and *Cities in Revolt: Urban Life in America, 1743-1776* (New York, 1955).

7

American Culture

The early immigrants to America brought with them few of their cherished possessions from the Old World, aside from a trunk or two of clothes and perhaps some household utensils. But these first colonists, and all who followed in their footsteps, brought intangible possessions as well — their ideas and customs — in short, their culture. The process of transplanting old ideas in the soil of the New World almost always led to an altered product. New England Puritanism, for instance, despite its origins in Old England, evolved along lines quite different from the religion of those Puritans who had remained behind in the old country. The impact of the New World environment upon Old World ideas largely determined the development of colonial American culture.

Because Americans came from varied European backgrounds, however, and because they settled in different parts of the American continent, regional differences in education, architecture, and religion, for instance, quickly developed. Well might one question whether, by 1760, there was indeed a single American culture at all.

Education and Science

As in all societies, education was of central importance to the cultural development of colonial America. In New England, where

Puritans believed that each man should be able to interpret the Scriptures for himself, the ability to read had a religious significance as well. Massachusetts Bay had, from the middle of the seventeenth century, required towns with more than 100 families to maintain both an elementary and a grammar school. Although numerous communities failed to comply, significant numbers of young Puritans acquired at least the rudiments of an education during the colonial period. These schools were maintained partly by taxation and partly by tuition charged to those parents who could afford it. Only children of the poor attended free. An elected school committee hired the teachers and established educational policy. At first, the curriculum included a considerable amount of religious instruction, but by the beginning of the eighteenth century these schools were predominantly secular in nature, focusing on the fundamentals of grammar and arithmetic. New England children probably received a better education than most children in the mother country.

In the middle colonies, however, public education was slow to develop. At the end of the seventeenth century, New York could boast of only one schoolteacher, and most young scholars in Pennsylvania had to rely on privately endowed schools until nearly the end of the colonial period, despite William Penn's efforts to establish a public system. Yet it was Benjamin Franklin who contributed the first significantly new ideas that shaped American education. In his *Proposals Relating to the Education of Youth in Pennsylvania* (1749), he argued that its students be taught "those things that are likely to be *most useful* and *most ornamental;* regard being had to the several professions for which they are intended." Young people should study history, he suggested, because it would teach them the importance of oratory, public religion, and constitutions. The great aim of all learning, Franklin maintained, was to develop the student's ability to serve mankind. Though public response to these ideas was slow at first, Franklin's emphasis on the practical pointed out a new direction for American education.

Population in the southern colonies was spread too thin for the establishment of public schools except in a few communities like Norfolk and Charleston. Some Anglican ministers offered instruction to neighboring planters' children on a tuition basis, and scattered throughout the region were a few privately operated institutions. Some planters hired tutors to live with the family and to instruct their youngsters, while others sent their sons to the best English schools. But the children of the middle-class farmers in the southern colonies had no such opportunity. Illiteracy stood as a class distinction throughout the colonial period.

Higher education gained relatively widespread public support, especially by the middle decades of the eighteenth century. Harvard, founded in 1636, continued to graduate a handful of young men each year, most of them bound for the ministry. Virginia's Anglicans established the College of William and Mary in 1693 to assure a supply of young men for their pulpits, while in 1701 Yale College began to train still more young men for the Congregational ministry. As the century progressed, Anglicans in New York sponsored King's College (later Columbia), Baptists set up Rhode Island College (renamed Brown) and Presbyterians the College of New Jersey (later Princeton) at Elizabethtown.

While denominational affiliations gave most colleges in colonial America their start, the secularization implicit in Franklin's proposals for an academy in 1749 had begun to affect higher education also. The charter of the College of Rhode Island stated that one purpose of the institution was the "preserving in the Community a Succession of Men duly qualified for discharging the Offices of Life with usefulness and reputation . . . ." The three earliest colleges were closely tied to their various colonial governments, dependent upon the legislatures for economic support. Yet the colonial colleges were in no sense "popular," since they served only a small fraction of Americans. Costs, the curriculum, and the farmer's need for his sons' labor at home all restricted college attendance to as few as one out of one thousand colonists up to the time of the Revolution. As historian Frederick Rudolph has pointed out, "the college had long been a necessity for society," as a source of political and church leadership, "but it had not become a necessity for the people."

For most colonists, the world of experience was their only classroom. As with many other peoples of the eighteenth century, most Americans were fascinated by their natural surroundings. Recording meteorological observations was a common hobby as men yearned for a more scientific explanation of the weather. A letter to Peter Collinson in 1755 concerning a small wind gust illustrates how inquisitive Benjamin Franklin could be. "It appeared in the form of a sugar-loaf . . . 40 or 50 feet high." Franklin was intrigued, and he pursued the whirlwind on horseback, trying to break it with his whip, to no avail. "I accompanied it about three quarters of a mile," he reported, "till some limbs of dead trees, broken off by the whirl, flying about, and falling near me, made me more apprehensive of danger."

One of America's first Newtonian scientists, Harvard Professor John Winthrop, taught his students and Bostonians in general that mysterious conditions and changes in the world around them resulted from natural law and not from a capricious God. It was man's duty to understand these laws, and Winthrop applied his knowledge of mathematics to this end. His work in astronomy gained his election to the Royal Society of London. Another mathematician, Philadelphia's David Rittenhouse, used his skills as an instrument maker to build an orrery, a working model of the solar system. The turn of a crank propelled each planet along its orbit around a large brass sun in the center, while three pointers indicated the hour, day, and year thus represented. This complicated mechanism in its own way epitomized the Americans' efforts to make understandable the natural world around them.

To both English and American botanists, the New World offered a fascinating display of flora and fauna unknown to Europeans. Philadelphia's father and son team, John and William Bartram, traveled throughout the colonies to make observations and to take collections for their botanical gardens. William's published account of a journey to the southern colonies included a description of a shrub which he and his father named *Franklinia,* in honor of their fellow Philadelphian. In the same volume, Bartram included his observations of the Cherokee Indians, a careful study remarkable for its objectivity.

Franklin's reputation as a scientist rested mainly on his work in the field of electricity. His letters to the Englishman Peter Collinson described in great detail the results of his efforts to generate and to store electricity as well as his experiments with the kite. Franklin was the first to realize the tentative nature of his findings. In August 1747, several months after sending Collinson two long descriptions of experiments, he was forced to admit that "I have [since] observ'd a Phenomenon or two that I cannot at present account for on the Principles of those Letters . . . . If there is no other Use discover'd of Electricity, this, however, is something considerable, that it may *help to make a vain man humble.*"

A number of Americans applied their scientific knowledge in a practical way to the field of medicine, struggling to overcome one of the most myth-ridden aspects of seventeenth- and eighteenth-century life. Among the most serious diseases were dysentery, measles, influenza, diptheria, and smallpox. Colonists had no miracle cures for these ills, but they experimented with herbs and other remedies learned from the Indians, sometimes with good effect. Quinine, ginseng, sassafras, and even tobacco had their adherents, although only the first-named proved particularly helpful. Most doctors were of little help to the seriously ill, for the vast majority of the practitioners were self-taught; only one in twenty was an M.D. But by the Revolution two medical schools had been established as well as several hospitals. Quarantine for the crews of incoming vessels had become a general practice, and the officials of larger communities had begun to show a concern for public sanitation.

The most noteworthy American contribution to the field of medicine was undoubtedly inoculation for smallpox, a practice first tried on a large scale in Boston in 1721, at the urging of the Reverend Cotton Mather. Despite considerable success, inoculation met with violent opposition from many inhabitants. Some worried about contracting the disease at all, of course; others were concerned about the legality of the practice. But a sizable number of colonists objected to inoculation as an interference into God's right to destroy those individuals and communities which displeased him. Not until the Revolution was inoculation widely accepted in America.

By the end of the colonial period, developments in education, science, and medicine reflected the general preference among Americans for the practical aspects of life rather than the theoretical. In virtually every field of learning, the colonists sought new ways to apply their knowledge. A people who in the next two centuries would become famous for their engineers had in their early history already demonstrated an aptitude for solving practical problems.

Reading and Writing

The paucity of formal education among the American colonists is somewhat misleading, for the ownership of books and the habit of reading were rather widespread according to most contemporary accounts. Only a few Americans possessed libraries as extensive as the nearly four thousand volumes owned by New England's Cotton

Mather or Virginia's William Byrd. But countless families could claim at least a Bible, a volume on household medicinal remedies, probably a classical history, and perhaps a volume or two on law. The more literate colonists would have added some modern history, a practical book such as *The Complete Gentleman* or *Of Domestical Duties*, and probably a guide to better agricultural methods or animal husbandry. Ministers of course held extensive collections of printed sermons and other theological tracts, while lawyers and government officials leaned toward works like Sir Thomas More's *Utopia* or Sir Edward Coke's *Reports*. Except for an occasional volume of poetry, perhaps by Anne Bradstreet or Michael Wigglesworth, the average colonist spared little time for diversionary reading, at least not until the generations of the later eighteenth century. The establishment of public libraries and perhaps more significant private "subscription" groups such as Franklin's famous Library Company of Philadelphia gave city dwellers access to far larger collections of books than they could possibly have accumulated for themselves.

While reading became increasingly popular with the advent of free time for many urban dwellers in the mid-eighteenth century, the skills of creative writing remained somewhat more elusive for most native Americans. Their concern with the practical aspects of life led a number of colonists to write histories of the New World, or at least of their own colony, often as a means of encouraging emigration from the Old World or to justify their position in some on-going dispute. The best of these histories is Thomas Hutchinson's *History of the Colony of Massachusetts Bay*, written at the end of the colonial period. As a long-time official of the colony and a member of one of its most distinguished families, Hutchinson had access to numerous historical documents upon which he based his colonial writing. Virginia's most accomplished historian, Robert Beverley, served for years in various official positions in the colony's government. His *History and Present State of Virginia*, published in 1705, was a frank appraisal of prominent planters and the colony they were building. The most famous colonial history, William Bradford's *Of Plymouth Plantation*, showed little effort on the part of Plymouth's first governor to achieve an objective view of that colony's first years. As an historical document in itself, however, Bradford's *History* gives an invaluable account of the Pilgrims' struggle for survival.

The most popular topic in the writings of colonial Americans was religion. The better known ministers published many of their sermons, while both ministers and laymen wrote all sorts of religious tracts in both prose and verse form extolling the virtues of a Christian life. The most ambitious undertaking, Cotton Mather's *Magnalia Christi Americana*, published in England in 1702, was a religious history of New England, its leaders, and its institutions. By extolling the greatness of New England's seventeenth century, Mather hoped to instill new zeal into the religious lives of generations to come. Later Jonathan Edwards, in his accounts of his experiences during the Great Awakening, strove toward a similar goal. Indeed, it would be difficult to exaggerate the dominance of religion as the principal theme in American literature, at least until the controversy with Great Britain after 1760 unleashed its flood of political tracts.

Another favorite theme of American writers was the Indian, and especially the colonists' relations with him. The "Indian captivity" story never failed to command a wide readership. Mary Rowlandson's account of her capture at Lancaster during King Philip's War, was republished in 1720 so that eighteenth-century readers could cringe with her. "Now is that dreadful hour come, that I have often heard of . . .," she related. "Some in our House were fighting for their lives, others wallowing in their Blood, the House on fire over our heads and the bloody Heathen ready to knock us on the head if we stirred out." Rowlandson and other chroniclers did not spare their readers a single gory detail in describing the brutalities of frontier war.

For better or for worse, the most widely read American writers were undoubtedly the compilers of almanacs and the editors of newspapers. Here, once more, America's preference for the practical dominated colonial tastes. Both of these kinds of publications gave the colonists the facts they needed to carry on their lives in the New World. To be sure, an inventive printer like Benjamin Franklin livened up his almanacs and newspapers with entertaining bits and pieces, but the main purpose of both publications was to satisfy his readers' craving for facts.

The most famous colonial almanac was of course *Poor Richard*, first published in 1733 by Franklin at Philadelphia. Because much of the information was regional in nature, such as times of sun and moon rise and high tide, printers in each of several major cities published almanacs for their own readers. Perhaps weather predictions took on greater authenticity in these regionalized editions, although it is doubtful that readers placed much dependence on this feature of the almanac. To men seeking the explanation of unpredictable occurrences in their lives, astrological data and the motions of the planets throughout the year had considerable appeal. Of more practical use were the dates of court sessions, Quaker meetings, and fairs. Many readers used their almanacs as miniature diaries, squeezing data about the weather and other occurrences into vacant spaces and along the margins. Franklin sold about 10,000 copies of *Poor Richard* each year despite the fact that rival printers published at least a half-dozen other almanacs in his area.

The first successful newspaper published in the colonies was the *Boston News-Letter*, founded in 1704 by John Campbell, who as postmaster had access to news from near and far. Scarcely more than 300 readers subscribed to the weekly in its early years, but, with aid from the General Court, Campbell remained in business. Within two decades newspapers were founded in both New York and Philadelphia, while the *News-Letter* acquired two local rivals. By mid-century, Maryland, Virginia, and South Carolina had their own journals, and a German-language paper was established in Pennsylvania. In 1764, at the beginning of the controversy with Great Britain that would bring an upsurge in circulation, there were twenty-three newspapers scattered throughout all the colonies save New Jersey and Delaware, with an average subscription list of over 500. Total readership was much higher, since each copy probably reached a half-dozen readers. Of course several newspapers failed to survive competition from rivals printed locally or in nearby cities, but Benjamin Franklin proved that a printer could indeed become moderately wealthy by combining the publication of a newspaper and an almanac with the office of public printer.

The typical colonial newspaper appeared weekly in a four-page format of small print generally in four columns. Headlines, illustrations, and editorials in their present form were unknown, and one had to read with great care to sort the wheat from the chaff. The front page was usually given over to a continuing excerpt from a moral essay or philosophical treatise lifted verbatim from an English edition. The inside pages contained the news, or "advices," generally beginning with "Foreign intelligence" ranging from the progress of the war between the Turks and the Russians, say, to the announcement of the safe delivery of the Duchess of Warsaw's thirteenth child. News from England included parliamentary proceedings, happenings at court, and such remarkable occurrences as the birth of a two-headed calf in Hampshire. The printer then turned to items from other American colonies, generally beginning with those most distant and working steadily closer to home. As in the case of foreign news, domestic advices were almost always copied verbatim from newspapers brought from distant parts by returning shipmasters or through the mails. Very little space was given to local news because communities were small enough for inhabitants to know what happened close to home. The last page of most newspapers contained four nearly solid columns of advertisements, some of them decorated with a standard cut of a runaway servant, a standing horse, or a sailing vessel, depending on the nature of the services sought or offered. Newspapers published in seaports also contained a marine list, cataloguing the arrival and departure of vessels. As in the case of other popular publications, the colonial newspapers provided information both necessary and interesting to the colonist who would keep abreast of the times.

The Arts

Colonists migrating to the New World from rural districts of the mother country brought with them the culture of rural England. In architecture, for instance, Puritan settlers longed to move out of the improvised shelters they had first constructed into two-storyed homes modeled after the Tudor houses they had remembered from the Old World. Very soon, however, New World conditions brought forth a distinctly American form of domestic architecture. Most seventeenth-century colonial homes had been dominated by a mammoth chimney, which served at first as one end of the house. As increasing wealth permitted, larger structures were built around a center chimney, with kitchen and chamber fireplaces providing both cooking and heating facilities. The saltbox house, common in the eighteenth century, was another development from simpler origins, achieved by extending the rear roof line almost to the ground to permit the addition of several back rooms.

For the most part, architectural styles remained relatively simple throughout the eighteenth century. The home of a prosperous farmer consisted of three or four rooms on each of two floors, but most colonists probably made do with two or three rooms altogether. Regional differences were reflected both in style and in building materials. The abundance of timber in New England made wood the almost universal material for domestic construction, but in the middle and southern colonies stone and brick houses were a more common sight. National differences also accounted for the varying architectural styles found, for instance, in New York and Pennsylvania, where Dutch and German influence remained strong.

In the seaports and on an occasional tidewater plantation one would find more pretentious structures reminiscent of the town houses of London or the country estates of Suffolk. Many a wealthy merchant or planter designed his own home with the generous assistance of English books on architecture. Philadelphia's Independence Hall was designed by the lawyer Andrew Hamilton; Peter Harrison, "the first American architect," was a merchant in Newport before he began designing buildings. The Redwood Library building and synagogue, both in Newport, and King's Chapel in Boston remain as monuments to his ability. Most public structures, perhaps even more than domestic structures, reflected styles prevailing in Georgian England. The Governor's Palace at Williamsburg, as well as the Capitol and the Wren Building at William and Mary, illustrate the style of the period.

In furnishings as in architecture the colonists owed much to English designs. Cabinetmakers relied heavily upon such books as Thomas Chippendale's *The Gentleman and Cabinetmaker's Directory*, but the best American craftsmen, like Benjamin Randolph of Philadelphia, and Newport's John and James Goddard, put something of themselves into each piece. For the common folk, Boston joiners turned out chairs and tables by the hundreds for export to other colonies, but Philadelphia's craftsmen remained preeminent in the field of furniture-making, even shipping hundreds of Windsor chairs to the New England colonies by the middle of the eighteenth century.

Because safe investments of commercial profits remained scarce during most of the colonial period, many merchants converted their earnings into silver. The surviving work of such masters as Joseph Richardson, John Coney, and Paul Revere are today mostly found in museums, but their original owners took great pride in using and displaying the knives, trays, and pitchers that represented the profits of a prosperous mercantile venture. The utensils used in most households, however, were wrought from pewter, brass, and iron. And in the country, of course, homemade wooden utensils were a commonplace.

The prints and paintings that adorned the walls of colonial mansions were mostly imported from England, for the colonies could boast of few really talented artists. In some of the major seaports, however, engravers like Paul Revere sold likenesses of prominent personages and views of historical events, such as the siege of Quebec or the Boston Massacre. Only two or three Americans achieved distinction as portrait painters during the colonial period. John Singleton Copley, the self-taught son of a tobacco shopkeeper, painted outstanding portraits of Boston's great citizens in the years just before the Revolution. Philadelphia-born Benjamin West gained his artistic reputation in London, where he welcomed other American artists such as Copley and Maryland's Charles Willson Peale as students. West, like Copley, never returned to his native country, although his influence over the development of American art remained strong.

As in the case of other art forms the not-so-great people of America had their own artists. Limners they were called, craftsmen of little training and often of still less skill, who offered their services to potential clients in cities and towns throughout colonial America. The resulting portraits more often than not had a woodenness to them that revealed little of the character or warmth of their human subjects. Almost all of these would-be artists painted shop signs and houses as a means of support when the portrait business was slow. For despite the vanity inherent in all men, not many Americans had either the time or the money to invest in portraits or to encourage those around them with true artistic talent.

Of the various art forms, probably the theater suffered most because of New World conditions. Seventeenth-century inhabitants found little time for such diversion, and besides, the Puritans in Virginia as well as those in New England strongly opposed theatrical entertainment. Nor did the Quakers regard the art any more kindly. By the beginning of the eighteenth century, however, traveling companies increasingly overcame these and other obstacles until by the 1750s New York, Charleston, Philadelphia, and Williamsburg, among other centers, boasted theaters. Despite the growing popularity of dramatic productions, Philadelphia's Thomas Godfrey stood alone as the colonies' only accomplished playwright. Other forms of entertainment offered the public included waxworks, elephants and other exotic animals, and teams of trapeze artists. Scientific demonstrations, particularly those involving electrical experiments, drew large audiences, as did a number of the lecturers who journeyed from town to town.

The most popular form of entertainment in colonial America was undoubtedly music. Psalm-singing played an important role in the church services of almost every major denomination in America except the Quakers. Because Puritan scruples did not permit the playing of musical instruments during religious services, the psalms were "lined out" by the minister or a member of the congregation. In 1640, New Englanders even published their own edition, popularly known as the "Bay Psalm Book," the first book printed in the English colonies. Anglicans and most other denominations encouraged the playing of music in church, and, after the turn of the century, the singing of hymns was accompanied by the organ.

Concerts and recitals, like theatrical performances, did not become popular in the colonies until the more leisurely decades of the eighteenth century. Thereafter traveling groups of musicians offered concerts in Boston, New York, and other urban centers. In 1762 interested citizens in Charleston founded the St. Cecilia Society to support a professional orchestra. American-born composers, however, were even more scarce than playwrights during the colonial period, though numerous amateurs dabbled with their own arrangements and variations of popular hymns.

By the eve of the Revolution, American craftsmen were producing the vast majority of furnishings, utensils, and other domestic tools used in the colonies, and of course all the buildings erected in America. In the skill of construction, if not in the originality of design, American artisans were the equal of their English and European counterparts. In the more decorative art forms like painting and in such fields of entertainment as theater and music, however, the colonists lagged far behind their European cousins. Once again the preference for the practical influenced the direction of creativity in colonial America.

Religion

American religious life in the eighteenth century was characterized by the appearance of a large number and variety of sects. This "latitudinarianism," as it was later called, resulted both from the policy of religious toleration practiced by several of the settled colonies and by the fact that there was an abundance of vacant space in which new communities could find homes. Meanwhile, in those colonies like Massachusetts Bay, first established upon religious principles, worldly concerns had since seriously tempered the spiritual zeal of the founding generation. Special exceptions had been made to the rules for membership to permit the less inspired descendants of the founding generation to participate in church affairs. Puritans were not the only ones experiencing such difficulties. Although Pennsylvania's Quakers maintained a strong hand in the political affairs of the colony, their religious principles continued to meet with severe opposition. In southern colonies, where religious institutions had never been strong, spiritual life declined still further. Bored by the style of religion that had once excited their ancestors, eighteenth-century Americans were ripe for a revolutionary change in the style of religious life.

That change came during the 1740s in a movement known as the Great Awakening. Through the early decades of the century, a revival had stirred thousands of ordinary Europeans to a new religious enthusiasm. Despite its European background, however, the Great Awakening was also distinctly American. The movement varied somewhat from colony to colony because it was everywhere the response of the common people to the conditions of their particular society. At the same time the Awakening had in all the colonies certain characteristics in common, in its origins and progress as well as in its effects.

Isolated outbursts of religious enthusiasm periodically disturbed the calm New England countryside during the 1720s. Then, in the middle of the next decade, a revival swept through the Connecticut Valley town of Northampton, where the young minister Jonathan Edwards had been calling for a return to the stricter Calvinism of the seventeenth century. Specifically, Edwards challenged the doctrine of "preparation," a kind of Arminianism that maintained man could by the use of his reason determine the will of God and thus prepare himself to become a more likely recipient of God's saving grace. The swelling ranks of the Anglican church, which had always been receptive toward Arminianism, stood as testimony to the appeal of this doctrine to many Americans. Edwards chose to fight this trend rather than to drift along with the tide as many of his fellow ministers were doing. By publicizing his stand and the startling effects it had on his congregation, Edwards prepared his many readers for the coming of change. He also suggested that the revival of religious spirit would bring the long-awaited millennium, the coming of God's Kingdom on earth.

What finally precipitated the Great Awakening in America was the arrival of George Whitefield in 1739. The work of this great English evangelist was already known in the colonies, and, beginning with his reception in South Carolina, his sermons generated an infectious enthusiasm wherever he went. When a Connecticut farmer learned that Whitefield was to preach in nearby Middletown one morning, "I was in my field at work," he later recalled. "I dropped my tool...and ran home to my wife telling her to make ready....I with my wife soon mounted the horse and went forward as fast as I thought the horse could bear...." As the pair approached Middletown they heard the rumbling of horses' hooves and saw a great cloud of dust rising over the valley. When they reached the meeting house several thousand people were already there, with hundreds more pressing on toward the town. "When I saw Mr. Whitefield come upon the scaffold," the farmer reported, "He looked as if he was clothed with authority from the Great God..., and my hearing him preach gave me a heart wound. By God's blessing, my old foundation was broken up," the farmer concluded, "and I saw that my righteousness would not save me." Here in the words of an ordinary Connecticut farmer was the sum and substance of the Great Awakening. For thousands of inhabitants throughout the colonies the "old foundations" were indeed broken up as they saw that "righteousness" was no guarantee of salvation.

The Great Awakening was more than a revival; it also stirred up a major religious controversy, as "Old Side" Presbyterians and "Old Light" Congregationalists dug in their heels against the winds of change. The Presbyterian Synod of Philadelphia insisted that all its ministers subscribe to certain articles of faith and refused to accept graduates from the Log College founded in Pennsylvania by the

Scots-Irish evangelist William Tennent in 1735. In New England the "Old Lights" fought to preserve the integrity of their church organization as "awakened" New Englanders forsook their former ministers to establish their own parishes under "New Light" leadership. Like their "New Side" Presbyterian brethren of the middle colonies, these men rejected outside control of their religious lives.

But the significance of the Great Awakening went far beyond these jurisdictional disputes. Boston's Charles Chauncy, spokesman for the opponents, challenged the revivalists' methods, particularly their appeal to the "passionate" side of man in preference to his reason. Thus the central theme of the Great Awakening was one of human psychology. "From the time of Calvin," as historian Perry Miller has pointed out, "the focus of Calvinist thought and of most Protestant thinking had been the will of God; the great divide that we call the Awakening forced both American parties, whether proponents or opponents, to shift the focus of analysis to the nature of man." For Edwards there was no arbitrary division between man's reason and his senses. Rather, man understands by his whole self being affected with "a sense of the heart," as he put it. In so arguing, Edwards anticipated the modern view of psychologists that man is a "living unit."

Anglicans, Establishment Congregationalists, and, less actively, the Quakers continued their defense of the *status quo* in the decades after the Great Awakening. But the future appeal of religion in America lay in the hands of those sects that gained strength from the Great Awakening — the Methodists, the Baptists, and the "New Side" Presbyterians. Chauncy's emphasis on reason led ultimately to William Ellery Channing's liberal Unitarianism in the early nineteenth century. But the line that had significance in the further democratizing of religion in America was that which could be traced from Edwards' broad concept of human psychology to the Transcendentalism of Ralph Waldo Emerson. In the words of historian Alan Heimert, "what was awakened in 1740 was the spirit of American democracy."

Even while the Great Awakening was running its course, a number of other significant developments brought more gradual change to the patterns of religion in colonial America. As a flood of immigrants continued to pour in from all corners of Europe, they strengthened older denominations and brought over new ones as well. By the middle of the eighteenth century Lutheran, Reformed, and Moravian joined the numerous Pietist sects already firmly implanted in the middle colonies. The ranks of Roman Catholicism also grew. One result was a gradual weakening of the domination exercised by established Congregational and Anglican churches. Religious toleration was crammed down the throats of reluctant defenders of the *status quo* until even the Congregationalists of Massachusetts had to permit dissenters to divert their compulsory religious taxes to their own churches. This was an important first step in weakening the bond between church and state, which ultimately led to the principle of free and voluntary exercise of religion, so important to the nation soon to emerge.

Defined in its narrowest sense, the culture of mid-eighteenth-century America still reflected its English origins. Most books came from the mother country, as did traveling theatrical groups and much of the music sung by the colonists. In the fields of architecture and the domestic arts, the styles set by Wren, Chippendale, and other leading craftsmen of Georgian England became the models for American artisans. Even so, the New World had begun to make subtle changes in many of the old English forms, changes which varied somewhat from region to region. The architecture of Virginia, for instance, differed from that of Pennsylvania, and the books read in Annapolis were not always those preferred by subscribers to Boston's circulating libraries. But running through the varieties of cultural styles found in the several colonies were certain common characteristics that reflected a distinctive American way of life. The importance of education as a means of getting ahead; a preference for the practical over the theoretical in the arts, reading habits, and the sciences; and a spirit of individualism and freedom in religion might be pointed out as peculiarly American values that were emerging by the middle of the eighteenth century.

FURTHER READINGS

Among the many useful surveys of colonial American culture are Louis B. Wright, *The Cultural Life of the American Colonies, 1607-1763* (New York, 1957); Thomas J. Wertenbaker, *The Golden Age of*

Colonial Culture (New York, 1942); and Michael Kraus, *Intercolonial Aspects of American Culture on the Eve of the Revolution*...(New York, 1928). The most helpful regional studies include Samuel E. Morison, *The Intellectual Life of Colonial New England* (2d ed., New York, 1956); Frederick B. Tolles, *James Logan and the Culture of Provincial America* (Boston, 1957); Louis B. Wright, *The First Gentlemen of Virginia*...(San Marino, 1940); and two works by Thomas J. Wertenbaker, *The Old South: The Founding of American Civilization* (New York, 1942) and *The Founding of American Civilization: The Middle Colonies* (New York, 1938). For education, see Bernard Bailyn, *Education in the Forming of American Society: Needs and Opportunities for Study* (Chapel Hill, 1960); Robert Middlekauff, *Ancients and Axioms: Secondary Education in Eighteenth-Century New England* (New Haven, 1963); Guy F. Wells, *Parish Education in Colonial Virginia* (New York, 1923); Edmund S. Morgan, *The Gentle Puritan: A Life of Ezra Stiles, 1727-1795* (New Haven, 1962); and Samuel E. Morison, *Three Centuries of Harvard, 1636-1936* (Cambridge, 1936). Two classic studies of early American literature are Vernon L. Parrington, *Main Currents in American Thought*..., Vol. I, *The Colonial Mind* (New York, 1927) Moses C. Tyler, *A History of American Literature, 1607-1765* (2 vols., New York, 1878). The writing and uses of history are the subjects of H. Trevor Colbourn, *The Lamp of Experience: Whig History and the Intellectual Origins of the American Revolution* (Chapel Hill, 1965) and Peter Gay, *A Loss of Mastery: Puritan Historians in Colonial America* (Berkeley, 1966). Three excellent introductions to early American science are Whitfield J. Bell, *Early American Science: Needs and Opportunities for Study* (Williamsburg, 1955); Brooke Hindle, *The Pursuit of Science in Revolutionary America* (Chapel Hill, 1956); and Raymond P. Stearns, *Science in the British Colonies of America* (Urbana, 1970). Medical matters are discussed in John B. Blake, *Public Health in the Town of Boston* (Cambridge, 1959) and Wyndham B. Blanton, *Medicine in Virginia in the Eighteenth Century* (Richmond, 1931). For art and architecture, see Walter M. Whitehill, *The Arts in Early American History: Needs and Opportunities for Study, An Essay* (Chapel Hill, 1965); Louis B. Wright, *et al.*, *The Arts in America: The Colonial Period* (New York, 1966); Hugh S. Morrison, *Early American Architecture: From the First Colonial Settlements to the*

National Period (New York, 1952); Carl Bridenbaugh, *Peter Harrison: First American Architect* (Chapel Hill, 1949); and the pioneering study by John W. Reps, *The Making of Urban America: A History of City Planning in the United States* (Princeton, 1965). Alan Heimert, *Religion and the American Mind from the Great Awakening to the Revolution* (Cambridge, 1966) provides a helpful overview, while more specialized studies of the Great Awakening are Wesley M. Gewehr, *The Great Awakening in Virginia, 1740-1790* (Durham, 1930) and Edwin S. Gaustad, *The Great Awakening in New England* (New York, 1957).

8

England and America
at Mid-Century

The British nation that would stand triumphant on the heights of Quebec in 1759 had undergone significant changes since the first band of colonists had left its shores more than 150 years before. Out of the revolutions of 1640 and 1688 emerged a stable system of government which despite obvious imperfections seemed to satisfy the vast majority of England's limited electorate throughout the eighteenth century. As a mercantile nation, England was without equal, and its navy was more powerful than the combined fleets of the next two powers, France and Spain. In short, Britannia had come of age as Europe's premier nation-state.

The English colonies in North America, meanwhile, had been developing partly in the image of the mother country, and partly in response to the different conditions of the New World. As American soldiers shared the triumph of their English compatriots in 1759, the two peoples stood at a crossroads. The major problem they faced concerned the British empire, which bound them together. What was the nature of this empire and how should it be administered? To comprehend the answers that the next generation offered to these questions, we must first examine the mother country and its colonies at mid-century.

The Colonial Wars

The eighteenth century was barely two years old when war broke out once again among the leading European powers, this time to settle the question of a successor to the throne of Spain. As in the case of the conflict between England and France just ended (The War of the League of Augsburg, or King William's War), the War of the Spanish Succession was also fought in America, where it was named for the reigning British monarch, Queen Anne. Now for the first time English southern colonies became embroiled, for Carolinians posed a threat to both Spanish and French interests in Florida and along the Gulf coast. To the north the war followed a now-familiar pattern. New Englanders captured Port Royal again, as they had done in 1690, but a climactic attack against Quebec once more ended in disaster. Of several fierce raids by France's Indian allies, perhaps the most memorable was that against the village of Deerfield, Massachusetts, in February 1703. Over one hundred of its inhabitants were taken into captivity, in the words of one of them "carried away from God's sanctuary, to go into a strange land . . . . the journey being at least three hundred miles . . . , the snow up to the knees . . . , the place we were to be carried to, a popish country."

Britain's most significant triumph during Queen Anne's War took place in the Caribbean, where her fleets established firm mastery of the seas. After a decade of struggle, both sides wearied of warfare, and a sweeping peace was signed at Utrecht in 1713. By its terms Great Britain obtained both Nova Scotia and Newfoundland, as well as recognition of her claims to Hudson's Bay. In addition, she retained Gibraltar and Minorca, both of which she had captured from Spain. England was well on her way to becoming the queen of the seas and the dominant colonial power in the New World.

To be sure, France had been ousted from her stronghold at Port Royal in Nova Scotia, but soon after the Treaty of Utrecht she established an even more formidable bastion at Louisbourg, on Cape Breton Island. Here she could defend the entrance to the St. Lawrence River effectively and send out privateers against New England shipping should war again break out with Great Britain. Retaining the right to dry fish on the shores of Newfoundland, the French fishing fleets once again swarmed over the Grand Banks to the consternation of English and Yankee mariners. Through her trading relations with Indian tribes of the interior, France could still command a sizable force of fighters for the kind of warfare that had characterized the struggle thus far. While the Treaty of Utrecht marked a turning of the tide in favor of Britain, in the battle for North America the French were not yet to be counted out.

An uneasy peace continued between the major European nations for twenty-five years, during which the rapidly maturing English colonies in America gained still greater strength both economically and in population. When the so-called War of Jenkins' Ear erupted between Spain and Great Britain in 1739 over maritime disputes, Americans under Georgia's founder, General James E. Oglethorpe, attacked Spanish Florida, though without success. Later in the war, over three thousand colonial troops joined a British expedition against Cartagena, the Spanish stronghold in New Granada (Colombia). The campaign ended in disastrous defeat, with some two thousand Americans dying in battle or from yellow fever. Colonists also outfitted privateers to prey on Spanish shipping. In 1744, France joined Spain in what then became the War of the Austrian Succession in Europe and King George's War in America. The scene of battle shifted once again to the Canadian frontier. The New England colonies promptly organized an expedition under the leadership of the New Hampshire merchant William Pepperrell to capture Louisbourg. Brilliant tactics and a good deal of luck brought success to the Yankee venture, and the French fortress fell after a campaign that lasted six weeks. Settlements along the New England and New York borders came under attack from France's Indian allies. But the greatest loss suffered by Americans took place at the peace table in 1748, when the British diplomats returned Louisbourg to the French in return for Madras, the province in India that had fallen to the enemy. New Englanders were understandably furious at this decision, and their enthusiasm for cooperating with the mother country in its perennial wars with France was at least temporarily dimmed.

The showdown between France and England in America came shortly after mid-century. While the struggle soon became merged with the Seven Years' War in Europe, its American version was more aptly called the French and Indian War. In general, of course, its causes lay in the century-old rivalry for domination of the North American continent. But while that struggle had previously been confined mainly to the New York and New England frontiers, in the years after 1750 the Ohio River valley became a new theater of battle. Here both England and France had equally plausible claims to sovereignty, for neither power had settlers in actual occupation of the disputed lands. Rather, traders of both nationalities traveled among the various Indian tribes selling their wares and purchasing furs. In 1752, the aggressive new governor of New France, the Marquis Duquesne de Menneville, decided to establish a chain of forts along the upper branches of the Ohio River in what is now western Pennsylvania. This move threatened the interests of the Ohio Company, a group of Virginians including Governor Robert Dinwiddie, who held patent to several hundred thousand acres in the area. Virginia's House of Burgesses reluctantly voted funds to construct rival forts in the region and authorized an expedition under Major George Washington to protect the workers from attack. But the young militia officer was met by a superior French force at his temporary encampment named Fort Necessity, and in July 1754 was obliged to retreat. The Ohio Valley remained in French hands, and it was to take a greater effort than that of one colony to dislodge them.

Great Britain was still at peace with France in Europe and had thus far shown little real interest in the outbreak of hostilities in western Pennsylvania. Many of the other English colonies in America were concerned, however, and delegates from seven of them met at Albany in the summer of 1754 to consider a defensive union. Although the conference adopted a plan drafted by Benjamin Franklin, none of the individual colonial legislatures would ratify it. When full-scale war broke out soon after, lack of coordination among the colonies as well as between British and American forces was once more a major hindrance to military success.

After Washington's defeat, however, British leaders took alarm at the spread of French power into the Ohio valley, and in early 1755 dispatched several regiments to America under the command of General Edward Braddock. The plan was to capture Fort Duquesne (later Pittsburgh) and three other French strongholds along the Canadian border before war was formally declared. In June Braddock was finally ready to launch an expedition against Fort Duquesne. With him were 2,500 troops including Thomas Gage and George Washington, who twenty years later would face each other as rival generals across the parapets at Boston. On 9 July, Gage led the vanguard of the expedition into a combined force of French and Indians, who promptly took to the woods on either side of the trail and caught the British in a withering crossfire. Utter confusion broke out among the Redcoats as one contingent after another blindly pressed into the pocket. At day's end, British and American casualties amounted to one thousand. Braddock was mortally wounded, and the remaining troops were in full retreat, hardly an auspicious beginning. French and Indian losses totaled less than sixty.

Expeditions against Fort Niagara in western New York and Crown Point on Lake Champlain also failed that year, although without the disastrous casualties experienced at Fort Duquesne. The attack on Fort Beauséjour, at the head of the Bay of Fundy, was the only successful British campaign of the year. And as a portent of further difficulties, several French ships bringing reinforcements slipped through the fog past British units blockading the Gulf of St. Lawrence. In 1756, the struggle became global in dimension, known as the Seven Years' War, and for two years British troops lost battles in Europe and India, as well as in America. Not until William Pitt became prime minister in 1758 did Great Britain gain the leadership it needed for successful prosecution of the war. With cool deliberation Pitt established long-range military objectives and kept to his overall plan. High on his list of priorities was the ambition to drive the French out of Canada altogether, leaving the war on the European continent to Britain's allies.

In 1758 the tide began to turn. An amphibious assault captured the French stronghold at Louisbourg, though with far greater casualties than experienced by Pepperrell's forces fourteen years before. Another expedition captured Fort Duquesne, which was promptly renamed Fort Pitt, in honor of Britain's prime minister. But these victories were only the beginning. The following year saw the British drive their opponents out of India, capture Fort Niagara, and establish control of the seas more firmly than ever. The stage was set for the climactic battle.

The capstone of Pitt's policy was a two-pronged invasion of the French capital at Quebec. Young General James Wolfe and his force of four thousand was skillfully transported up the St. Lawrence, but the expedition under Major General Jeffrey Amherst driving up the Lake Champlain route became stalled after capturing both Crown

Point and Fort Ticonderoga. Wolfe had to assault alone the nearly impregnable defenses held by some ten thousand French troops. After establishing strong points downstream of the city, the British general forced the French into open battle by putting his men ashore on the Plains of Abraham, just west of the city gates. In the sharp contest that followed on 13 September 1759, the British troops won a decisive victory. Although Wolfe was killed, the French promptly surrendered the city. Off the French coast later that fall the British turned back a fleet intending to bring reinforcements to Canada, and the conquest of New France was complete.

With the fall of Quebec, the fighting in North America ended, although not until 1763 were the final peace terms settled. By the Peace of Paris, France surrendered all its North American possessions except two small islands off Newfoundland and several of its sugar islands in the Caribbean, while from Spain Britain acquired East Florida. In addition, France turned over to its Spanish allies its vast domain in Louisiana. Although the French thus withdrew as a power in the New World, they would make their presence felt on this side of the Atlantic in decisive fashion during the American Revolution.

England at Mid-Century

The British nation that emerged from the Seven Years' War as the world's greatest power was not particularly large. England, Wales, and Scotland together embraced a population of about eight million in 1760, a figure that had increased only slightly during the previous one hundred years. Ireland had an additional three million people, but they were not regarded in the popular mind as "British." While Englishmen still lived on the land as farmers, London had become a crowded metropolis of 750,000 people. No other city in Great Britain topped one hundred thousand, although Bristol and Edinburgh were large. The movement from country to city was only just beginning to transform midland towns like Manchester, Birmingham, and Sheffield into major industrial centers. Every county had its market towns, with their cluster of shops and stalls, where farmers from the nearby villages brought their wares and made their purchases on market days.

Agriculture reigned supreme in eighteenth-century England as it had one hundred years before. But the life of the farmer in many parts of the realm underwent steady change during this period. The enclosure movement had by 1760 replaced the older open-field system in still more counties. Taking advantage of the kind of large-scale operations that enclosure permitted, some forward-looking landowners encouraged the development of new uses and methods for their holdings. Crop rotation, fertilizing, and manuring improved the soil in parts of Essex, Norfolk, and Suffolk, particularly. Drainage of swampy lands opened new fields in Lincolnshire. In several ways, enterprising farmers increased the yield of the land, especially in the cultivation of wheat. Major improvements were also made in the raising of livestock. New breeds of sheep were developed to provide meat rather than fleece. Beef cattle were the subject of other experiments. Sturdy work horses began to replace oxen on many farms in the middle and south of England. In the northern areas of the realm, as well as in Scotland, such changes came more slowly.

By 1760, England stood poised on the brink of an industrial revolution. The factory had not yet replaced the domestic system of production in textiles, but the home jenny increased output as did new machines in many other industries. Another development was the movement toward standardizing such handmade products as pottery and furniture, an important forerunner of mass production. The manufacture of cotton goods, centered at Manchester, was growing slowly and was not yet a threat to the supremacy of Yorkshire woolens. Laborers worked at home, weaving cloth, forging nails, or firing pottery from materials supplied by the capitalists. But numerous hardware goods and particularly heavy ironware could not be produced by the domestic system. As demand for these and other goods increased through the latter half of the century, the factory began to replace the home as the center of production in England.

While the vast majority of eighteenth-century Englishmen were farmers, industrial workers, or craftsmen (and sometimes a combination of these), a much smaller but equally important group sailed the seas. The English trader carried the surplus products of his countrymen — their woolens, pottery, and hardware — to scores of overseas markets in Scandinavia, on the European continent, and of course throughout the growing British empire. English ships returned with such luxuries and necessaries as tea, wines, cordage, linen, and naval stores. The men who manned the merchant and fishing fleets were also able, if not always willing, to serve aboard His Majesty's ships of war. Trade was important to England in yet another way. Government officials had discovered years ago that customs and excise taxes were a far less painful means of raising revenue than steady increases in the land tax. As a result, duties on commerce constituted a major source of income for the British government.

England of the mid-eighteenth century was, despite the gradual changes taking place in its economy, still a relatively stable society presided over by the landed gentry. The turmoil of the 1600s had ended, and the disruptions of the industrial revolution were still to come. The rigid lines that continued to separate one class from another were recognized by both sides. As one foreign commentator pointed out in 1755, "the Englishman always has in his hands an accurate pair of scales in which he scrupulously weighs up the birth, rank, and above all, the wealth of the people he meets, in order to adjust his behavior towards them accordingly." Upward mobility was only a little less difficult than a hundred years before. Essential in the process was still the acquisition of a country estate upon which to establish a basis for local influence. The ownership of land and the resultant income from rents enabled many gentlemen to pursue lives of leisure while wielding an impressive degree of power over the lives of other Englishmen, most of whom lived off the land or in country villages.

The landed squire and his children had almost exclusive access to the full range of educational opportunities. Private tutors prepared the sons for one of the independent grammar schools like Eton or Winchester, from whence the more scholarly went up to Oxford or Cambridge, though rarely staying long enough to take a degree. Only the gentry had the leisure and the money to spend time in London, the cultural center of the kingdom, returning to their country seats with an impressive veneer of the latest fads and fashions and, occasionally, new ideas about agriculture, education, or some other subject of concern to their neighbors. The squire also dominated the religious life of the community through his traditional power to place his own choice in the parish "living," as the local church position was called. As the wealthiest man in the neighborhood, the squire could, through his charities, shape its cultural values, reward the "industrious poor" with his support while ignoring the indolent, and in many other ways play the role of paternal leader.

More important than the squire's economic and social influence was the political power that resulted from it. Almost all the justices of the peace were in fact gentlemen, for one had to possess an estate that earned at least £100 a year to hold the office. Justices were appointed by the king, generally for life. Individually, each one sat as a local court to enforce the laws and to settle disputes among his neighbors. Collectively, the justices of each county sat as a court of quarter sessions. Since the king chose the county's other important officials, the lord lieutenant and the high sheriff, from the ranks of the squirearchy as well, the landed gentry completely controlled local and regional government. The only check to their power was the parish vestry, generally a self-perpetuating body, which established and collected the poor rate and served as fiscal watchdog over the local officials appointed by the justice. Practically speaking, however, a justice of England was left entirely free from interference by local or national officials. His only guide was his sense of duty to maintain the king's peace, with fairness to all.

The structure of local government differed from that of the counties, but the effect was often the same. A number of towns were in fact small villages controlled by the local squire. Most of the rest were run by a small group of wealthy tradesmen who formed the "corporation" and controlled the council and board of aldermen. In many towns these were self-perpetuating groups whose members sat for life, and who exercised not only the powers of justices of the peace but wielded considerable influence over the economic affairs of the community. In a few boroughs, London most notably, local government was broadly based among the shopkeepers and craftsmen, who elected members of the Court of Common Council or similar body. But most urban dwellers, like their country cousins, had no such choice of local officials. In the mid-eighteenth century, most Englishmen accordingly had no more control over the level of government that most influenced their daily lives than had their ancestors one hundred years before.

In the century and a half since the founding of England's first American colonies, the structure of national government had undergone several major changes. The dominant position enjoyed by the Stuart monarchs of the early seventeenth century fell victim (as did the king himself) to the forces of Parliament in the revolution of 1640. Parliament could not successfully rule alone, however, and the monarchy was restored in 1660. But the division of authority between the crown and Parliament was no clearer than before. Not until the settlement of the revolution of 1688 was a stable basis for national government re-established. Governmental authority was thereafter described as residing with the "King in Parliament," or with "the Crown, Lords, and Commons." In this compôte it was understood that the House of Commons took the dominant role. The king still chose the ministers of state, however, and although he had to select those who could command a majority of Parliament, at the same time he had a number of ways at his disposal to assure majority support for the ministers he chose. A powerful minister like Robert Walpole, for instance, owed much of his strength to the patronage of the crown, but Parliament could repudiate any leadership it distrusted, and therein lay the realm's first defense against centralized tyranny.

The House of Commons was dominated, though not controlled, by the landed gentry, who usually held about one-third of the seats. A few boroughs returned men of trade, but only about ten percent of the House was composed of businessmen. Army and naval officers formed a somewhat larger bloc, while two other groups, lawyers and officeholders, each held another ten percent of the seats. Scots, Welsh, a handful of West Indian planters, and even a few Americans were among other members. A member of Parliament was not required to be a resident in the constituency for which he stood.

Members for the county were chosen by the forty-shilling freeholders, who varied in number from Yorkshire's 20,000 to fewer than 1,000 in other counties, with about 4,000 the average. The freeholders almost invariably supported the neighboring squire or his candidate. Results in borough elections were often less predictable because qualifications for voting varied so widely. In about half of England's 203 boroughs the franchise was open to all freemen, a distinction, however, which was conferred by the ruling oligarchy. In some "freeman" boroughs, as many as 1,000 men could vote, but electorates under 100 were not uncommon. In the "scot and lot" boroughs, payment of the poor rates gave one the vote, while in a few others any householder not himself on poor relief could vote.

Finally, there was a group of boroughs with no electorate at all, boroughs in which the vote resided in a particular piece of property and was exercised by the owner.

Under such circumstances it is not surprising that in most elections many seats went uncontested altogether. In the election of 1761, for instance, only fifty-three of 298 boroughs and counties offered electors a choice of candidates. Rarely did ideological issues separate the candidates; rather, the contest was among rival families or other political interests. Victory sometimes cost more than £5,000. By one means or another the country gentlemen and the borough oligarchies strove to control their various constituencies. But these men themselves were not always their own political masters. Many a squire was under the thumb of a still larger land-holder, often a noble like the Duke of Newcastle. Loyalty was often best expressed by supporting the candidate favored by one's patron. In the small "corporation" boroughs, the local oligarchy sometimes gave at least one of their seats to a government candidate, in expectation of a naval contract perhaps, or some other plum.

In practice, Parliament's primary function was not to represent the people of England, not even its geographical parts, but rather to serve as a forum in which spokesmen for the various interests of the realm discussed major policies of state. It was only just that the landed interest be so dominant in such a body, theorists and apologists argued, because so many Englishmen lived on the land. By the same token, the commercial interest and the military interest, for instance, had their spokesmen as well. No matter that Manchester and Birmingham had no members, for the concerns of those towns were well represented by members from other boroughs with commercial enterprise. What difference that the member for a northern rural constituency hailed from some other county so long as he represented the agricultural interest of his electorate?

Because the landed interest was intensely jealous of its control over local affairs, it stoutly opposed every real or imagined extension of central government into county and borough affairs. Just such an expansion under Walpole during the first half of the eighteenth century produced an avalanche of pamphlets and essays in opposition. As historian Bernard Bailyn has pointed out, the secret of England's constitution was that it "had harnessed the use of power." To stay in office, a government needed not only the approval of the king but also the support of a chronically suspicious Parliament. Under these circumstances the king's ministers played up to the landed gentry whenever possible. By these indirect means, then, government policy usually reflected the views of a predominantly agricultural nation, modified somewhat by the concerns of merchants, industrialists, and other minority interests.

The Empire at Mid-Century

The imperial structure that bound Great Britain's colonies to the mother country in the middle of the eighteenth century was built from an accumulation of economic and political practices. Although from time to time the nature of this empire had been the subject of study by one or another pamphleteer, no one British ministry had taken the time and trouble to re-examine the principles and practices of the empire since its founding more than 150 years before. It is only fair to say that no American colonists, aside from Benjamin Franklin in his Albany Plan of Union in 1754, had thought much about imperial principles either. Under these circumstances, then, it is not surprising that Englishmen and Americans would soon disagree as to the nature of the British empire and the distribution of rights, powers, and responsibilities within it.

Although the term *mercantilism* itself was not in general use, both Englishmen and colonists would probably have agreed that the main function of the empire was to protect and encourage the economic self-sufficiency of the mother country. The purpose of colonies was to further this end. We have already seen how the Navigation Acts channeled much of the commerce of the colonies through the mother country often to their distinct benefit. Not only did membership in the empire mean a fairly stable market for their produce but the colonists also gained the protection of the world's most powerful naval fleet, a significant advantage during this era of global war. Equally valuable was the provision that colonial-built ships counted as English in the carrying trade of the empire. The mother country also offered bounties for the production of strategic commodities like masts and naval stores and encouraged the colonies to export pig and bar iron to England.

But the mercantile coin had another side to it. Parliament successively passed the Wool Act (1699), the Hat Act (1732), and the Iron Act (1750) in an effort to preserve the colonies as a market for British manufactures. To the same end, Americans had long since been required to clear through the mother country any foreign manufactures like French textiles or Dutch gin. There, of course, they were subjected to heavy taxation. By terms of the Molasses Act of 1733, colonial rum manufacturers were expected to pay a prohibitive duty when purchasing molasses from the French West Indies rather than from the British islands.

The affairs of the empire were in practice administered almost entirely by the king and his Privy Council. The King in Council appointed the royal governors, attorneys general, collectors of customs, and all other important executive officers in most of the colonies. This body also drew up instructions binding colonial officials, approved the appointment of councilors, received petitions from and settled disputes between the various colonies, reviewed all laws enacted by colonial assemblies, and heard appeals from colonial courts. The King in Council could thus disallow any piece of colonial legislation; it could control the membership of the governor's council (in all royal colonies but Massachusetts); and he could instruct his appointed governors to pursue certain policies in their respective provinces. Some matters the council handled alone, but in most cases it sought the advice of an appropriate executive department or committee, such as the admiralty, the Attorney and Solicitor General, and particularly the Board of Trade and Plantations.

William III created the Board in 1696 to check an attempt by Parliament to extend its authority over commerce and the colonies. Its eight members, joined occasionally by knowledgeable outsiders, periodically examined the trade and fisheries of the empire and "inquired into" the condition of the colonies, their administration, and their potential development. In practice, the Board of Trade made nominations for most of the colonial officials theoretically appointed by the Privy Council; therefore, its effective powers were considerable. They were guided in most of their decisions by a mercantilist point of view, determined to keep the colonies subordinate to and dependent upon the mother country indefinitely.

In one way or another, most of the other major administrative boards were also involved in colonial affairs. The Commissioners of

Customs supervised the work of the collectors in customs districts throughout the colonies, while the Treasury disbursed funds for salaries, Indian trade, and other activities. The admiralty provided defense for the colonial trade, patrolled against pirates and smugglers, and licensed American merchant vessels as letters of marque during wartime. Along with the War Office, the admiralty awarded contracts for victualing its forces, constructing facilities, and supplying various equipment. The competition for such favors among colonial merchants was often fierce, for a fat wartime contract could be the beginning of a fortune.

The principal link between the King in Council and its advisers, on the one hand, and the royal colonies, on the other, was the governor. Among the men who served in this position during the colonial period were peers, knights, Oxonians, lawyers, and former members of Parliament. The great majority of governors had similar experience in the governing class of the mother country and performed their duties with competence. But they worked under the severe handicap of receiving their directions from men 3,000 miles away in London, virtually none of whom had been in America or had the slightest interest in making the voyage. By the mid-eighteenth century, royal instructions more often than not failed to take into consideration the political realities of the American colonies, to say nothing of the interests of its inhabitants. Maintaining that the colonial assemblies existed only at the pleasure of the king, for instance, the Board of Trade and Privy Council bent every effort to thwart the ambitions of those legislatures to emulate the rise of Parliament in the mother country.

So unsatisfactory at times was the operation of imperial government that the colonists constantly strove to circumvent the system. Legislatures often paid no attention to the ruling that upper houses had the power to amend money bills, ignored the suspending clause that bound colonies not to enforce certain acts until approved by the King in Council, and re-enacted laws that had been disallowed. In a more positive vein, the colonial legislatures circumvented the governor's office as a channel of communication by sending their own representatives to London. The first colonial agents were sent only occasionally, to present the colony's case on a particular issue. But by the end of the seventeenth century, the colonists came to realize the value of maintaining agents in London on a permanent basis.

Thereafter the agents played an important role in the day-to-day administration of colonial affairs in London, where governmental officials acknowledged their value. The agents testified before the Privy Council, they discussed matters concerning their colonies with the major departments of the government, and they maintained close contact with the Board of Trade. The agents occasionally testified before parliamentary committees and lobbied for legislation favorable to their clients in America. By the middle of the eighteenth century, colonial administration had become so complex that the best agents had to master the art of expediting documents and other materials necessary for prompt decisions, serving the bureaucrats as well as their colonies in the process. Even more important, the successful agent required a wide circle of acquaintanceship among London's officialdom. In choosing their agent, therefore most legislatures favored English merchants and lawyers with colonial connections or colonists concerned in Anglo-American affairs.

In short, the agents represented the interests of their colonies. When agents for the New England colonies, for instance, opposed passage of the Molasses Act in 1733, they were merely representing the particular interest of their clients (distillers) in opposition to the interest of West Indian sugar planters. "Interest" politics had long been the *modus operandi* of the English governmental system, and only the agents could represent the colonies in the game. At mid-century, the American legislatures were fortunate to have competent agents who were in turn respected by the government in London. Surely the British empire could have functioned without them, but not without a price — the price ultimately paid by the mother country when later in the century its ministers no longer listened to the Americans' point of view as expressed through their only representatives — the colonial agents.

The Colonies at Mid-Century

At the close of the French and Indian War in 1763, the population of the thirteen continental colonies stood at a little over one and one-half million, of whom one-fifth were enslaved blacks. These figures were about double those of just twenty-five years earlier. Steady arrivals from the British Isles, the European continent, and Africa promised far greater numbers in the years ahead. Virtually all the good land in the eastern part of the colonies had long since been taken up, and those immigrants who did not settle in the cities joined native Americans in their relentless push into the interior searching for cheap land. American commerce with the mother country had more than doubled, and other trade routes reflected similar growth. More important than these quantitative changes in the American scene, however, were the more subtle qualitative developments that gave shape to the total life style of the Americans.

By the middle of the eighteenth century, most colonists took for granted the large measure of self-rule that had come to characterize their political lives. Strong local government flourished in virtually every colony. In contrast to the domination over local affairs exercised by the squirearchy in England, the broadly based electorate in the American colonies chose the officials who managed almost all the affairs of towns, parishes, and counties. Among the most significant functions they performed were the assessment of property, determination of tax rates, and establishment of an annual budget for the community. Control of the school system, care of the poor, and regulation of markets were also in the hands of local officials.

One of the relatively few ways in which a colonist became aware of other levels of government was in the annual election of representatives to the colonial legislature. Here the flow of practical political power from the grass-roots level below met the line of theoretical authority stemming from the king above, through the royal governor, and his appointed advisers, the Council. We have already seen that from fear of what the governor might do rather than for any abstract right of self-government, legislators in many colonies bent every effort to restrict the exercise of the executive's power. One unintended result was to make the lower houses of assembly permanently more powerful than their governors. Another outcome, equally unplanned, was to encourage Americans to be suspicious of all political authority not directly under their own control. The natural desire of numerous legislatures to model their assemblies after the House of Commons gave further impetus to the rise of the lower houses.

In the middle years of the century, Americans could see all around them signs of the growing strength and power of their country. Although the gulf between rich and poor widened somewhat as the economy expanded, the general standard of living for all free colonists rose steadily throughout the period. Furthermore, the opportunity for individual advancement remained high relative to European standards. The number of white colonists permanently consigned to a life of poverty was never large, although for blacks America as the land of opportunity remained an ironic concept indeed.

One of the most significant developments was the steady change in colonial agriculture. The market economy created by the growth and concentration of population made farming a profitable business as well as a way of life for thousands of colonists. At the same time, of course, the availability of foodstuffs made the rise of urban cities possible in the first place. This interdependence of city and farm did not always foster friendly relations, but it was perhaps an inevitable result of the fact that the colonists were growing steadily more self-sufficient. Fortune also smiled on southern planters during the middle decades of the eighteenth century. The market for tobacco, indigo, and rice moderately improved, while farmers in the middle colonies and around the Chesapeake who harvested wheat made still greater gains. Rising agricultural prosperity brought new faces into the ranks of political and social leaders. Increased purchasing power among planters and farmers created a demand for the goods and services of colonial artisans in a score of fields.

At the same time, the rising prosperity of the farmers contributed also to the growth of American commerce. Not only did the gradual increase in exports enable merchants to expand their trade with other parts of the empire, but the planters and farmers became an important market for goods from abroad. Reckoned on the basis of the white population per capita, imports from England alone rose by about 40 percent during the first half of the eighteenth century. Increased trade of course brought expanding prosperity to merchants, shipbuilders, and most other inhabitants of colonial seaports. Many of these men, like the newly wealthy planters and other landowners, worked their way into positions of political power, first on the local level and then through the general assembly of their colony.

America's expanding maritime economy had other significant results. The merchants of the northern and middle colonies came to know one another and to know many of the southern planters as well because of the rapidly growing coastwise trade. While their correspondence was generally confined to business matters, they occasionally commented on political affairs too. Northern merchants also established contacts with important mercantile houses overseas, not only in the mother country but in Holland, Spain, Portugal, and to a lesser extent France. Furthermore, the fact that thousands of Americans earned their livelihood on the sea was in itself significant, for these men had the experience necessary to man privateers during the numerous wars with France and Spain. Finally, there developed a pattern of illicit trade that pitted some of the most prominent merchants and shipmasters against the king's representatives — the governor, the custom officials, and naval commanders. Such overt flouting of the Acts of Navigation further diminished the colonists' respect for imperial authority.

Despite the gradual emergence of a distinctly American culture by mid-eighteenth century, one could still argue, as did the visiting British cleric Andrew Burnaby, that the American colonies were so disparate that union among them was an impossibility. Burnaby cited the prevalence of slavery in the southern colonies, the dominance of the commercial interest in the northern provinces, the different national backgrounds and religions among the settlers, and the petty jealousies that pitted one colony against another in power struggles. Burnaby was wrong to conclude that the colonies could not unite, but why? Historians have ever since struggled to determine what common factors among the continental American colonies at mid-century made possible the political union of the 1770s.

Certain obvious preconditions were necessary to begin with. Geographic propinquity and a growing ease of transportation encouraged the exchange of people, ideas, and goods. A common English heritage underlay the political and cultural institutions of the colonies, despite New World modifications. Of course all the provinces had since their founding been subject to the same rules and regulations of the empire, and they had occasionally even worked together in defense against Indians and French. But the historian must look beyond these shared conditions and experiences to find the common grounds for subsequent union.

Americans of the mid-eighteenth century shared a number of values. The principle of self-government, particularly the right of property holders to a voice in their own taxation through elected representatives, was by then a tradition. So too was the virtual autonomy of local government. Freedom from external control in church affairs was another cherished idea in most communities. The chronic shortage of labor and the prevailing Protestant Ethic combined to emphasize the value of work and enhanced the belief that a man should be judged by what he had done and not by his family's pedigree. The expanding economy, the availability of cheap land, and the absence of an hereditary aristocracy, which in England monopolized the sources of power, made economic and social advancement at least theoretically possible for most colonists. The manifest improvement in the lives of some inspired others, until striving to "get ahead" became a common characteristic. Indeed, even today it is difficult to convince Americans that not all people have this ambition, and its absence is thought somehow to be "un-American."

The mass of colonists who aspired to a better life were unconsciously expressing faith in the future — their own and that of their family's. The pioneer, who moved to the frontier, for instance, realized that it would take years of toil before he could clear his land and establish a secure foothold; yet he was willing to make short-term sacrifices for the long-term gain for himself and his children. The successful urban craftsman, instead of spending all he earned, ploughed some of his profits back into the shop, for more tools and materials, perhaps, or for the services of another apprentice. Some resourceful artisans invested in commerce, ultimately rising to the status of merchant, while merchants in turn purchased more vessels and expanded their businesses. One of the most common investments for Americans was land speculation. The pioneer in the wilderness and the craftsman in the city, the merchant and the landowner, were all taking risks to improve themselves. In so doing they were literally betting their lives and their fortunes on the future.

The fact that thousands of colonists did indeed improve themselves not only whetted the ambitions of others but it encouraged the idea that America was the land of the future, where opportunity was offered to all. Thus in 1751 Benjamin Franklin hailed the New World as a place

Where the sick Stranger joys to find a Home
Where casual Ill, maim'd Labour, freely come;
Those worn with Age, Infirmity or Care
Find Rest, Relief, and Health returning fair . . . . [1]

[1] [Benjamin Franklin,] *Poor Richard Improved, 1752*, as quoted in Max Savelle, *Seeds of Liberty* (New York, 1948), p. 567.

And looking into the future for the readers of his almanac, Nathaniel Ames observed in 1758 that "the Progress of Humane Literature (like the Sun) is from the East to the West; thus has it travelled thro' Asia and Europe, and now is arrived at the Eastern Shore of *America*. As the Celestial Light of the Gospel was directed here by the Finger of God, it will doubtless, finally drive the long! Long! Night of Heathenish Darkness from *America:* — So Arts and Sciences will change the Face of Nature in their Tour from Hence over the Appalachian Mountains to the Western Ocean...."

The Puritans had viewed America as a New Canaan, a chosen land favored by God and Nature and destined to future greatness. But the concept lost much of its original meaning in the years that followed the first settlements. By the middle of the eighteenth century, however, increasing numbers of colonists believed that America, in contrast to the Old World, was the land of opportunity. Franklin's prediction in 1751 that within a hundred years the majority of Englishmen would be living in the New World is as much a comment about England's future as about America's. This shared faith in America, as distinct from the Old World, was the most important belief that the colonists had in common after the middle of the eighteenth century.

FURTHER READINGS

The definitive study of the British empire at mid-century is Lawrence H. Gipson, *The British Empire Before the American Revolution* (15 vols., Caldwell and New York, 1936-1970). The best short survey of the Anglo-French rivalry in North America is Howard H. Peckham, *The Colonial Wars, 1689-1762* (New Haven, 1933), but for sheer pleasure the student should also read one or more of the books of Francis Parkman. Other works include Douglas E. Leach, *The Northern Colonial Frontier, 1607-1763* (New York, 1966); Richard Pares, *War and Trade in the West Indies, 1739-1763* (Oxford, 1936); and Wilbur R. Jacobs, *Diplomacy and Indian Gifts: Anglo-French Rivalry Along the Ohio and Northwest Frontiers, 1748-1763* (Stanford, 1950). For England at mid-century, see Dorothy Marshall, *Eighteenth Century England* (London, 1962); Sir Lewis Namier, *The Structure of British Politics at the Accession of*

George III (2d ed., London, 1957); and Caroline Robbins, *The Eighteenth-Century Commonwealthman...* (Cambridge, 1959). For matters concerning the empire at mid-century, Charles M. Andrews, *The Colonial Background of the American Revolution: Four Essays in American Colonial History* (rev. ed., New Haven, 1931) is still useful. More recent studies include Michael G. Kammen, *A Rope of Sand: The Colonial Agents, British Politics, and the American Revolution* (Ithaca, 1968) and *Empire and Interest: The American Colonies and the Politics of Mercantilism* (Philadelphia, 1970); Thomas C. Barrow, *Trade and Empire: The British Customs Service in Colonial America, 1660-1775* (Cambridge, 1967); and Carl Bridenbaugh, *Mitre and Sceptre: Transatlantic Faiths, Ideas, Personalities, and Politics, 1689-1775* (New York, 1962). A variety of views of the colonies at mid-century are found in early parts of Howard M. Jones, *O Strange New World. American Culture: The Formative Years* (New York, 1964), and in Louis B. Wright, *The Dream of Prosperity in Colonial America* (New York, 1965) and Richard L. Merritt, *Symbols of American Community, 1735-1775* (New Haven, 1966).

Part III

The Revolutionary Era

9

A Decade of Crisis, 1763-73

With the triumphant ending to the French and Indian War, colonial Americans looked with pride on their membership in the world's most powerful empire. Their blessings were numerous. They shared with their British cousins the long heritage of political freedom and civil rights guaranteed by that amorphous collection of documents and precedents — the British Constitution. Economically, Americans as a group were every bit as prosperous as their British counterparts. But if the American colonists believed in 1763 that they lived in the best of all possible worlds, why then was it that within a dozen years many of them would risk their lives and fortunes to sever connections with the mother country? The answer is to be found in the events of that most critical period in American history, the years 1763-76.

Prologue to Revolution

Despite the spectacular military successes of 1759-60, the British found the cost of continuing the war prohibitive and welcomed the peace overtures made by the French in 1761. As the price of a lasting treaty, however, the English realized they would have to surrender at the conference table at least some of the territory won on the battlefield. The choice soon narrowed to one between the West Indian island of Guadeloupe and French Canada, and the question was widely debated in pamphlets and newspapers even before the conference convened at Paris. Urging the retention of Guadeloupe for its rich sugar crop, old-school mercantilists argued that colonies were primarily valuable as sources of raw materials. Guadeloupe admirably fitted this role. More recent mercantilist thought, however, considered the colonies as important markets for the manufactures of the mother country, like woolens and hardware. Guadeloupe, with its small white population, offered little promise in this respect. French Canada, on the other hand, though thinly populated in 1760, might one day become a major market for a wide variety of British goods. The fact that the value of its fur and timber amounted to only a fraction of Guadeloupe's sugar was of minor importance to the new thinkers. Furthermore, the retention of Canada would secure the English colonies in North America from the threat of continuing French attack. In the end, the British ministry chose to retain Canada, and in so doing incurred the obligation to administer this extensive territory and to protect it against hostile Indians and a possible invasion by French forces.

In 1763 Great Britain faced a major financial crisis, for the price of victory over France was high. In addition to interest payments on the soaring national debt, the government was faced with the cost of protecting its newly conquered territories. For the Caribbean islands, the maintenance of a first-class fleet was necessary; for the North American colonies, the stationing of ten thousand troops was called for to defend the frontiers from possible attacks by revenge-seeking French and Indians. At the cessation of hostilities, Yankees began pouring into the unsettled parts of northern New England. To the southward, other colonists moved across the mountains into western Pennsylvania and the vast areas beyond claimed by the colony of Virginia. In reaction to these threats, Indians under Chief Pontiac attacked English forts and settlements throughout the Ohio territory in the spring and summer of 1763. Only after the death or capture of 2,000 soldiers and settlers did the British succeed in quelling the uprising.

Pontiac's War convinced most Americans that the western forts needed to be garrisoned. But the colonial militia consisted of citizen-soldiers who were willing to leave their farms only during an actual emergency. Garrison duty they gladly left to the professional British army whenever they could. But the expense of maintaining such a force, over £200,000 annually, seemed unnecessarily burdensome to England's landed gentry, who bore the brunt of taxation in Great Britain. As George III's new first minister, George Grenville, looked around for new sources of revenue in 1763, he concluded that the Americans might reasonably be expected to contribute to the cost of their own defense. Although Parliament had not previously taxed the colonists, there was no doubt in the minds of most Britons of its right to do so.

Looking back on the years before the outbreak of the revolutionary crisis, historians can now conclude that all was not serene between American colonists and British authorities. We have already seen that friction between colonial legislatures and royal governors was a commonplace. Some of these crises resulted from personality differences, others from the clash of political factions, but underlying the contest in most of the colonies was the fact that the legislators derived their authority from the people, while the governor represented the distant sovereignty of the crown. While Americans loved their king in an abstract, patriotic fashion, they had also been brought up on the basic Whig doctrine that political power was self-corrupting and therefore to be regarded with deep suspicion. In a widely circulated sermon, *A Discourse Concerning Unlimited Submission...*, published in 1750, the New England minister Jonathan Mayhew wrote, "The people know for what end they set up and maintain their governors; and they are the proper judges when they execute their *trust* as they ought to do it.... To say," he continued, "that subjects in general are not proper judges when their governors oppress them and play the tyrant... is as great *treason* as ever man uttered." Here is standard Whig doctrine born of John Locke and matured under the care of eighteenth-century writers like John Trenchard and Thomas Gordon.

Quite apart from this ideological basis for American suspicions of British political power were certain attitudes that separated the mother country from her colonies. The British had long held a rather condescending view of Americans in general. After all, many colonists were descendants of Puritans who had deserted England during the seventeenth-century struggles with the Stuarts. Other colonists were of Scots-Irish ancestry, and still others of German peasant stock. To status-conscious Englishmen of the ruling class, these ethnic origins were hardly worthy of respect. For their part, Americans increasingly came to view the mother country as old-fashioned and even decadent, an attitude reinforced by reports from numerous colonists, like Benjamin Franklin, who visited the mother country.

Some of the Englishmen who had actually been in America as army officers, governors, or other officeholders held a more charitable view toward the colonists than the average Briton, but equal numbers of these returned home with a strong anticolonial bias. This was particularly true of regular army officers, who looked down on American militiamen as blundering amateurs. General Braddock's crushing defeat in 1755, on the other hand, did little to encourage colonial confidence in British military leadership, and by the end of the French and Indian War, American troops could only with difficulty be persuaded to fight under British generals. British insistence that even the most recently appointed officers holding royal commissions preceded all provincials of the same rank angered many Americans, especially when they realized that most royal officers had purchased their commissions, while Americans were either elected by their men or appointed by their governors.

Overlaying both the ideological and attitudinal differences that divided the mother country and the colonies at mid-century were a number of concrete disputes that historians have come to view as signs of future trouble. The issues varied from colony to colony. In Pennsylvania sparks flew when the Privy Council vetoed an act of the Assembly granting the province's judiciary tenure during good behavior rather than during the king's pleasure only. Disallowance of Virginia's Two-Penny Act in 1759 loosed a storm of resentment against the Anglican clergy. The arrival of the Reverend East Apthorp at Boston in 1760 strengthened the convictions of some Americans that the Church of England was about to establish an American episcopate. In Massachusetts Bay, a controversy raged over the issuance of "writs of assistance," warrants granting customs officers in search of smuggled goods carte blanche to enter the cellars, warehouses, and ships of merchants. To colonists heading westward over the Alleghenies, the Proclamation of 1763, temporarily prohibiting settlement beyond the mountains, was still another grievance. American resentment over these and other issues was not very strong, however, nor was it yet focused on the Parliament, the crown, or any other particular instrument of British rule. But by the early 1760s, enough Americans were suspicious of British intentions to create a potentially hostile atmosphere in the colonies.

So long as Great Britain's policy toward its colonies remained essentially passive, the relatively minor issues that irritated Americans had little chance of precipitating an imperial crisis. Unfortunately, however, it was at just this moment that George Grenville succeeded Lord Bute as George III's first minister. We have already seen that Great Britain's finances were in serious straits as a result of the costly Seven Years' War. The ministry urgently sought a new source of funds to defray the expenses of defending its overseas possessions, and it seemed only logical that the Americans be required to make a significant contribution to this end.

But a new look at the colonies appealed to Grenville for another and perhaps even more important reason. In 1763, the Board of Trade decided to investigate reports of widespread smuggling throughout the American colonies. Not only was the Molasses Act of 1733 regularly evaded, the board found, but far more serious, the colonists were importing quantities of manufactured goods from Holland, Hamburg, and other continental ports. Most annoying was the continuation of trade between the French Caribbean islands and North America during the Seven Years' War. When asked to comment on the situation, the Customs Commissioners pointed out that not only was the revenue collected in America "very small and inconsiderable" but that widespread smuggling by the colonists made the proper regulation of their trade of immediate necessity, before it was too late. Grenville thereupon put his assistants to work drawing up legislation that would reform colonial trade as well as raise a revenue.

In March 1764, Grenville laid before Parliament the comprehensive proposals that ultimately became the Sugar Act of 1764. Among them was a lowering of the long-ignored duty on foreign molasses imported into the colonies from six pence to three, the idea being to make evasion no longer profitable. Duties were also levied upon wine, sugar, indigo, and coffee. While its authors hoped to net upward of £100,000 annually from these various levies, the measure in fact brought in only one-fourth of that sum in its first years, and it never exceeded £ 42,000 in any year thereafter. Viewed from another perspective, however, the Sugar Act proved far more successful than any other effort to collect a revenue in America, accounting for nearly ninety percent of the total sum raised. More ominously, most of the burden fell on five or six ports only, Massachusetts alone paying more than twenty-five percent of the total.

The Sugar Act also contained major revisions in the enforcement of the acts of trade in America. The master of virtually every little coasting vessel was required to obtain special documents — for a fee — covering his cargo, and those engaged in foreign trade faced an avalanche of paperwork at both ends of their voyage. A new vice-admiralty court with sweeping jurisdiction was established at Halifax. In this court there would be no juries, and the burden of proving compliance with the law rested on the accused, who had to pay court costs even if acquitted. Conviction meant the loss of vessel and cargo, which was then divided equally between the crown, the governor, and those who had informed against the vessel in the first place. No wonder historian Oliver Dickerson has concluded that the Sugar Act of 1764 ushered in an "era of customs racketeering."

The Stamp Act Crisis

Although many colonists had known ahead of time about the Sugar Act, their protests came too late to prevent its passage. Furthermore, their arguments were confined to economic issues: nowhere did they challenge Parliament's right to raise a revenue in the colonies. After the passage of the Sugar Act, however, colonial views began to harden. For one thing, they discovered for the first time that the act was far more than a revenue measure. But the main reason for this change in attitude stemmed from yet another clause of the Sugar Act, one providing for a stamp tax modeled on a method of taxation long a fixture on the English scene. At the time his revenue measures were being considered in March 1764, Grenville asked for a one-year delay in enactment of the stamp tax proposal, ostensibly to allow the colonists to propose an alternative means of raising a revenue. In fact, however, he had already determined upon the measure and probably sought the additional time only to work out the details.

This time the colonists did not wait for passage of the new bill to protest, and now the arguments took a new direction. In the most widely read political pamphlet of the period, *The Rights of the British Colonies Asserted and Proved* (1764), the eccentric James Otis argued that the imposition of taxes in America by Parliament "is absolutely irreconcilable with the rights of the colonists as British subjects and as men..." because they were not represented in that body. "No taxation without representation" would become a rallying cry for protest throughout America. Otis recognized no difference between an external and an internal tax, between the duties on foreign molasses and the proposed stamp tax. In Otis's view, Parliament had been misled by malicious people who doubted the colonists' loyalty and who urged that they be made more dependent upon the mother country. Although it was their duty to obey, Otis recommended that the Americans seek repeal by pointing out to Parliament their mistaken assumptions. Another way out of the dilemma, he proposed, was for Americans to be granted representation in Parliament. But not many colonists endorsed this idea, and Otis himself later repudiated the suggestion.

Neither the protests of colonial pamphleteers, nor the more official complaints of several colonial assemblies and their agents could alter Grenville's determination to impose a stamp duty upon the American colonies. The act itself, as finally adopted in March 1765, affixed duties on a variety of legal documents ranging from ship clearances, deeds, and mortgages, to college diplomas. Almanacs, pamphlets, and newspapers were also to be printed on stamped paper. Worse still, the duties were payable in specie, always difficult to obtain, although the funds collected were to be expended in the colonies and the act would not therefore result in draining hard currency from America, as some argued. Still another unpopular feature was that the law could be enforced in the dreaded admiralty courts without a jury trial, a provision that Englishmen themselves would have protested vigorously if it were applied to their own stamp tax.

Grenville did not let the arguments of Otis and other colonial pamphleteers go unanswered. In 1765 he had one of his assistants, Thomas Whately, draft a defense of the British program entitled *The Regulations Lately Made Concerning the Colonies.* Whately defended the government position on the ground that the Americans were "virtually" represented in Parliament, even though they did not elect any of its members. Whately's logic, if it can be called that, stemmed from the idea that "every Member of Parliament sits in the House, not as Representative of his own Constituents, but as one of that august Assembly by which all the Commons of Great Britain are represented." He pointed out that the Americans' position was not different from that of many Englishmen without the franchise, such as the inhabitants of Manchester and Birmingham, who were similarly subject to parliamentary taxation.

The doctrine of "virtual representation" may have satisfied those disenfranchised in England, where the members of Parliament did not have to be residents of the boroughs in which they stood for election. But in most American colonies a representative to the legislature was a delegate elected by his fellow townsmen and was often bound by specific instructions from his constituency. Whately's argument therefore failed to convince the colonists that Parliament had the right to tax them. Daniel Dulany, a conservative lawyer of Maryland wrote a stinging rebuttal, *Considerations on the Propriety of Imposing Taxes in the British Colonies* . . . in 1765. "We claim an exemption from all parliamentary impositions, that we may enjoy those securities of our rights and properties, which we are entitled to by the constitution," said Dulany. "For those securities are derived to the subject from the principle *that he is not to be taxed without his own consent.*"

As the day approached in the autumn of 1765 for the Stamp Act to go into effect, the protest movement grew both in strength and breadth throughout colonial America. Representatives of royal government designated to become stamp distributors were subjected to intimidation and worse by crowds of people. In Boston, Andrew Oliver agreed to resign his commission after his elegant home had been gutted by angry townspeople. Two weeks later the crowd turned on Thomas Hutchinson, scion of a respected American family, who was both chief justice and lieutenant governor of Massachusetts Bay. Hutchinson personally disapproved of the Stamp Act, and in fact had secretly written a pamphlet in the spring of 1764 claiming the colonies should be exempted from taxation by other than their own representatives. In every essential point Hutchinson agreed with the arguments advanced by James Otis several months later. Because of his official position in Massachusetts Bay, however, Hutchinson refused to make his views public. Partly because he had tried to prevent the sacking of Oliver's house, Hutchinson became the people's next victim. They broke into his house, destroyed most of its furnishings, slashed paintings, and threw the contents of his priceless library into the gutter. Turning next to the grounds, they trampled the garden and broke down a number of lovely fruit trees. Not until dawn did the crowd disperse, carrying away those valuables not already destroyed. Whatever ideological sympathy Hutchinson may have had with the colonial cause was lost in the rubble of his home. Meanwhile, unpleasant outbreaks occurred in other colonies, particularly in Rhode Island and New York. When the day arrived to issue the stamped paper, hardly a distributor could be found willing to perform his duties.

While some colonists used violence in the name of patriotism, others sought more peaceful means to protest Parliament's program. Throughout 1765, various colonial legislatures adopted strongly worded resolutions denying Parliament's right to tax Americans and calling for repeal of the obnoxious Stamp Act. Some of the strongest of these came from Virginia's House of Burgesses at the end of May. At the suggestion of Massachusetts, delegates from nine colonies met in New York in October to adopt joint resolutions drafted by Pennsylvania's John Dickinson. After pledging their devotion and loyalty to George III and acknowledging "all due Subordination to that August Body the Parliament," the delegates stated their case against the Stamp Act. The now familiar protest against taxation without consent was joined by an insistence on the right of trial by jury and a claim that the recent restrictions on colonial commerce were a hardship. The Resolves concluded with a call for a repeal of the Stamp Act, all legislation extending the jurisdiction of the admiralty courts, and other acts that had restricted American commerce.

Few patriots were confident that protest alone would bring about repeal, for such methods had not prevented enactment of the Stamp Act in the first place. Rather, some means of direct pressure on Parliament seemed necessary. While Americans had no voice in that body, British merchants did, particularly after the summer of 1765, when Grenville was replaced as first minister by the more tractable

Marquis of Rockingham, whose ministry depended in part on the support of Britain's mercantile interests. When groups of American importers informed their English correspondents to ship no more goods to America until the Stamp Act was rescinded, British merchants bombarded Parliament with petitions calling for repeal. William Pitt gave his support to the demand from the floor of the House of Commons, and the movement gained momentum. Behind the scenes, the colonial agents spared no effort to discuss the issue with members of the ministry and other important governmental officials. Benjamin Franklin, acting as agent for several colonies, gave brilliant if rather too clever testimony before the House of Commons in February 1766 against the Stamp Act.

It soon became apparent that Lord Rockingham could muster a majority in favor of repeal only if a strong statement of parliamentary supremacy over the colonies was issued first. A resolution was therefore adopted which became the Declaratory Act, denying the claim of colonial legislatures to the exclusive right of taxation in America. Instead, the act stated, the colonies were "subordinate unto, and dependent upon" the crown and Parliament and that Parliament had "full power and authority to make laws and statutes . . . to bind the colonies and people of America subjects of the Crown of Great Britain in all cases whatsoever . . . ." With the adoption of that sweeping statement, Rockingham led Parliament into a repeal of the Stamp Act. Later that spring, the colonial agents and London merchants also succeeded in persuading Parliament to lower the molasses duty from threepence to one, but molasses from British as well as foreign islands now became subject to the levy. The duty thereby lost whatever disguise it previously had as a trade regulation and stood revealed as a revenue measure.

Although the immediate crisis had ended, the seeds of future discord had been sown; for Americans considered repeal of the Stamp Act a vindication of their claim to exemption from Parliamentary taxation, a triumph won, they thought, by the boycott threatened against importation of English goods. Englishmen, on the other hand, far from considering repeal a recognition of colonial claims, thought that the Declaratory Act spoke for itself and that their right to tax the Americans was in no way compromised. For the next two decades Americans and Britons would argue their incompatible principles in peace and in war.

The Townshend Crisis

In the long run, repeal of the Stamp Act settled nothing. Several disputes between the mother country and her colonies continued to fester. One stemmed from the Currency Act of 1764, in which Parliament prohibited the American colonies from issuing legal tender currency and required the prompt retirement of such bills from circulation. The measure particularly burdened the middle and southern colonies, which were dependent on paper currency to supplement their meager supply of hard money. In the spring of 1766, several of these colonies complained of the deflationary effects of the bill. Their agents in London began to press members of the ministry, and for a brief moment in the spring of 1767 it looked as if repeal of the Currency Act was a distinct possibility. Then the issue became tangled with the question of raising a revenue in America, and all chance of repeal was lost. For the next nine years, the Currency Act remained a sore point in the relations between Great Britain and her continental American colonies.

Another issue, potentially even more explosive, erupted over application of England's Mutiny Act to the colonies. This law required citizens to provide barracks or other accommodations and certain basic provisions for any British troops within their colony. Thomas Gage, the commanding general of Britain's forces in America, had chosen New York as his headquarters because of its central location. In the early summer of 1766, the New York Assembly refused to comply with terms of the act. When word reached London, feeling began to mount against the province. The Rockingham ministry had fallen and William Pitt nominally headed a new group whose attitude toward the colonies was far less conciliatory. After long delay, the ministry concluded that something had to be done, and in May 1767, Parliament in effect suspended the New York Assembly by prohibiting the governor from approving any of its bills until the Mutiny Act was accepted. Such intervention into the internal affairs of a colony marked yet another departure in British policy toward America.

But the most serious problem concerning British-American relations remained that of finances. The new Chancellor of the Exchequer, responsible for presenting an acceptable budget, was young Charles Townshend. Like Grenville before him, Townshend realized the necessity of a new source of revenue, and he pledged to the opening session of Parliament in January 1767, that he would eventually find new funds in America. The financial crisis deepened when the government failed to agree on a plan to procure a revenue from the East India Company. Then the Opposition succeeded in driving through a reduction of the land tax from its wartime level to three shillings in the pound. Townshend had to bring a new program immediately or resign.

The chancellor's idea was to impose duties on imports into the colonies of paper, glass, lead, paint, and tea. In addition to meeting some of the costs of defending the colonies as the Stamp Act had been designed to do, Townshend's Act had a new purpose — "defraying the charge of the administration of justice and the support of civil government...." In short the proposed scheme would free royal officials from dependence upon the colonial legislatures for their salaries. Townshend hoped to take advantage of an ostensible distinction between "internal" taxes like the stamp levy and "external" taxes collected at the ports by customs officials. Like most Britons he believed that Parliament had the right to levy either kind of tax. What he failed to realize was that the Americans objected as much to external as to internal taxation.

Along with suspending the New York Assembly and adopting the Townshend duties to support a civil list, Parliament, in the spring of 1767, undertook yet another innovation relative to America. The collection of customs duties in the colonies had long faced discouraging obstacles. To make the service more efficient, Parliament authorized the establishment of an American Board of Customs Commissioners to sit at Boston. At the same time came a reorganization of the vice-admiralty court structure. Additional courts were set up at Boston, Philadelphia, and Charleston, in addition to the one already sitting at Halifax. Finally, a new office of cabinet rank, called the Secretary of State for the Plantations, was created to give special attention to the administration of the colonies. The idea of such an office was in itself a step forward, but its first occupant, Lord Hillsborough was not. He lacked the cool head the job required, and like other members of the Bedfordite faction, he relied on force as the best way to handle the colonies.

When the colonists learned that the new revenue scheme was to go into effect in September 1767, they not surprisingly adopted the tactics they thought had brought about repeal of the Stamp Act the year before. John Dickinson once again turned his literary talents to a reasoned statement of the colonial position, this time in a series of essays entitled *Letters from a Farmer in Pennsylvania*. In looking over the Townshend Act, Dickinson wrote, "we observe an authority expressly claimed and exerted to impose duties on these colonies; not for the regulation of trade..., but, for the single purpose of levying money upon us. This I call an innovation." Thousands of colonists who read his essays in the newspapers or in pamphlet form agreed. The weapon they most counted on to bring about repeal of the Townshend duties was the refusal to import British goods. Though slow to organize, merchants in ports from Maine to Georgia began to enter into nonimportation agreements during the fall of 1768; housewives in inland towns and villages pledged to forego the purchase of dutied articles, and colonists throughout America turned with patriotic fervor to whatever native substitutes they could develop for products formerly imported from the mother country.

Enforcement of the nonimportation agreements depended solely on the pressure of public opinion brought to bear against violators. Any uncooperative merchant or shopkeeper was listed in the local journal as an "enemy of his country" and could expect a nocturnal visit from a delegation of local patriots bent on intimidation. Sometimes his house was smeared with paint, either of the common variety or of that called "Hillsborough paint," the contents of outhouses named after the hated Secretary for the Plantations. Particular concern was shown for the importation of dutied tea, because the beverage was so popular in the colonies. Numerous communities celebrated public tea-burnings and boasted of their ladies' preference for "labradore" tea or some other native herb as a substitute. Lists of citizens refusing to give up the habit were posted on town-house doors, where they might bear the scorn of more patriotic citizens.

Although there were a number of merchants strong enough to ignore the nonimportation agreements with impunity, by and large the boycott of English goods was effectively enforced, and once again acting in self-interest, the merchants of Great Britain petitioned Parliament for repeal of legislation harmful to Anglo-American trade. A motion to rescind the Townshend Act in the spring of 1769 failed to carry. But shortly thereafter the Pitt-Grafton ministry concluded that most of the duties were "uncommercial," inasmuch as they simply increased the price of the taxed commodities and angered the colonists, without producing a revenue nearly large enough to be worth the trouble. The cabinet decided to call for the repeal of all the duties save that on tea at the next session of Parliament. The decision to retain the duty on tea would prove fateful indeed. In proposing only partial repeal to Parliament as scheduled in March 1770, the new prime minister, Frederick, Lord North, argued that this was no time to grant concessions to the Americans by a total repeal. "The properest time to exert our right of taxation is when the right is refused." Parliament agreed by retaining the duty on tea as a symbol of its authority to tax the colonists.

When the news of Parliament's action reached America, the colonists were in quandary. The original nonimportation agreements had as their objective total repeal, and the principle of no taxation without representation could hardly have permitted the continuation of one Townshend duty on the statute books. Yet the agreements became increasingly difficult to enforce as the summer drew on; importers were eager to order their winter goods from London. One by one groups of merchants in the major cities abandoned their boycott of British goods. As a face-saving device most ports retained a nominal ban on the importation of dutied tea, but otherwise the gates were flung open once more to trade with the mother country. And thus, by the autumn of 1770, five years of colonial protest and resistance came to an end. For the next three years a relative calm settled over Great Britain and her American colonies.

The Road to Revolution

Looking back on the preceding seven years, a colonist of 1770 must have been astonished by the abrupt change that had taken place in the attitude that he and his fellow Americans felt toward the mother country. This change John Adams would much later describe as "the real American Revolution." In 1763 the colonies had sung the praises of Great Britain and showed evident pride in their membership in the empire. But during the next seven years, American newspapers and American legislative halls began to feature one denunciation after another of the mother country and its colonial policies.

If the object of his fellow citizens' anger surprised him, the colonist of 1770 would have found nothing new in the violent tactics by which Americans expressed their disagreement. Although relatively rare in the seventeenth century, except for Bacon's Rebellion and the disturbances accompanying the revolution of 1688, mob activity became quite common in the colonies by the eighteenth century, as it had much earlier found a permanent place in the political life of the mother country. Sometimes the mob's purpose was to obstruct some disfavored governmental action. Thus attempts to impress Americans into the Royal Navy often met with violent resistance. On other occasions, the people turned to violence not in opposition to authority but as a means of supplementing it, as in Boston, when bawdy houses were several times attacked by indignant citizens.

The colonists took matters into their own hands most commonly in protest to overzealous enforcement of the Acts of Trade. Anyone who informed on a smuggler in hope, perhaps, of sharing in the confiscated goods, had to reckon with the violent reaction of his neighbors. The customs officials stood as ready-made targets of the crowd's displeasure. These hapless individuals were faced with an impossible assignment — to enforce unpopular laws without an adequate staff under their own direction. While both army and naval detachments were on hand to assist, far too often coordination between the various groups was nonexistent. For the most part, customs officials bore the brunt of American resentment alone, with neither support nor encouragement from other representatives of the crown. After one particularly severe beating, an official in Philadelphia complained of "a constant pain in my breast...besides a kind of inward favour [fever] which hangs about me, no appetite to my victuals, and spirits very much depressed."

A serious riot broke out at Boston in the spring of 1768, when a customs official, Joseph Harrison, and his son seized John Hancock's sloop *Liberty* on suspicion of illegally importing a cargo of Madiera wine. Harrison and his son had to run through a gauntlet of stones, brickbats, and sticks for nearly 200 yards. Only by the aid of friendly hands did the two escape with minor wounds. By late summer, conditions had become so bad in Boston, in the eyes of the authorities, that General Gage was ordered to send two regiments of troops from New York to help keep order, to be joined later by two more. This was an extraordinary step, for although regular soldiers were used in England to maintain the peace, such an assignment had never before been made in America. The troops arrived in October, amid the catcalls of the people, while the Governor's Council dragged its feet on whether to provide them with barracks. Not until the snows of winter began to fly were the troops finally quartered in rented warehouses and other buildings.

Not surprisingly, the presence of troops in Boston soon proved to have the opposite effect to the intended role of keeping the peace. By the following winter, fistfights and other confrontations between citizens and soldiers became almost daily occurrences. It was freely predicted that a showdown would soon become inevitable. Then, on the night of 5 March 1770, it happened. A gang of youths started taunting a sentry standing guard in front of the Customhouse. He clouted one of them with his musket. "Damned rascally scoundrel lobster son of a bitch," they yelled back. A swelling crowd began throwing chunks of ice at the soldier, shouting "Kill him, kill him." From across the way the captain of the guard ordered out a corporal and six tall grenadiers to the rescue and followed in their wake. They reached the sentry safely, only to be cut off from headquarters by the crowd. With loaded muskets the band stood against the pressure — against the snowballs, the shrieks, and the never-ending taunts. "Damn you, you sons of bitches. Fire!" cried the mob. A club came hurling through the air and knocked one of the grenadiers flat. He struggled to his feet and fired his musket, apparently into the air. The crowd reeled back, but after a pause came more shots. And men began to fall, mortally wounded, onto the icy street.

The Boston Massacre quickly became the symbol of British oppression; each year its anniversary occasioned an inflammatory address from one or another of the Boston patriots. In 1772, for instance, Joseph Warren recalled for his fellow townsmen "the horrors of that dreadful night... when our streets were stained with the blood of our brethren... and our eyes tormented with the sight of the mangled bodies of the dead." The massacre prompted Governor Thomas Hutchinson to withdraw the soldiers to Castle William, in the middle of Boston harbor, where they remained until the spring of 1774. This action effectively ended the clashes between citizens and soldiers, to be sure, but when the governor felt the need of troops during the Tea Party crisis in December 1773, they were too far from the center of town to be of any help to him. By that time the streets of Boston belonged to the people — or at least to some of them.

Historians know less than they should about the activities of mobs during the revolutionary crisis. Some older historians have remarked on how orderly American mobs seemed in comparison to those of Europe, especially, those of the French Revolution. They have explained this moderation by suggesting the people were always under the control of leaders, who "used" the mob for political purposes. More recent research suggests that European mobs were not much more wantonly destructive than their American counterparts. Younger historians of the "New Left" school have objected to the idea that the actions of crowds in the American revolutionary crisis were in any way directed or manipulated by individual leaders. And yet at the same time they insist that these mobs (in fact they object to the word mob itself as pejorative) behaved in a rational manner. Such sweeping generalizations on both sides of the argument suggest the need for more thorough investigation of the nature and role of the crowd during the American revolutionary crisis.

Throughout the decade 1765-75, certain groups of patriots in the leading towns at least thought they were exerting some influence on the behavior of the crowd, and most contemporary observers seemed also to believe that political action by mobs was usually something less than spontaneous. Among the self-proclaimed leaders of the people were Ebenezer McIntosh, a Boston shoemaker, Benjamin Edes, printer of the Boston Gazette, Captain Isaac Sears and Alexander McDougall, of New York, and Charles Thomson in Philadelphia. Without much doubt the most successful and certainly best known popular leader was Samuel Adams. A graduate of Harvard in 1740, Adams had failed in one profession after another, from an abortive attempt at the study of law to service as Boston's tax collector, in which position ineptitude rather than dishonesty led to a shortage of £ 8,000 in his accounts by 1764. As the revolutionary movement began, Sam Adams was a forty-two-year-old failure, unable even to give adequate support to his family. But one talent he did have, a gift for politics, and he soon became the leader of Boston's popular faction in its struggles against first Governor Sir Francis Bernard and then Governor Thomas Hutchinson. Personalities rather than principles gave Adams his start, but by the end of the Stamp Act crisis he was convinced that the British ministry was consciously bent on a policy of tyranny over the American colonies. By the fall of 1772, he had gained control of Boston town meeting and thereafter made effective use of this position to remind the people of the issues still unresolved between Great Britain and America.

The campaign that Adams and others waged against the policies of Great Britain would have had little or no effect on the people had not most American newspapers been in the hands of printers sympathetic to the American cause. Letters espousing the popular viewpoint outnumbered those from more conservative commentators severalfold. Resolutions and speeches in defense of the American position were invariably printed, while the efforts of colonists more sympathetic to Great Britain's point of view received little attention. But history shows us very few protest movements that were sustained by words alone, and writers who have suggested that the American Revolution was mainly the work of propagandists seriously misunderstand its nature.

Though public concern flagged somewhat in the two years after the Boston Massacre, very real grievances remained. An interesting compilation of them, entitled "A List of Infringements and Violations of Rights," was assembled by Sam Adams for Boston town meeting in November 1772 and circulated to the other towns of the province by the newly formed Boston Committee of Correspondence. The Declaratory Act, Parliament's taxation of the colonies, the great increase in number and powers of customs officers, and the use of vice-admiralty courts and the armed forces to help collect the revenue were high on Adams's list. He dwelled at length on the fact that some of this revenue was used to support royal officials. "It has always been held that the dependence of the Governor of this Province upon the General Assembly for his support," he wrote, "was necessary for the preservation of [that] equilibrium . . . without which we cannot continue in a free state." Adams complained also of excessive interference in provincial affairs by royal instructions to the governor. He singled out three specific restraints on American economic enterprise, those prohibiting slitting mills, the export of hats, and the shipment of wool by water. Interestingly enough, Adams made no mention of the Navigation

Laws in general. After expressing fear that an American episcopate was about to be established, Adams concluded with a relatively minor complaint about the continual alteration of colonial boundaries by king and council.

The grievances that Samuel Adams thought it necessary to remind his fellow Americans of in the winter of 1772-73 emphasize the fact that none of the basic issues between mother country and the colonies had yet been settled. This failure on the part of British officials to take advantage of the lull in public affairs to review their policy toward America was symptomatic of their particular myopia, not the result of a plot to enslave the colonies, as many Americans were convinced. British government officials simply failed to understand what developments had been taking place in the colonies since their settlement over a century before. Those who did have an inkling — men like William Pitt, Colonel Isaac Barré, and Governor Thomas Pownall — all contended that Americans had developed a large measure of local self-government and that the ministry and Parliament should not attempt to interfere with their internal affairs. But those in authority, from George III down through most of his principal ministers, were unable to recognize that the colonists were no longer to be treated as children. This paternalistic attitude had irritated Benjamin Franklin as early as 1767. "Every man in England seems to consider himself a piece of a sovereign over America," he noted, "[and] seems to jostle himself into the throne with the King and talks of *our subjects in the colonies . . . .*"

The king and his ministers were sincere in their conviction that Parliament had the right to collect a revenue in the American colonies, and only a handful of Englishmen disagreed. Their mistake, perhaps, was to insist on exercising this right so soon after the Stamp Act crisis, rather than to remain content with its expression in principle only through the Declaratory Act. The amount of revenue involved, "a mere peppercorn," some called it, was hardly worth the trouble of collection, but once the colonists renewed their challenge to Parliament's claims of authority, the issue became one of principle rather than simply of practicalities.

In the period 1770-73 the British government had an opportunity to revise, without the risk of losing face, its over-all policy and administration concerning the colonies in light of the recent disturbances. The new Secretary for the Plantations, William Legge, the second Earl of Dartmouth, enjoyed the confidence of most Americans in London such as Ben Franklin, but he had neither the imagination nor the initiative to force through major reforms. While Sam Adams struggled to keep the revolutionary spirit alive in America, British leaders made no real effort to remove the remaining points of irritation. Instead, they blundered their way into the final crisis with no awareness of the consequences of their actions.

FURTHER READINGS

Perhaps the best short survey of the entire Revolutionary period is Edmund S. Morgan, *The Birth of the Republic, 1763-1789* (Chicago, 1956). Others include Esmond Wright, *The Fabric of Freedom, 1763-1800* (New York, 1961); Eric Robson, *The American Revolution in its Political and Military Aspects, 1763-1783* (Hamden, 1965); Dan Lacy, *The Meaning of the American Revolution* (New York, 1964); John Alden, *A History of the American Revolution* (New York, 1969); and Ian Christie, *Crisis of Empire: Great Britain and the American Colonies, 1754-1783* (New York, 1966). Of several collections of essays concerning the Revolution and its interpretation the best are Richard B. Morris, ed., *The Era of the American Revolution* (New York, 1939); Esmond Wright, ed., *Causes and Consequences of the American Revolution* (Chicago, 1966); and Jack P. Greene, ed., *The Reinterpretation of the American Revolution, 1763-1789* (New York, 1968). The most comprehensive recent book on the coming of the Revolution is Merrill Jensen, *The Founding of a Nation: A History of the American Revolution, 1763-1776* (New York, 1968), while different interpretations will be found in Lawrence H. Gipson, *The Coming of the Revolution, 1763-1775* (New York, 1954); Bernhard Knollenberg, *Origin of the American Revolution, 1759-1766* (New York, 1960); and John C. Miller, *Origins of the American Revolution* (Boston, 1943), to note only three. Aspects of the British scene are examined in Sir Lewis Namier, *England in the Age of the American Revolution* (2d ed., London, 1961); John Brooke, *The Chatham Administration, 1766-1768* (London, 1956); Sir Lewis Namier and John Brooke, *The History of Parliament: The House of Commons, 1754-1790* (3 vols., London, 1964) and their *Charles Townshend* (London, 1964); Thomas C. Barrow, *Trade and*

Empire: The British Customs Service in Colonial America, 1600-1775 (Cambridge, 1967); B.D. Bargar, *Lord Dartmouth and the American Revolution* (Columbia, 1965); Franklin B. Wickwire, *British Subministers and Colonial America, 1763-1783* (Princeton, 1966); Jack M. Sosin, *Agents and Merchants: British Colonial Policy and the Origins of the American Revolution, 1763-1775* (Lincoln, 1965); Charles R. Ritcheson, *British Politics and the American Revolution* (Norman, 1954); George H. Guttridge, *English Whiggism and the American Revolution* (Berkeley, 1942); Margaret M. Spector, *The American Department of the British Government, 1768-1782* (New York, 1940); and Richard Pares, *King George III and the Politicians* (London, 1953). For more specialized topics, see Arthur M. Schlesinger, *Prelude to Independence: The Newspaper War on Britain, 1764-1776* (New York, 1958), and *The Colonial Merchants and the American Revolution, 1763-1776* (New York, 1918); Carl Ubbelohde, *The Vice-Admiralty Courts and the American Revolution* (Chapel Hill, 1960); Oliver M. Dickerson, *The Navigation Acts and the American Revolution* (Philadelphia, 1951); Bernard Bailyn, *The Ideological Origins of the American Revolution* (Cambridge, 1967); Randolph G. Adams, *The Political Ideas of the American Revolution* (Durham, 1922); Jack M. Sosin, *Whitehall and the Wilderness: The Middle West in British Colonial Policy, 1760-1775* (Lincoln, 1961); and Philip G. Davidson, *Propaganda and the American Revolution, 1763-1783* (Chapel Hill, 1941). Edmund S. and Helen M. Morgan, *The Stamp Act Crisis: Prologue to Revolution* (Chapel Hill, 1953) is the definitive study of that key episode. Another important event is the subject of Hiller B. Zobel, *The Boston Massacre* (New York, 1970), while Richard D. Brown, *Revolutionary Politics in Massachusetts: The Boston Committee of Correspondence and the Towns, 1772-1774* (Cambridge, 1970) reexamines the work of Samuel Adams.

10

The Road to Revolution,
1773-76

Although the years 1770-73 have been called a period of calm, we know that beneath the surface many Americans remained anxious about British policies that might affect the colonies. Occasional bursts of violence, as in the burning of the royal revenue cutter *Gaspée* off Providence in 1772, reminded authorities that they were still deeply resented by those in the seaports. Virtually the only issue that was potentially dangerous in all the colonies was the question of parliamentary taxation. To be sure, the crown continued to collect a variety of revenues in America. The importation of molasses seemed to continue unabated, netting an annual average of about £16,000 in duties. Although most of the tea consumed in America during the period was probably smuggled from Holland, enough came in from England to net about £3,000 a year in duties. While not all colonists took a "business as usual" attitude, nevertheless most seemed content to go about their daily affairs in peace and quiet. But should the British ministry once again threaten to exercise its principle of parliamentary taxation, serious consequences would surely follow. In the spring of 1773, this is precisely what an unwitting Lord North and his ministry did.

The Boston Tea Party

During the years immediately following the Seven Years' War, Britain's famed East India Company fell into serious financial difficulty, partly owing to expensive military operations and corruption in Bengal, partly to mismanagement at home. Among the privileges long enjoyed by the company was a monopoly of all British trade east of the Cape of Good Hope. Throughout most of the eighteenth century, the mainstay of this commerce was the importation of tea from China. But because of the high duties charged by the government upon its entry into Great Britain, the company's tea could not compete with the Dutch variety smuggled into England from Amsterdam in ever-mounting quantities. Americans also found it cheaper to obtain their tea in Holland or France. In an effort to undercut the smugglers, Parliament, for a five-year trial period starting in 1767, lowered the inland duty on the company's tea consumed in England and allowed a full drawback of all duties on tea exported to America. The act helped at first, until the Townshend duty on tea enacted later that year destroyed whatever chance the company had of building up its American market. By 1773 the East India Company had a surplus of seventeen million pounds of tea in its London warehouses.

Hoping to convert this liability into a much-needed asset, in January 1773, an obscure stockholder of the company made an interesting suggestion to the directors. If the government would allow the company to re-export some of this surplus to markets abroad, first granting a drawback on the customs duty collected on importation, perhaps most of the tea could be sold on the European continent. After a brief investigation, the directors concluded that the abundance of Dutch tea in Europe would make a profit there difficult. Instead they asked Parliament's permission to ship the tea to America, where they planned to have it sold wholesale at the lowest possible prices. When the issue came before the House of Commons in the spring, the irascible leader of the Opposition, William Dowdeswell, urged that repeal of the remaining Townshend duty on tea be a part of the bill. "I tell the Noble Lord now," he addressed Lord North, "if he don't take off the duty they won't take the tea." But the first minister once again refused to permit removal of the tea duty. Even though he would still have had the one-pence molasses duty, Lord North insisted on retaining a more visible manifestation of Parliament's claim to the right of taxation in America. Never in the crisis between England and America would a single act of ministerial stubbornness have graver consequences for its authors.

Upon passage of the bill, the East India Company laid plans for the undertaking. It was first decided to make an initial shipment of six hundred thousand pounds to the four major ports of Boston, New York, Philadelphia, and Charleston. After considerable difficulty, ships were chartered for the passage, and on the advice of London exporters, a group of American merchants with experience in the tea trade was chosen in each of the ports to receive the shipments on consignment. The first vessels left for the colonies in early autumn, but not before word of their impending arrival had preceded them across the Atlantic.

Some of the opposition to the East India Company's plan came from the fear that, if successful, the arrangement would be extended to include other commodities, thus confronting the American merchant with a monopolistic competitor. Since the company planned to sell the tea in large lots at wholesale only, however, this suspicion was not realistic. Among other opponents of the plan were undoubtedly the smugglers of New York and Philadelphia, who feared that the company's tea would undersell the tea they brought in from Holland. By far the greatest source of opposition, however, stemmed from the fact that this tea would be subject to the Townshend duty. Thousands of Americans saw a ministerial plot to force them into acceding to the hated principle of parliamentary taxation. While the ministry surely hoped that Americans would accept the dutied tea, this was hardly the purpose of the plan.

The patriots of New York and Philadelphia were the first to respond to the threat, but by mid-October inhabitants of all four chosen ports were determined not to permit the tea to land. By forcing the consignees to refuse their commissions (which most of them had not yet received) and by persuading the ship captains to turn back to England without landing the detested tea, local patriots hoped to prevent payment of the Townshend duty. At both New York and Philadelphia the harbor pilots were warned at their peril not to bring the tea ships into harbor. Letters in the press and resolutions at open meetings repeated the theme again and again — to accept the East India Company's tea was to concede the validity of Parliament taxing America. Larger duties on other commodities were sure to follow. The consignees at New York, Philadelphia, and Charleston either resigned their commissions outright or at least agreed not to press their cause with either the citizenry or the government.

But the situation at Boston was different. Throughout November, the patriot leaders there had tried every possible means of persuasion, both peaceful and violent, to force the consignees to reject their commissions. But these gentlemen steadfastly refused to give in, mainly because among them were two sons of Governor Thomas Hutchinson, who was determined to use all the powers of his office to support the consignees. Ever since the Stamp Act crisis eight years before, Hutchinson had been waiting for a chance to face down his tormentors. Relations between the governor and the patriots had worsened in January 1773, when Hutchinson took the opportunity to lecture the General Court on the supremacy of Parliament over the American legislatures, hardly a topic to soothe ruffled feelings. Then in the summer the patriots retaliated by publishing some of the governor's private correspondence purporting to show that he favored stricter control by the mother country. When the General Court then filed impeachment proceedings against Hutchinson, relations had passed the point of reconciliation.

When the *Dartmouth* arrived at Boston in late November, followed a few days later by two other vessels laden with East India Company tea, the crisis was at hand. Because the vessels had entered the customs district, they could not properly be given a clearance to leave until their cargoes were landed and the Townshend duty paid. But at two successive mass meetings at the end of November, the people voted that the vessels should be sent back without unloading the tea. The patriots then put guards on board the vessels at Griffin's Wharf to prevent the tea from being landed surreptitiously, for they knew that once the cargo was ashore, the dutied tea would be offered for sale at prices too attractive for many lukewarm patriots to resist.

A final mass assembly was held at Old South Meeting House on 16 December. There the owner of the *Dartmouth* was instructed to demand a pass from Governor Hutchinson so that his vessel could depart with the tea. But the governor knew that under the regulations customs officials would be free to seize the tea for nonpayment of the duties the next day (the twenty-day-grace period having expired) and "compel" payment by the consignees, who, of course, would be all too willing. Hutchinson, therefore, saw no reason to capitulate on the eve of his long-awaited triumph over the patriots. Upon learning of the governor's decision, the meeting at Old South broke up midst cries of "Boston Harbor a tea-pot tonight!" "Hurrah for Griffin's Wharf!" Meanwhile, small bands of patriots were busily disguising themselves with daubs of paint and old blankets and began converging on the wharf as the meeting ended. Altogether perhaps sixty men climbed aboard the three tea ships under cover of darkness, while thousands of citizens stood by to watch. Without fanfare they went about the business of hoisting 340 chests of tea out of the holds and dumping their contents into the harbor. When the job was done three hours later, about 90,000 pounds of tea worth nearly £10,000 sterling was destroyed.

The rest of the colonists received the news of the Boston Tea Party with mixed feelings. Conservatives of course were shocked at the wanton destruction of property and defiance of royal authority. But even many patriots seemed chagrined at the outbreak of violence at Boston, action that stood in contrast to the peaceful resolution of the problem at the other ports. In Philadelphia the governor refused to take a firm stand, as Hutchinson had done, and the captain of the tea ship readily agreed to return to London with his cargo. At Charleston the patriots finally permitted the tea to be landed and stored in the customhouse, where it gradually rotted away without the duty being paid. New York's tea ship was blown off the coast by a December gale, but when it finally arrived in April 1774, its captain was persuaded not to land his cargo. Because the officials backed away from a showdown in these other ports, then, the inhabitants won the day by peaceful means. Only at Boston were the patriots faced with a determined governor. Thus it was that they found themselves confronted with a choice between capitulation to their arch foe Hutchinson or destruction of the tea. By choosing the latter they precipitated the final crisis between the mother country and the colonies.

The British Reaction

In late January 1774, news of the Boston Tea Party reached Great Britain, where public reaction was one of anger and a desire for vengeance. As a friend to the American cause, Lord Dartmouth had only recently expressed the hope that Parliament would soon repeal the tea duty, but when he learned of Boston's "outrageous madness" as he termed it, the Colonial Secretary became the first official to suggest that the town be punished. Within a few weeks Lord North had a plan for retaliation and reform ready to put before the Parliament. The first measure was the Boston Port Bill, providing that after June 1774, all regular commerce in Boston harbor was to end except for coastwise vessels bringing food and fuel to the inhabitants. The port of Boston was to remain closed until full compensation was paid the East India Company for its loss and the town's inhabitants could convince George III that in the future it would be on its good behavior. Debate on the bill was for the most part perfunctory. Few members stood up for the colony, and those that did were greeted with derisive coughing fits from the back benches. Once reliable friends of America like Colonel Isaac Barré spoke in support of the punitive measure, and the bill passed with no significant opposition.

In the next few weeks the ministry rammed through two other measures designed to curb apparent abuses in the government and administration of justice in Massachusetts Bay. The Massachusetts Government Act altered the colony's charter so as to provide for the appointment of the Governor's Council by the crown, as in other royal colonies, rather than by election, as had been the practice in the Bay colony. Also, town meetings were limited to a single annual electoral session in order to halt their use as a means of rallying public opinion against the mother country. The Administration of Justice Act permitted the governor to send home to England for trial all government officers accused of crimes committed in the execution of their duties. It was expected that these men could better preserve the peace and execute the laws if freed from the apprehension of trial by an American jury if they performed their duties overzealously. The latter bills were designed more for reform than retribution, as was a fourth measure, the Quartering Act, which authorized the seizure of barns and other unoccupied buildings for billeting British troops in America. Upon passage, all four bills together became known as the Coercive or Intolerable Acts. In the summer, Parliament passed the Quebec Act, in reality a farseeing law providing enlightened government for Canada. But under the circumstances, the Americans greatly resented the fact that the law incorporated into "Quebec" western territories claimed by Virginia and other colonies.

Although the Port bill had met with virtually no resistance on the floor of Parliament in March, by the time the ministry introduced its other measures, the Opposition began to pull itself together and made an effort to block adoption of both the Government and Administration of Justice Acts. Some members of Parliament cited the sanctity of charters in speaking against the Massachusetts Government bill, while others felt that, at the least, the colonists deserved a hearing. After explaining his support of the Boston Port bill as "a bad way of doing right," Colonel Isaac Barré attacked the Administration of Justice Act as unnecessarily provocative. "You are becoming the aggressors," he warned the ministry, "and offering the last of human outrages to the people of America by subjecting them in effect to military execution." In another notable speech, the ailing William Pitt, now Lord Chatham, spoke in opposition to the ministry's entire colonial policy and closed with these prophetic words:

My lords, I am an old man, and would advise the noble lords in office to adopt a more gentle mode of governing America; for the day is not far distant, when America may vie with these kingdoms, not only in arms, but in arts also. It is an established fact, that the principal towns in America are learned and polite, and understand the constitution of the empire as well as the noble lords who are now in office; and consequently, they will have a watchful eye over their liberties, to prevent the least encroachment of their hereditary rights.[1]

But none of the ministry took Lord Chatham's warning. Nor did he and others of the Opposition find significant support among the English public. Indeed, throughout the spring and summer of 1774, public opinion in Great Britain ran strongly against the Americans in general and the Bostonians in particular. Virtually, every commentator insisted that the colonists owed allegiance to Parliament, not just to the crown. They justified the Coercive Acts in terms of parental correction. "Spare the rod and spoil the child," warned one observer, without much originality. Even William Dowdeswell

[1] Hansard, *Parliamentary History of England* (London, 1815) XVII, 1355.

referred to the colonists as children, but as he did so, he reminded Parliament that just as there were "forward children" so too were there "peevish parents." The more often parents demanded "You shall do it," the more likely children would answer "I won't," he cautioned.

If almost all Britons agreed that Parliament enjoyed legislative authority over the American colonies, they disagreed over the best means by which to exercise this authority. Among members of Parliament coercion was obviously the most popular method of handling disobedient colonies, as evidenced by the overwhelming adoption of the Coercive Acts. Leniency had been tried in the repeal of the Stamp Act and most of the Townshend duties, with no success, they argued. Therefore it was time for harsher measures. Numerous letters calling for severe punishment of the Bostonians appeared in the London press. One writer proposed that they be prohibited from building ships, from engaging in foreign and coastwise trade, and from fishing on the banks off Newfoundland. Another suggested that "about one hundred of these Puritanical Rebels" ought to be hanged, while a third proposed that if Massachusetts Bay continued its disobedience, its charter should be annulled altogether, with half the province going to New York, and the other half to Nova Scotia. Most authors of such severe measures believed the Bostonians to be in a state of actual rebellion. Fleets, armies, and artillery trains were the only responses the Americans would understand. "The Boston rioters will scamper behind their counter . . .," sneered one commentator, "then assume an affecting hypocritical air, clasp their hands, cast up their eyes to Heaven, [and] wonder if the King knows their oppressed condition."

In the great debate on colonial policy, all arguments ultimately led to the question of Parliamentary taxation of America. When a member moved repeal of the tea duty in April, the House of Commons had an opportunity to discuss the issue at length. The leading speaker was Edmund Burke, whose famous speech on the subject was subsequently published under the title *On American Taxation.* He pointed out that by the principles of the Navigation Acts the colonies contributed to the mother country through their commerce. Direct revenue by taxation was never seriously contemplated by Parliament until the Grenville ministry's proposals. Americans complained about the Navigation Laws, and even evaded them, but so too did Britons at home. The Americans did not deny the validity of the acts, however; only when a new system of revenue was combined with the familiar system of commercial regulation did they complain. Burke urged repeal of the tea duty and a return to the old system. But the motion lost, 182 to 49. Although this was the highest proportion of votes gained by the Opposition forces during the course of the debates on colonial policy, the margin was still nearly four to one against the Americans. Yet another opportunity for conciliation was rejected.

The Continental Congress

When the colonists learned of the Port Act in mid-May 1774, a spontaneous wave of sympathy for the plight of Boston swept through the continent. Inhabitants of southern colonies, none too kindly disposed toward the Boston Yankees in earlier years, put aside petty jealousies and came to the aid of the beleaguered town. George Washington spoke for many cautious Americans when he wrote that "the cause of Boston . . . now is and ever will be considered as the cause of America (not that we approve their conduct in destroy [in] g the Tea.)" From southern ports and inland towns, from villages throughout the thirteen colonies, came aid in the form of livestock, foodstuffs, and money, all representing the willing sacrifice of countless Americans able for the first time to play at least a minor role in the struggle against a British ministry which each day appeared more tyrannical. And echoed in the resolutions accompanying their gifts were the words of Washington, that Boston's cause was the cause of all America. Within a few weeks, the magnitude of the ministry's blunder had become apparent. Instead of serving as a warning to other colonists not to follow in the steps of rebellious Boston, the closing of the port did more to bring about American unity than all the efforts of Samuel Adams and his friends. By mid-June, it was agreed throughout the colonies that another congress like that prompted by the Stamp Act should be held to determine a joint policy of action.

During the summer of 1774, towns, counties, and colonies held conventions to decide how to elect their delegates to the coming meeting at Philadelphia, and what instructions if any to give them.

Interestingly enough, both strong patriots and more cautious conservatives welcomed the idea of a congress, the former as a way of focusing public opinion against the ministry, the latter as a chance of confining American reaction to mere words. In some colonies, like Rhode Island and Massachusetts, the patriots succeeded in naming the delegates without difficulty, while in New York and Pennsylvania, moderates and conservatives maintained considerable influence in the selection process. Nor was there any consistent method of choosing delegates from colony to colony. In some, the legislature made the choice; in others the selection was made by an *ad hoc* convention of towns and counties.

By translating the idea of a congress into a reality, the colonists had achieved a truly remarkable accomplishment. For the decision was made on the grass-roots level by thousands of colonists. Furthermore, most of the Americans taking part in these proceedings had decided what they wanted their congress to do. First, they expected the body to support the Bostonians in rejecting the terms of their punishment for the Tea Party. Second, they instructed their delegates to state the rights of the colonists as they saw them and to petition for a redress of grievances. Finally, most of them recommended that congress exert some sort of economic pressure on Great Britain, by a cessation of trade or the threat of it, in order to force an acceptance of colonial demands. The delegates from at least eight of the colonies were either specifically instructed to support a commercial boycott, or at least they personally favored such action themselves.

The First Continental Congress met at Philadelphia's Carpenter's Hall in early September 1774. The climate of opinion toward the mother country had changed markedly in the nine years since the Stamp Act Congress of 1765. Among the more popular political pamphlets making the rounds in the late summer of 1774 was *A Summary View*, by the young Virginian, Thomas Jefferson. For the first time, a major American spokesman openly denied the validity of the Navigation Acts and other parliamentary measures affecting the economy of the colonies. Jefferson did not base his argument on the injustice of these measures. Rather, he wrote, "the true ground on which we declare these acts void is, that the British Parliament has no right to exercise authority over us." The Pennsylvania lawyer, James Wilson, shared Jefferson's position concerning Parliament in his *Considerations on the Authority of Parliament,* published at about the same time. Both Jefferson and Wilson had carried the old "no taxation without representation" argument to its logical conclusion. But the Virginian went a step further in *Summary View* by criticising the king himself for continuing to exercise the ancient right of veto over colonial legislation long after he had given up the practice concerning acts of Parliament. While Wilson and other commentators clearly stated that Americans owed allegiance to the crown, Jefferson contented himself with appealing to the king as "chief magistrate of the British empire."

Within the first two weeks the Continental Congress determined on a strong stand against Great Britain when the assembly endorsed the Suffolk Resolves, a set of resolutions adopted by Suffolk County Massachusetts earlier in the month. That county, which included the town of Boston, recommended that the people commence military training, confining themselves to defensive measures "so long as such conduct may be vindicated by reason and the principles of self-preservation, and no longer." Then the congress rejected by a narrow margin a conciliatory plan of union offered by Pennsylvania's Joseph Galloway. This scheme would have established a Grand Council of representatives from all the colonies to raise a revenue and otherwise to oversee American affairs. But the council would admittedly be a body inferior to and dependent upon the British Parliament, and by the autumn of 1774 such an arrangement was no longer acceptable to many Americans.

Next, the delegates accepted a series of resolutions that came to be known as the Declaration of Colonial Rights and Grievances. Among them was a clause written by John Adams asserting the colonists' right to self-government in matters of taxation and internal law. The resolution did grant that by consent, not by right, Parliament might regulate the commerce of the empire to the advantage of the mother country, provided no attempts were made to raise a revenue thereby. Consistent with this statement, the declaration ruled that all existing acts of Parliament that taxed the colonists were infringements on American rights. So too were the Coercive Acts, the Quebec Act, and several other laws, all of which the delegates called upon Parliament to repeal.

Having made their demands, the delegates then adopted a program of action. They agreed to ban all importations from Great

Britain and Ireland after 1 December 1774 and resolved that, unless American grievances were redressed by 10 September 1775, exports from America to Great Britain, Ireland, and the West Indies would stop as well. To enforce this program of economic retaliation known as the Continental Association, the Continental Congress authorized groups of patriots in each town or county to interfere in the private affairs of all citizens. With the adoption of addresses to the king and to the people of Great Britain stating their case, the First Continental Congress adjourned in late October, after providing that another congress be convened in May 1775, unless the colonists' grievances were redressed before that date.

Committees of Safety and Inspection sprang up in all parts of the colonies to form with existing committees of correspondence a network of extralegal government. Not only did these revolutionary groups enforce provisions of the Continental Association but they also organized militia units, ordered gunpowder and other munitions, and stood ready for come what may. In some colonies, members of these extralegal bodies altogether superseded royal officials as the effective government. In Massachusetts, General Thomas Gage, who had replaced Thomas Hutchinson as governor in May 1774, refused to convene the newly elected legislature in the fall. But its members met anyway, declared themselves a provincial congress, and prepared for war. In Virginia, Patrick Henry told delegates at a special convention that the time had arrived for a military defense of American rights.

As the spring of 1775 approached, General Gage found his position in Boston increasingly dangerous. Rebellious inhabitants in nearby Portsmouth, New Hampshire, had seized the gunpowder stored in Fort William and Mary by a bloodless assault, and an expedition Gage had sent to capture patriot military supplies in Salem was ignominiously thwarted by a band of local minutemen. His instructions from Lord Dartmouth made it clear that he was expected to take the offensive to halt the spread of rebellion in the countryside around Boston. When he learned that the patriots had a major store of munitions at Concord, therefore, he prepared a force of nearly a thousand regulars to seize or destroy them. The resulting skirmishes at Lexington and Concord might well have been conveniently forgotten like the two earlier clashes, had the leaders of Great Britain and America strongly wished to preserve the peace. In fact, General Gage, in reporting the day's events to the Secretary of War, appended his account casually to a routine report: "I have now nothing to trouble your Lordship with but of an affair that happened here on the 19th instant . . . ." But the Americans were decidedly unwilling to forget the episode and made every effort to assure that the shots fired that day would indeed be heard "round the world."

Messengers carried the news of Lexington and Concord to the inhabitants of other colonies, while the minutemen of Massachusetts beseiged the British troops in Boston and prepared themselves for further action. When the Americans took positions on strategic Breed's Hill overlooking the town, Gage finally succeeded in dislodging them after the costly Battle of Bunker Hill. While Gage tried to improve his position in Massachusetts, Lord John Murray, fourth Earl of Dunmore, governor of Virginia, was having equal difficulty controlling the rising rebellion in his domain. By the summer of 1775, the Second Continental Congress, which had convened as scheduled in May, appointed George Washington commander in chief of the Continental forces and did what it could to supply him with the necessary arms and men. In a ringing proclamation called "The Causes and Necessity of Taking Up Arms," the Congress traced the course of recent events to the present crisis. The king and Parliament had both ignored the petition of grievances submitted by the First Continental Congress; General Gage had made "an unprovoked assault on the inhabitants" of Massachusetts; his troops had wantonly burnt the town of Charlestown (during the Battle of Bunker Hill). "We have taken up arms," the delegates proclaimed, "in defense of the freedom that is our birthright . . . . We shall lay them down when hostilities shall cease on the part of the aggressors . . . and not before." And so the dispute between Great Britain and the colonies was to be settled on the battlefield.

British Policy

England had learned of the decisions of the First Continental Congress in late autumn 1774. King George's speech opening Parliament in November assured the assemblage that strengthening the supreme authority of that body in America was uppermost in his mind. Not surprisingly colonial affairs played an important role in the session that followed. Parliament had no sooner returned from its Christmas holiday when William Pitt (Lord Chatham) proposed in the upper house that Great Britain withdraw its troops from Boston as a first step toward re-establishing American confidence in the mother country. He also called for the immediate repeal of these acts which the Congress complained of, predicting that sooner or later they would have to be repealed, and Pitt was right, for most of the detested acts would be rescinded by 1778. But both of his proposals for reconciliation lost by overwhelming margins. Within a month, Parliament voted to increase His Majesty's military and naval forces.

Meanwhile, the House of Commons turned its back on petitions from various groups of English merchants pleading for a restoration of peace and harmony between the mother country and its colonies. After many days of debate, both Houses agreed that rebellion in fact existed within Massachusetts Bay and urged "the most effectual measures to enforce due obedience to the laws and authority of the supreme legislature." One of those measures was the so-called New England Restraining Act, which limited the commerce of all four New England colonies to Great Britain, Ireland, and the British West Indies (the very regions, of course, which all colonists had agreed to boycott in the Continental Association). More significantly, they were also prohibited from fishing on the banks off Newfoundland, the cornerstone of New England trade. A handful of America's friends in Parliament protested that the measure would confront thousands of innocent colonists with the prospect of starvation, but the measure easily passed in late March.

To counterbalance these efforts to coerce the colonies into submission, in late February 1775, Lord North brought in what have been called his "Conciliatory Propositions." The heart of the proposal was that Parliament should refrain from levying taxes in any colony that agreed to make voluntary contributions for the support of its own defense. Immunity would last only as long as the grants continued. While some of the hard-liners were baffled by the ministry's apparent leniency, Colonel Barré and Edmund Burke had no trouble seeing through to the real purpose of the proposal — to divide the weaker colonies from the stronger without making any meaningful concessions to either group. The resolution was adopted by a margin of three to one and sent on to the governors in America for submission to the colonial legislatures.

It was Edmund Burke who picked up the olive branch of reconciliation offered by Lord Chatham in January. Burke's speech, "On Conciliation," before the House of Commons on March 22, 1775, remains a classic. He pointed out that the real value of the American colonies was as a market for exports from the mother country, worth in 1772 over £6,000,000, far more than could be obtained by insisting on the right to tax them. He recognized as so few other Britons did, that the colonies had matured greatly and could no longer be treated as dependent children. Because of their English descent, their religion, manners, form of government, and remoteness from the mother country, Burke noted, have combined to make "the spirit of liberty ... stronger in the English colonies probably than in any other people of the earth." Burke thought it very unlikely that Great Britain could change this spirit and that it would be foolish for it to try.

Burke defined an empire as "the aggregate of many states under one common head." The line between the privileges and immunities of the subordinate parts and the supreme common authority was difficult to draw. Rather than argue over matters of right, the mother country should seek to compromise its differences with the colonies in the name of humanity, reason, and justice. Rather than attempting to hold the empire together by coercion, the mother country should foster "the close affection which grows from common names, from kindred blood, from similar privileges, and equal protection. . . ." Instead of insisting on Parliament's right to tax the colonies, or demanding that the individual legislatures vote regular supplies, Burke simply pointed out that when the crown had in the past called upon the colonies to make such grants, they had cheerfully done so. He then proposed the repeal of all the revenue and coercive measures passed since 1763 as a first step toward peaceful reconciliation.

Most of Burke's fellow members of Parliament could not perceive the kind of empire Burke had in mind. Instead, they insisted that the supremacy of Parliament be upheld under all circumstances and denied that the American assemblies ever had the legal power to grant monies to the crown. This was a privilege of Parliament only, won in the glorious revolution of 1688. To give it up, of course, would have meant the surrender of Parliament's exclusive domination over the king. Burke's motion lost 270 to 78, and the last real chance for reconciliation was lost with it. For within two months Great Britain learned of the outbreak of hostilities at Lexington and Concord. Thereafter the king, ministry, and Parliament looked to still stronger measures of coercion.

Even as early as the previous autumn, George III had found it difficult to think in terms of compromise. In September 1774, he had exclaimed "the dye [sic] is now cast, the Colonies must either submit or triumph." And two months later, he said of the Americans that "we must either master them, or totally leave them to themselves and treat them as Aliens." Such an "either-or" attitude left little room for meeting the colonists part way. One reason for this intractable position was the conviction widely held in England that the Americans, despite their frequent denials, were in reality plotting for independence. How better to explain the rebellious behavior at Boston and elsewhere? Many supporters of the king shared his view that "there are evil spirits walking among ourselves who . . . are the chief instruments in misleading the deluded populance of America . . ." How better to explain difficulties abroad than by blaming the Opposition party at home? To compromise with the Americans would not only be abetting their intentions to declare independence but it would also give victory to the king's domestic opponents.

News of the outbreak of hostilities at Lexington and Concord convinced still more Britons of the Americans' intentions and made compromise still less likely. "Treating with Rebels, while they have Arms in their Hands," wrote one observer, "would demonstrate a Weakness in Government which no Victory could compensate for. If they are sincere, let them lay down their Arms, and implore Pardon," he concluded. Otherwise, as Lord North had argued in February, "they must be reduced to unconditional obedience." Throughout the year 1775 Great Britain escalated its commitment of force to bring the war to the general American population. Thus, in early spring, the New England Restraining Act was extended to include New Jersey, Pennsylvania, Maryland, Virginia, and South Carolina. And month by month the king increased his land and naval forces and assured himself that whatever action was taken in America would not be interrupted by foreign intervention.

The low opinion which many Britons had of the colonists made such a policy easier to adopt. "Shall illustrious Britannia meanly truckle to an upstart province of her own creation and nutrition," sneered one commentator; "[and] submit to be governed by a rebel rout of fanatick, canting hypocrites; a meaner lower class of her own bastard subjects, composed of a medley, the refuse of this and all nations?" How unlikely it was that those Britons who held a similar view of the colonists would accept a compromise settlement, such as Burke's, which suggested a degree of equality between the English and the Americans. Much more likely were they to accept the virtual declaration of war issued by Parliament in the late autumn of 1775, when the American Prohibitory Act authorized the seizure of all American vessels found engaged in any form of commerce, "as if the same were the ships and effects of open enemies."

The Coming of Independence

While the ministry of Great Britain moved steadily away from any real effort at reconciliation, the Continental Congress vacillated between policies of firmness and leniency. Two days after adopting the outspoken "Causes and Necessity of Taking Up Arms," in early July 1775, for instance, the Congress endorsed the so-called Olive Branch Petition, again beseeching George III to intercede in behalf of the Americans. "We solemnly assure your Majesty that we...most ardently desire the former harmony between [Great Britain] and the colonies." The petition was drafted by John Dickinson and was strongly supported by moderate delegates still hopeful of reconciliation, although in fact it conceded nothing of substance to the mother country. At the end of July, however, the Congress rejected out of hand Lord North's "Conciliatory Propositions." Great Britain would have to offer more than tentative suspension of the *practice* of taxation on Americans. By the summer of 1775, most delegates to the Congress would not have settled for anything less than abandonment of Parliament's right to tax them.

John Adams and other more extreme patriots thought another petition from the Congress to the king useless, and indeed when Lord Dartmouth was handed the Olive Branch Petition in September, he told the colonial agents that he would not even present it to the king.

Adams preferred to negotiate from strength. Privately, he believed the Congress should draw up a constitution, establish a navy, open American ports to all nations, and arrest loyalists and royal officials as hostages for the inhabitants of Boston. Then perhaps negotiations with Great Britain might result in a meaningful reconciliation. Adams knew that these views were not yet widely enough shared in the summer of 1775 for him to propose such a program to the Congress.

Throughout 1775, Americans in general, like the Congress that represented them, were genuinely hopeful of a reconciliation with the mother country. For the loyalists, who did not share the suspicions of British intentions that concerned other colonists, reconciliation was the primary goal. But for many Americans, the preservation of liberty was far more important. The major question for them was how best to protect their freedoms from what they considered an all-out attack by the British ministry. The answer for most Americans probably lay somewhere between Dickinson's faith in petitioning and Adams's reliance on strenuous measures. Like all middle ground, this one was difficult to define in its own terms. Beyond containing General Gage's forces in Boston, continuing the boycott against British trade, and strengthening the armed forces, there was little more that most Americans felt could be done.

As the year 1775 drew to a close, however, a few Americans began to discuss publicly what some of them had been considering privately for months — a declaration of American independence from Great Britain. Ironically, British observers had been insisting since the imperial crisis began that the Americans really intended all along to break free from the mother country. But in fact one can find only isolated expressions favoring independence in either the private correspondence or public prints of the Americans until well into the summer of 1775. As the hostilities continued, however, independence became at least an acceptable topic of public discussion. Several actions on the part of Great Britain made it increasingly difficult for the loyalists and moderates to hold the line. In October 1775 a small British fleet bombarded Falmouth (now Portland, Maine) and destroyed much of the town. Subsequently, other New England seaports were raided. In November, Virginia's Governor Dunmore granted freedom to all slaves and indentured servants who would join his troops. In early January 1776, his forces burned the town of

Norfolk. At about the same time, Americans learned of the king's address to Parliament declaring them all rebels, and they heard it rumored that he was arranging to hire German and Russian mercenaries.

Then, in mid-January 1776, came the publication of a pamphlet which stated the case for independence far more persuasively than any previous letter or document. *Common Sense* was written by an Englishman, Thomas Paine, who had arrived at Philadelphia in 1774 after an earlier life spent fighting against what he considered the tyranny of British government at home. By the summer of 1776, over one hundred thousand copies of *Common Sense* had been sold in the thirteen colonies and in England as well. Paine recognized that many Americans still held a strong sense of loyalty to King George, and he set out to demonstrate how misplaced their faith really was. Referring to the monarch as the "Royal Brute," Paine pointed out that as long as the colonies remained under George III "he will have a negative over the whole legislation of this continent. And as he hath shown himself such an inveterate enemy to liberty, and discovered such a thirst for arbitrary power; is he, or is he not, a proper man to say to these colonies, '*You shall make no laws but what I please.*'"

As the spring of 1776 arrived, increasing numbers of colonists came to support the idea of independence, though not all for the same reasons, perhaps. Some Americans rationalized their decision in Lockean terms — that the king had already violated the compact between ruler and ruled by various transgressions and therefore the colonists (like Englishmen of 1688) were absolved from further obligations of loyalty. Some Americans looked around them and saw that in most colonies royal government was no longer in effective power. For them, a declaration of independence would be an accurate description of the real state of political affairs. Still others supported independence because they believed that after so many months of warfare it was too late to turn back, that the mother country would take advantage of any negotiated peace to adopt repressive measures far more severe than the Coercive Acts.

Most of the Americans who came to favor independence during the spring of 1776 saw the move as a means to an end rather than as an end in itself. Time and time again commentators in private and public correspondence viewed independence as a last resort, as the only way they saw left by which to preserve American liberties from British tyranny. A handful of colonists regarded independence as the fulfillment of some natural destiny of America and its inhabitants, although some of them were uncertain that 1776 was the proper time for America to go its own way. The Scots poet Thomas Blacklock had an interesting observation concerning independence. In a pamphlet published in early 1776 entitled *Remarks on the Nature and Extent of Liberty,* he pointed out that "America is wise enough to see that the independence of a state must be intrinsic and can never derive permanence or security from political negotiations alone." In other words, any meaningful independence would have to be won by American power, for as Thomas Paine put it in *Common Sense,* "If /the British/ cannot conquer us, they cannot govern us."

During the spring of 1776, other events combined to give the movement for independence increasing momentum. As the fighting became more intense, naturally feelings became more bitter. The British evacuation of Boston in March meant that for several months not a British soldier stood on American soil. Individual colonies like New Hampshire and South Carolina quickly set up new governments as royal authority dwindled away. In April, the Continental Congress voted to throw open the ports of America to the ships and goods of all nations, a virtual declaration of economic independence. In May, the Congress called on all the provinces to establish stable governments, and from Philadelphia John Adams wrote that "every post and every day rolls in upon us Independence like a torrent." Towns and counties both in New England and in the southern colonies called upon the Congress to declare independence. Only the middle colonies hung back. In June, the delegates adopted a resolution proposing a declaration of independence, the formation of foreign alliances, and the establishment of a confederation among the American states.

The moderates, headed by John Dickinson, managed to postpone consideration of independence until 1 July. Meanwhile, Virginia's Thomas Jefferson was given the task, along with John Adams and Benjamin Franklin, to draft a declaration in the event that the Congress so decided. When the delegates reconvened, they learned that New Jersey had elected new representatives, that Maryland's delegation had swung in favor of separation, and that Pennsylvania had removed earlier restrictions prohibiting its delegation from supporting independence. Dickinson rose to state once more the case against the Declaration. Perhaps the quarrel could be settled by compromise. Perhaps the British commander reported arriving at New York had new terms to offer from the ministry. Should we not wait until we learned what France would think of independence? Why hurry? It appeared to John Adams and others favoring the break that they had already delayed long enough. A declaration would inspire the soldiers, encourage foreign assistance, and forestall Britain's attempt to divide and conquer the colonies, Adams argued in rebuttal to Dickinson. On a poll of all the delegations later that day, however, only nine voted in favor of independence. The decision was postponed until 2 July. Then, with New York still abstaining, all the others joined in declaring the American colonies free and independent states. Now they must *win* their freedom.

FURTHER READINGS

See suggested readings at the end of Chapter 9. In addition, Benjamin W. Labaree, *The Boston Tea Party* (New York, 1964) studies an important event in the coming of war, while Bernard Donoughue, *British Politics and the American Revolution 1773-1775* (London, 1964) focuses on the Coercive Acts and other aspects of the British reaction, and Gerald S. Brown, *The American Secretary: The Colonial Policy of Lord George Germain, 1775-1778* (Ann Arbor, 1963) carries the British side of the crisis into the war itself. Michael G. Kammen, *A Rope of Sand: The Colonial Agents, British Politics, and the American Revolution* (Ithaca, 1968) and Jack M. Sosin, *Agents and Merchants: British Colonial Policy and the Origins of the American Revolution, 1763-1775* (Lincoln, 1965) discuss efforts to hold the dividing empire together. John Shy, *Toward Lexington: The Role of the British Army and the Coming American Revolution* (Princeton, 1965) focuses on another factor. Edmund C. Burnett, *The Continental Congress* (New York, 1941) and Carl Becker, *The Declaration of Independence* (New York, 1922) are two classics on their subjects, while in John M. Head, *A Time to Rend: An Essay on the Decision for American Independence* (Madison, 1968) a new interpretation is offered.

11

War and Peace, 1775-83

What makes the military aspect of the revolutionary war of enduring significance is the fact that the Americans had to *fight* for their independence. In 1774, a British pamphleteer, Josiah Tucker, in his *Four Tracts Together with Two Sermons,* proposed that Great Britain simply declare the colonies free, then and there, not because he wanted the mother country to be rid of them, but because he knew that if *given* their freedom, the colonies would soon quarrel among themselves and have difficulty making their own way in the rough world of the late eighteenth century. Within a few years, he predicted, they would be begging their way back into the empire on any terms demanded by Great Britain. The Scottish poet, Thomas Blacklock, made the same observation in his *Remarks on the Nature and Extent of Liberty,* when he explained that "Every independence...which the colonies cannot acquire and maintain by their own internal force is evanescent and fluctuating." Like the manhood rites of many tribes, colonial independence had to be *won* in order to have any meaning. The fact that the American colonists had to fight for their independence from the mother country made all the difference, not only to the revolutionary generation, but to generations of Americans who have followed. The War of Independence was the wellspring of American nationalism, a common endeavor that knit together the inhabitants of thirteen colonies and made possible the sublimation, for nearly a century, of their very real differences.

The Loyalists

For a significant minority of Americans, the Revolution was a civil war before it became a war of independence. These were the Loyalists, men and women who ultimately decided that they could not condone armed resistance against their king or support the Declaration of Independence. A number of Loyalists, like Thomas Hutchinson, had in fact defied the American patriots even before the Stamp Act crisis in 1765. Others, such as Maryland's Robert Alexander, supported the patriots' cause until American independence became virtually inevitable in early 1776. The moment of decision for thousands of other colonists came at some time between these dates. Few if any Loyalists completely approved of all the measures adopted by Great Britain as the crisis deepened. But they were faced with a take-it-or-leave-it decision, and they chose to take continued membership in the empire rather than independence.

Colonists became Loyalists for a great variety of reasons. Most inhabitants who held appointive positions with the royal government of their colony remained loyal to the king. Not only were oaths of office taken seriously, but self-interest usually dictated drawing one's salary and commissions as long as one could. Other members of the Establishment, merchants who profited from British army contracts, lawyers who prosecuted cases for the king, and the wide network of others dependent on the royal governors' favors for income or self-esteem, or both, had good reason to remain loyal. Not surprisingly, British-born inhabitants of the colonies were more likely to be Loyalists than native-born Americans, although there were numerous exceptions each way. Thomas Paine, Horatio Gates, and John Paul Jones, were all recent immigrants at the outbreak of the Revolution, while Thomas Hutchinson was only one of many Loyalists descended from early American settlers. Expediency persuaded some to remain loyal, those who were convinced the Americans could not win; and fear of the future compelled others to oppose the changes that were taking place all around them. In particular, members of the upper class, content with the *status quo* that found them on top, saw nothing good in turning out British authority.

As with many patriots, ideology as well as expediency accounted for the decision made by a number of Loyalists. Many sincerely regarded the British constitution as the best possible form of government. They pointed to the great progress and prosperity achieved by the American colonies while under British protection, and they saw no reason to change. They dreaded the possibility of anarchy and civil chaos, which they were convinced would become permanent features of the republican form of government espoused by most patriots. Some Loyalists had already suffered at the hands of unruly crowds. They had good reason to condemn the inability (or the unwillingness?) of the patriots to enforce respect for the rights of their opponents. The danger to their liberties, they believed, came not from Great Britain but from the excesses of democracy which they identified with the revolutionary movement. One Pennsylvania Loyalist entered a poem in his diary which included the following stanza:

> In order God has wisely rang'd the whole
> And animates that order, as the Soul;
> In due gradation, ev'ry rank must be,
> Some high, some low, but all in their degree.[1]

Many colonists who shared this belief that God ordered peoples into superior and inferior ranks also believed the colonies to be naturally and permanently subordinate to the mother country.

For a number of Americans, the issues between Great Britain and the colonies were of secondary importance in determining their loyalism. More significant were ancient quarrels which had divided inhabitants long before the dispute with the mother country. In Connecticut, for instance, sharp theological differences divided New Light and Old Light Congregationalists, and the split was worsened by the fact that many of the New Lights hailed from the eastern end of the colony and were involved together in a controversial company speculating in land along Pennsylvania's Susquehanna River. When Old Lights seemed to acquiesce in the Stamp Act, the New Lights

[1] "Short notes on the Life of Robert Proud, Written by himself, 1806," Proud Papers, (Historical Society of Pennsylvania).

seized this opportunity to combine politics with religion and economics and charged their opponents with lack of patriotism. After losing control of the colony's government in the election of 1766, many Old Lights drifted toward loyalism as a means of continuing their opposition to the party now in power. In New York, some of the small farmers long oppressed by wealthy landowning families who became patriots took out their frustrations by supporting the cause of Great Britain. Numerous frontiersmen in the Carolinas and Virginia similarly looked to the mother country to protect them from the domination of easterners, many of whom were ranking patriots. Historians no longer view the distinction between Loyalists and patriots in terms of rich vs. poor, or merchant vs. farmer. The factors that made the American Revolution a civil war are too diverse to be explained so simply.

In their ideological struggle with the patriots, Loyalists faced almost insurmountable odds. In the first place, most colonial printers sympathized with the anti-British cause, making it difficult for Loyalists to find outlets for their views. As a minority, Loyalists could not easily use the public platforms of town and county meetings as did the patriots. Another problem was that Loyalists had no affirmative ground to stand upon. Most of them personally disapproved of at least some of Britain's actions toward America. How to oppose the patriots, then, without appearing to endorse the ministry became a challenging task indeed. The Loyalists were limited to arguing that the patriots' actions would somehow bring ruin upon the colonies. But "the prophets of doom and gloom" have never been very influential in changing the ways of perennially optimistic Americans. Furthermore, the Loyalists had no program of action. It is always easier to gain the support of people if one can give them some way to participate, like the nonimportation agreements and boycotts organized by the patriots. But the nature of the Loyalist cause precluded such popular programs. Finally, with each new act of taxation or coercion, the British ministry cut more ground out from under the Loyalists. Except for Frederick Lord North's "Conciliatory Propositions," the ministry offered nothing to which Loyalists could point as evidence of the mother country's good will. They were thus left the hapless defenders of a policy they themselves found exceedingly difficult to support.

Loyalists had, of course, come under intermittent pressure from local groups of patriots since the Stamp Act crisis of 1765. For the most part, however, royal officials and seaport merchants bore the brunt of the patriots' displeasure. But as the controversy with Great Britain intensified, so too did the pressure on other Loyalists, and those living in the interior, who had previously escaped attention, now began to pay a price for their minority opinions. Under terms of the Continental Association, localities established Committees of Inspection, which required compliance to the various prohibitions of the Association. Increasingly, reluctant inhabitants were branded "enemies to their country," found their business falling off, and often faced physical intimidation or worse. With the outbreak of hostilities in the spring of 1775, conditions became far more desperate, especially in Massachusetts, where most of the early fighting took place. There many Loyalist families took refuge with General Thomas Gage in Boston. Connecticut's Loyalists flocked to New York City, where their rights were generally accorded somewhat wider respect than in the countryside. There they could remain safely until the end of the war, while those who had fled to Boston were forced to leave when the British evacuated the city in March 1776. Whether fleeing to exile abroad, joining the Redcoats to take up arms against their fellow Americans, or lying low in neutral retirement, Loyalists faced years of uncertainty, for their lives, their families, and their property.

The War's First Phase, 1775-77

General Gage's troops and the minutemen who met them on Lexington Green in the early morning mist of 19 April 1775 fulfilled the prediction made the previous autumn by George III that "Blows must decide whether they /the New England governments/ are to be subject to this country or independent." The controversy between Great Britain and America entered a new stage that day. From 1764 on, British governors had occasionally used troops to maintain order and naval power to enforce the Navigation Acts. And the inhabitants of various colonies had often resorted to violence in opposition to the ministry's recent policies. It was the direct confrontation and exchange of gunfire between the British regulars and American militiamen, however, that marked Lexington and Concord major turning points. While debate would continue for another year, the fate of English America was to be settled on its battlefields and in its coastal waters.

Many of the advantages and disadvantages facing each adversary in the War of American Independence became apparent in the first year of battle. First, the Americans depended on militia serving short terms under amateur leadership, while the British employed regular troops led by professionals. The British could also expect intermittent support from bands of Loyalist troops and from various Indian tribes. By mid-1776, the first of several regiments of Hessian and other European mercenary troops joined the British. Second, the basic strategy of the war unfolded during the early fighting. Many of the coastal towns, already centers of royal government, were in British hands through much of the war, while the Americans controlled most of the countryside. The British objective should necessarily have been to capture or destroy all organized military opposition to their authority in America. The Americans, on the other hand, had to maintain both the means and the will to continue resistance. As illustrated by the fighting in New England during 1775, the war was one of cautious movement, the British sallying forth from their bases along the coast and in Canada, the Americans keeping up a constant harassment and occasionally attempting to dislodge the enemy from the port cities.

A third factor of significance was the British possession of Canada, for it gave them control of the frontier areas from Maine to Virginia. As a result, many backwoodsmen chose to defend their own homes against possible Indian attacks rather than to join the Continental forces against the mother country. Furthermore, the capture, or as patriots put it, the liberation, of Canada became an obsession for which scarce American resources were gambled and lost on several occasions. Finally, the British navy controlled the seas throughout most of the war except for a few critical months. The colonists had only a few naval vessels, and while their privateers hampered the flow of British maritime commerce, losses of American vessels were even more severe.

An American patriot reviewing in June 1776 the events of the war's first year could afford a measure of cautious optimism, for British troops occupied not a single square foot of territory within the thirteen rebellious colonies. One month after the mauling given

Gage's Concord expedition in April 1775, a daring band of volunteers led by the legendary Ethan Allen captured Ticonderoga, the strategic fort located at the junction of Lake Champlain and Lake George. In June came the bloody battle of Bunker Hill, which prompted one Briton to observe that many more "victories" such as that one would cost his country the war. Late in the summer of 1775, the Americans launched twin drives into Canada. One led by General Richard Montgomery followed the Lake Champlain route and culminated in the capture of Montreal in the autumn. The other, under Benedict Arnold, slashed through the Maine woods to the gates of Quebec City, where the two forces joined. In the furious assault that followed, Montgomery was killed and the expedition to capture the city failed, but the Americans remained in Canada until late in the spring of 1776. Meanwhile, troops under General Henry Knox had dragged cannons from Fort Ticonderoga through the northern woods to the outskirts of Boston, where they were placed on Dorchester Heights, commanding the occupied port. In March, the British, along with over a thousand Loyalists, abandoned the city to the patriots.

Americans in the southern colonies were no less successful. A force of Loyalists in the Carolina back country were put to rout at Moore's Creek Bridge in February 1776, and in June patriots repulsed an attempted British landing at Charleston. More important than these victories was the fact that in each colony a patriot government was in firm control of both civil and military affairs. Likewise, the Second Continental Congress was beginning to provide necessary central administration of military affairs. From the naming of George Washington as commander in chief to the purchase of military supplies abroad, the Congress was prepared to commit the colonies' last resources to the war. With the Declaration of Independence in July 1776, American fortunes reached a peak not again attained for two more years.

The patriots' determination to achieve independence in fact was almost immediately put to test, for as the Congress issued its Declaration, General Sir William Howe arrived at New York in command of a formidable army of British regulars and German mercenaries. He and his brother Admiral Lord Richard Howe, who soon joined him, served also as commissioners from the crown empowered to make peace with the colonists provided those in rebellion first laid down their arms. Only then were the Howes to disclose their terms of settlement. Among them was a provision for American contributions to the cost of colonial defense by requisition rather than by parliamentary taxation. But self-government for Americans even within the structure of the empire was not mentioned, and of course independence was out of the question. Furthermore, there was no real certainty that the amnesty offered the rebel leaders by the Howes would in fact be honored by their superiors in London. And so, after intermittent discussions and a conference with the Howes, the patriots refused to lay down their arms and concentrated on achieving military victory instead.

General William Howe had already landed his force of over 30,000 men on Staten Island in July, and from there he quickly overran New York's feeble outer defenses in the Battle of Long Island (August 1776), forcing Washington to evacuate the city altogether to avoid further losses. For the next eighteen months, American partisans had little to cheer about. Only the approach of winter seemed to favor the American cause. General Sir Guy Carleton, commanding British forces in Canada, abandoned his drive down the Lake Champlain route until spring after being delayed by a motley fleet of "warships" on the Lake under the command of Benedict Arnold. General Howe settled into a life of gracious luxury among his many admirers in loyalist New York. Washington, in the meantime, had retreated across New Jersey and down into Pennsylvania. In late December 1776, however, he struck back across the Delaware River and captured more than a thousand Hessian troops at Trenton. In another brilliant maneuver, he dealt a stinging blow to the British force pursuing him near Princeton. With these victories for consolation, Washington withdrew into the hills around Morristown, New Jersey, to await the coming of the spring of 1777.

The contrast between the respective winter quarters of Howe and Washington was more than symbolic of the differing circumstances surrounding the two armies. New York, New Jersey, and to a lesser extent Pennsylvania, were centers of loyalism. In occupying the strategic port of New York, Howe received far more aid and comfort from its inhabitants than did Washington from the farmers and villagers of the middle states. As the fortunes of war turned against the patriot army after July 1776, support from the general population dwindled. Morale sagged as supplies ran low, and short-

term militiamen refused to extend their enlistments. The ultimate
success of military resistance depended upon things spiritual as well
as material, and in the winter of 1776-77, despair ran high in the
American camp. Once more the pen of Thomas Paine went to work in
a series of essays entitled *The Crisis*, that appeared in newspapers
and as a pamphlet throughout the continent. "These are the times
that try men's souls," Paine wrote. "The summer soldier and the
sunshine patriot will, in this crisis shrink from the service of his
country, but he that stands it now, deserves the love and thanks of
man and woman." The effect of *The Crisis* papers is more difficult to
assess than that of *Common Sense*, but with the coming of spring,
American forces throughout the continent were prepared for a year of
the war's hardest fighting.

The Turning Point, 1777-78

The patriots faced attack in three major areas during 1777. First and
potentially most dangerous was the twin-pronged British drive from
Canada toward New York City, with the isolation of New England
from the rest of the continent the objective. Throughout the spring
and summer, General John Burgoyne cautiously edged his way down
the historic Lake Champlain route, easily overrunning Fort
Ticonderoga in July. At the same time, an army of regulars and
Indians under Colonel Barry St. Leger pushed through the Mohawk
Valley toward a rendezvous with Burgoyne near Albany. The two
forces were then to drive down the Hudson Valley to meet General
Howe coming north from New York.

But the plan did not succeed. First, an American force under
Benedict Arnold stopped St. Leger by recapturing Fort Stanwix on
the upper Mohawk River in late August. Then, as Burgoyne moved
south from Ticonderoga, hordes of New England militia began
flocking to support the Continental forces now under the command
of General Horatio Gates, formerly a British army officer, who had
come to the colonies in 1774. Gates took up strong defensive
positions south of the village of Saratoga, where, in late September,
he repulsed Burgoyne, who suffered heavy losses. Meanwhile,
General Sir Henry Clinton belatedly moved out of New York with re-
enforcements, but his force was too small to reach Burgoyne in time.

In early October, Arnold led another punishing assault against the British, who were then surrounded in Saratoga and forced to surrender on 13 October, 1775. Over five thousand British and German troops marched off to return to England, under pledge not to fight again in the war.

Part of the blame for Burgoyne's defeat must rest with General Howe. Instead of sending a force up the Hudson to meet the British drive coming south and therefore dividing the attention of the Americans, Howe committed most of his troops to his own pet scheme, an attack on Philadelphia. His fleet did not leave New York until late July, and a change of plans en route meant a passage of more than a month before his force landed at the head of Chesapeake Bay. Washington attempted to halt Howe at Brandywine Creek without success, and in late September 1777, the British occupied Philadelphia, the American capital. Although the Congress had already fled to Lancaster and most of the supplies of military value had been evacuated, the loss of Philadelphia was a blow to the Americans' pride, nonetheless. But it took Howe so long to launch his invasion fleet and capture the city that he was unable to spare sufficient troops to relieve Burgoyne's straitened circumstances.

Howe would have to do more than occupy America's ports if he hoped to put down the rebellion. He had either to capture Washington's army, which he had tried unsuccessfully to do first at Long Island and then at the Brandywine, or he would have to devise some other strategy to break up organized resistance to British forces. In this sense the most effective campaign against the Americans in 1777 was waged not by the British troops but by the Indians. Bands of Cherokees in the south and Iroquois in the north, together with other tribes, inflamed the back country from Maine to Georgia. Thousands of frontiersmen, desperately needed by Washington's Continental army, were tied up in the defense of their homes in the western mountain valleys. On several occasions Washington diverted some of his regular troops to reinforce the frontier militia. These men were as effectively removed from the major theaters of the war as though they did not exist at all.

After an unsuccessful assault on the British defenses near Germantown, Washington withdrew his forces and finally set up camp at Valley Forge. The winter of 1777-78 that Washington spent with his army at Valley Forge has become symbolic of how desperate the American situation was. True enough, the troops were ill-fed and ill-clothed, but these conditions were more a result of incompetent and corrupt suppliers than of country-wide shortages. While cold, the winter was not nearly so severe as that of 1779-80. Refusal on the part of the men to extend enlistments and outright desertions of troops ran at no higher rates than during the previous winter. What has given the ordeal at Valley Forge its real significance was that Washington's troops still stood alone against the British. It was not until spring 1778 that France came to the support of the Americans.

Ever since its resounding defeat in the Seven Years' War and the resultant loss of Canada, France had been looking for the opportunity to settle old scores with her arch enemy Great Britain. When hostilities first broke out between England and her American colonies, France remained officially neutral. But through Pierre Augustin Caron de Beaumarchais and others, the Americans received valuable munitions and other supplies. What finally brought the French openly into the war was a combination of the American success at Saratoga and the failure of General Howe to capture Washington's army at Philadelphia. It remained for the clever Benjamin Franklin, sent by Congress as special envoy to Paris, to make the most of these facts. Franklin had many friends and admirers in France, among them Louis XVI's foreign minister, the Comte de Vergennes. In early February 1778, France recognized the United States, and the two countries entered an alliance to continue the war against Great Britain until American independence was no longer in doubt. What had begun at Lexington and Concord in April 1775 as a skirmish between colonial militia and a detachment of British regulars had mushroomed into a conflict of global proportions.

News of Burgoyne's defeat at Saratoga brought about a change in British military strategy. Lord George Germain, Secretary for the Plantations, concluded that Great Britain could not commit the additional troops deemed necessary for subjugating the rebels in the northern provinces without dangerously exposing the home island in the event of a French war. On his recommendation, therefore, the ministry agreed to rely more on naval power to bring the Americans to their knees. Destruction of the seaports and shipping became the new strategy, even at the cost of evacuating Philadelphia. Perhaps land operations could later be undertaken in the southern provinces. But the British fleet was in no condition to carry on such an offensive as envisioned by the ministry. Lord Sandwich, head of the admiralty, reported in December 1777 that he had only forty-two ships-of-the-line in operational condition, most of which would have to remain in European waters as a defense against a possible French attack.

The defeat at Saratoga and the certain knowledge of American negotiations with France resulted also in a change in British political strategy. Hard pressed by severe criticism within and without Parliament and wracked by self-doubts, the prime minister Lord North longed to resign from the government. But George III would not hear of it. In desperation, therefore, Lord North searched for a way to make peace with the colonists before France could take full advantage of Great Britain's adversity. He laid new conciliatory proposals before the House of Commons in February 1778. England would renounce the right to tax the colonists, although retaining the right to regulate imperial commerce. The Tea Act and the Massachusetts Government Act were to be repealed, and commissioners were appointed to negotiate with the Americans on any terms short of permanent recognition of their independence. Amnesty for the rebels would be guaranteed and a new relationship with the mother country drawn up to assure the colonies of virtual home rule.

These proposals had much in common with those of Edmund Burke in 1775, and in some significant ways they anticipated the kind of British empire that emerged in the nineteenth century. Had the plan been offered by the ministry three years before, it might well have cut the ground out from under the extremists and strengthened the hand of moderates like John Dickinson enough to assure its acceptance by the Continental Congress. But now in the spring of 1778 it came too late. The commission, which took its name from one of its members, the Earl of Carlisle, arrived at Philadelphia just as the city was being evacuated by the new British commander in chief, Sir Henry Clinton. The commissioners were furious at not having been told of this decision upon their departure from England. Their bargaining power was weakened still further by the fact that the Americans had just learned of their treaty with France. The Congress turned aside the British overtures in favor of the French alliance. Several appeals over the heads of the Congress to the

American people failed to generate any popular groundswell in favor of accepting the British terms. In the autumn, the Carlisle Commission departed empty-handed for Great Britain as the war entered its decisive stage.

Final Victory, 1778-82

The new British commander, Sir Henry Clinton, carried out the ministry's revised strategy by evacuating Philadelphia and concentrating his forces in New York. But fearful of Franco-American attacks on his base there, Clinton was careful for the next year or two not to commit his troops to any major offensive campaigns. Except for occasional thrusts up the Hudson or raids against American-held ports, war in the northern states ground to a virtual standstill.

Meanwhile, the war at sea increased in intensity. American privateers, now free to operate from bases in France, mauled British shipping from the mouth of the Thames to the Mediterranean, but not without heavy losses themselves. The newest American hero was a native Scot born John Paul, who had fled to the colonies from a charge of murder and added "Jones" to his name. In 1778, John Paul Jones carried the war to British waters, sinking several vessels within sight of land and launching a daring raid on the English town of Whitehaven, just south of the Scottish border county of his birth. As a result of these activities, the British admiralty was obliged to increase that part of its fleet assigned to home defense. Even so, Jones gave American morale a great boost when, in August 1779, his flagship *Bonhomme Richard* defeated the larger British ship *Serapis*.

Already committed to stations in Mediterranean, African, and Indian waters, the once invincible British navy was no longer capable of maintaining supremacy of the seas. In the Caribbean, vessels of the French navy captured the valuable sugar islands of Dominica, St. Vincent, and Grenada. In North America, the British were forced to evacuate the strategic harbor of Newport, Rhode Island, which was promptly occupied by the French and Americans. To make matters worse, Spain joined with France (but not with the United States) and proceeded to lay seige to the British base at Gibraltar. Spain and France put together a fleet to invade the British bases at Portsmouth and Plymouth. Only incredibly bad planning prevented the allies from carrying out their plans. Most of the maritime nations of northern Europe, eager to settle old scores against the bully of the sea lanes, aligned themselves against Great Britain. Not since the Dutch wars of the previous century had British supremacy been so gravely threatened.

Thwarted in their military efforts in the northern colonies by Washington's army, the British turned to the southern provinces, where they anticipated considerable support from Loyalists. From their base at Savannah, captured at the end of 1778, the British launched a futile attack against Charleston the following spring. A combined Franco-American force was equally unsuccessful in its effort to retake Savannah that fall. Then in February 1780, Sir Henry Clinton arrived off Charleston with an invasion force. General Benjamin Lincoln, a bulky man from Massachusetts, held them off until mid-May, but was then forced to surrender both the city itself and his army of over 5,000 troops. He had no real alternative, for he realized the political consequences of a New Englander withdrawing his troops and leaving an important southern city to the mercy of the enemy.

After the fall of Charleston, Clinton returned to New York, leaving the job of securing the southern colonies to Lord Cornwallis. The task was more difficult than the British first imagined. The great distances between British seacoast bases and interior communities made lines of communication difficult to maintain. Loyalist troops often proved undependable in their support of military operations. Still worse, patriot guerrillas, under such leaders as Thomas Sumter and Francis Marion ("The Swamp Fox") kept the pressure on the British. A small force of regulars under General Horatio Gates, the hero of Saratoga, posed a still more serious threat to Cornwallis's plans. But in August 1780, the British general routed the Americans at Camden (S.C.), inflicting over 800 casualties and taking 1,000 prisoners. Gates was humiliated, and the way now seemed clear for Cornwallis to move through North Carolina and into Virginia.

Matters had been going no better for the Americans in the northern theater of war during the years 1779 and 1780. While Washington managed to keep Clinton pinned down in New York, his own army suffered from serious supply shortages and sagging morale. The Connecticut troops mutinied in the spring of 1779, and during the following winter both the Pennsylvania and New Jersey lines rebelled. The mutineers charged that they were being kept in service beyond their enlistments, were poorly fed and clothed, and had not been paid in over a year. Only with extreme difficulty were the troubles settled, but still half the veteran troops from Pennsylvania went home in disgust. Equally discouraging was the disclosure in September 1779 of Benedict Arnold's treason. Over his head in debt and faced with a humiliating court-martial for his personal conduct while in command of Philadelphia, Arnold had agreed with the British to surrender his new post at West Point for £10,000. When the plot was discovered, the Americans lost the services of a skillful if erratic field general. One of the few bright spots during these dismal months was the arrival, in July 1780, of 5,000 French troops under Comte de Rochambeau. But he cautiously kept his troops out of action at Newport until the French fleet should return from the Caribbean and re-establish command of northern waters. The year 1780 closed with little cause for optimism in the allies' northern headquarters.

In replacing Gates as commander of the southern army in October 1780, the Congress took George Washington's advice and appointed the brilliant Rhode Islander, General Nathanael Greene. Even before he took effective command, American backwoodsmen defeated a force of Loyalists at King's Mountain (S.C.), preventing Cornwallis from following up his victory at Camden. The showdown in the southern theater would come in 1781.

With the new year, the British moved obliquely through the back country into North Carolina. But first Colonel Bonastre Tarleton's force of Loyalists suffered punishing losses to a rag, tag, and bobtail band under General Daniel Morgan at the Battle of Cowpens in January 1781. Greene and Morgan then retreated north, with Cornwallis in hot pursuit. Taking a stand at Guilford Courthouse in mid-March, the Americans again inflicted heavy casualties on the British, though forced to withdraw from the battleground themselves. While Cornwallis nursed his wounds at Wilmington, North Carolina, awaiting re-enforcements, Greene launched a campaign that by the end of the summer cleared the British from all of South Carolina except Charleston and its vicinity.

Lord Cornwallis had long maintained that Virginia was the key to control of the American south, and he wished to become the conqueror of the Old Dominion himself. After notifying Clinton of his intentions, but not waiting for orders, Cornwallis broke camp in April 1781 and led his troops north. He joined British units already at Petersburg, Virginia, and by the end of May, Cornwallis had an army of 7,500 troops under his command. The Americans were divided into two smaller groups, one under the Marquis de Lafayette and the other under Baron Friedrich von Steuben. In June, Colonel Tarleton's cavalry put the Virginia legislature to flight from its capital in Charlottesville, nearly capturing Governor Thomas Jefferson at Monticello. Cornwallis then received orders from Clinton to send him 2,000 troops to assist in the defense of New York, which the British suspected was about to be attacked by a combined Franco-American force.

While Cornwallis finally chose the Yorktown peninsula for his main base in Virginia, the allied armies under Washington and Rochambeau joined at White Plains, north of New York. There they discovered how strong Clinton's defenses of the city were. When Washington learned that the French fleet under Comte François de Grasse, with 3,000 troops, was heading for the Chesapeake area instead of New York, he agreed to a new plan — to pounce upon Cornwallis's army in Virginia. After convincing Clinton that a seige of New York was their objective, Washington and Rochambeau marched southward through New Jersey, Pennsylvania, and Maryland toward a rendezvous with the allied forces which had pinned down Cornwallis at Yorktown. Meanwhile, Admiral de Grasse had arrived in the Chesapeake at the end of August, landed his troops, and stationed his vessels off both the James and York Rivers. The British finally sent a fleet down under command of Admiral Thomas Graves, but indecision doomed to failure his desultory effort to dislodge the French from Chesapeake Bay in early September. This "decision at the Chesapeake" sealed the fate of Lord Cornwallis, for as long as the French fleet maintained command of the sea, he could neither receive re-enforcements by water nor escape by that route himself.

De Grasse met the armies of Washington and Rochambeau at the head of the bay and transported the troops to the James River, from whence they quickly took up seige positions around Cornwallis's camp at Yorktown at the end of September. Confronted with an enemy more than twice the size of his own force of 7,000 troops,

Cornwallis's will to fight on seemed slowly to drain away. Upon learning in New York of the Earl's predicament, Clinton acknowledged that "If Lord Cornwallis's army falls, I should have little hope of seeing British Dominion re-established in America, as our country cannot replace that Army." He hastily prepared a relief force to be sent by sea, but delays in refitting Graves's fleet postponed its departure until mid-October. By then it was too late.

Cornwallis was forced to evacuate his outer defenses on September 30; two weeks later he lost two more key positions by assault. Meanwhile, American and French artillery were bombarding his encampment night and day. His artillery had exhausted its ammunition, and an effort to evacuate his force across the York River by cover of night was thwarted by a vicious rainstorm. On October 19, therefore, not knowing that a relief force was on the way, Lord Cornwallis surrendered his beleaguered army of some 7,000 troops to General Washington, as the band allegedly played "The World Turned Upside Down." Clinton was right; the loss of Cornwallis's army ended all hope of re-establishing British control over its former North American colonies. Although skirmishes continued intermittently for another year, the scene of action now turned to the peace table at Paris.

In England, the news of Yorktown brought down the tottering North government. Its successor, under Rockingham, was authorized to make peace on the basis of recognizing American independence. To Paris came the envoys of Great Britain, Spain, and the United States to meet with representatives of the French government under the Comte de Vergennes. Benjamin Franklin, John Adams, and John Jay, joined later by Henry Laurens, were the principal negotiators for the new nation, and each represented a different American interest. Adams, for instance, showed great concern for freedom of the Grand Banks off Newfoundland, where New Englanders had fished for generations. John Jay emphasized a commercial settlement between the belligerents. Franklin, on the other hand, valued the land beyond the Appalachians, and was willing to sacrifice the other points for a generous western boundary. France did not relish a strong United States, and its support at the peace table proved noticeably less strong than during the war itself.

In negotiating with Lord Rockingham, and after his death in mid-1782, with Lord Shelburne, the Americans were dealing with Britons who had opposed most of the measures that had led to the outbreak of the Revolution seven years before. Furthermore, the Americans gained from the fact that Great Britain had to fend off the demands of France and Spain, particularly the latter's hope of winning Gibraltar at the peace table. Thus, the United States not only gained clear recognition of its independence, a *sine qua non* of the negotiations, but rights to the fishing grounds and generous western boundaries to the Mississippi River as well. In return, the Americans were obligated to honor all debts owed British citizens and the Congress was to "earnestly recommend" that the state legislatures fully restore the Loyalists' estates and civil rights. Although somewhat miffed that the Americans had proceeded to make a separate agreement with the British, Vergennes accepted Franklin's explanation in good spirit. The birth of the new American nation thus received legitimacy, nearly seven war-weary years after the event.

FURTHER READINGS

For the Loyalists see, Leonard W. Labaree, *Conservatism in Early American History* (New York, 1948); William H. Nelson, *The American Tory* (New York, 1961); and Wallace Brown, *The King's Friends* (Providence, 1966) and *The Good Americans: The Loyalists in the American Revolution* (New York, 1969). There are several fine accounts of the war itself, including Willard M. Wallace, *Appeal to Arms: A Military History of the American Revolution* (New York, 1951); Chistopher Ward, *War of the Revolution* (2 vols., New York, 1952); John Alden, *The American Revolution 1775-1783* (New York, 1954); Howard H. Peckham, *The War for Independence* (Chicago, 1958); and more recently Piers Mackesy, *The War for America, 1775-1783* (Cambridge, 1964). The war in the west is discussed in Jack M. Sosin, *The Revolutionary Frontier, 1763-1783* (New York, 1967). More interpretative is Eric Robson, *The American Revolution, 1763-1783* (London, 1955). For short studies of the military leaders on both sides see George A. Billias, ed., *George Washington's Generals* (New York, 1964) and his *George Washington's Opponents* (New York, 1969). The diplomatic aspects of the war are the subject of Samuel F. Bemis, *The Diplomacy of the American Revolution* (New

York, 1935) and Richard W. Van Alstyne, *Empire and Independence: The International History of the American Revolution* (New York, 1965). The definitive study of the Treaty of Paris is Richard B. Morris, *The Peacemakers: The Great Powers and American Independence* (New York, 1965).

12

The New Nation, 1776-89

Neither the act of declaring American independence in 1776 nor its confirmation in the Treaty of Paris in 1783 marked the true end of the Revolution. For most Americans of this era, as we have seen, independence was only a means to the specific goal of regaining and preserving the liberty enjoyed by previous generations of colonists. The best way to measure the relative success of the Revolution is to examine the kind of society that emerged during the first years of independence. The period itself takes its name from the Articles of Confederation, a frame of national government finally adopted by the Congress in 1781 and ultimately replaced in 1789 by the Federal Constitution. Although most of the political changes that took place during these years resulted from the conscious decisions of thousands of inhabitants on the grass-roots level, economic and social conditions particularly were altered as well by the factors far beyond the control of individuals or small groups. A revolution evoked in the name of preserving old values, in short, also produced important changes.

State Government

Since the Revolution was conceived and fought primarily in political terms, the most significant early fruits were naturally political. And since the goal was to preserve rather than innovate, the state governments that emerged after the Declaration not surprisingly bore strong resemblance to their colonial antecedents. The idea that the purpose of government was to protect the rights of the people was, of course, well established in eighteenth-century America. To insure this end, Americans of the revolutionary generation in each colony insisted first on the establishment of a written constitution in which the powers of the government were specifically enumerated. In most states the task was done by the legislature and put into effect without ratification by the people, though generally this procedure was itself approved by the inhabitants. In Connecticut and Rhode Island, the job was simple; since the colonial charters already provided for elected governors and councils, these documents were simply taken over as state constitutions. In Massachusetts, the inhabitants took seriously what their General Court had declared in January 1776: "In every Government there must exist, somewhere, a supreme, sovereign, absolute, and uncontrollable power; but this power resides, always, in the body of the people . . . ." The inhabitants of Concord, for instance, suggested that a convention of delegates chosen by the state's adult males should draw up the constitution. When the General Court failed to take this advice, the electorate rejected their proposed frame of government. Not until 1780, therefore, did Massachusetts finally get a new constitution, one that was drawn up by a popularly elected convention and approved by a majority of the adult males of each town who cared to vote on the matter.

Another protection for the rights of the people was the bill of rights which preceded the actual constitution in most states. Modeled for the most part after the Declaration of Rights drawn up by George Mason, for the state of Virginia, these documents typically asserted the individual's right to trial by a jury of his peers, that he not be deprived of life, liberty, or property except by due process of law, and that he not be compelled to testify against himself. Most states also guaranteed freedom of speech, of the press, and in some cases of religion too.

As further assurance that the new governments would protect rather than threaten the liberties of freeborn Americans, the framers of each state constitution made certain that the locus of political power remained, as it had resided on the eve of the Revolution, in the lower house of the legislature. Traditional features that assured truly representative assemblies were retained, such as the principle that legislators act as delegates of their respective constituents subject to letters of instruction and to annual election. The new constitutions drawn up in the period 1776-80 carefully preserved this close relationship between the sovereign people and their delegates. In many states, the legislatures were made more representative by a broadening of the franchise to include all male taxpayers. Generally, however, there was some minimum property qualification for voters. It is interesting to note that the constitution of Massachusetts, as approved by the free adult males, in fact disqualified some of those same men from becoming voters by its relatively high property qualifications. For the most part, however, only younger adults getting started were deprived of the vote, and very few residents were permanently disenfranchised by these restrictions.

Virginia and the many states that followed its example further strengthened their legislatures by reducing the powers of the governors. Typically, the governor was chosen by the assemblies, had no veto power, and could make no decisions without the advice and consent of a council, again chosen by the legislature. Pennsylvania had no governor at all, executive powers residing instead in a council, one of whose members served as president. These constitutions incorporated a number of other changes calculated to enhance the power of the popular branch of government. In some, the legislatures appointed the judges; the houses were reapportioned more accurately to reflect population; property qualifications for holding office were lowered or dropped altogether; and in some states, delegates were compensated for their services.

The dominance of legislatures in many of the states was simply a natural continuation of their rising influence during the colonial period. Writers of state constitutions were reacting against the days when the royal governor had seemed a formidable antagonist. Another reason was the continuing influence of John Locke, who had emphasized — in a different context — the supremacy of Parliament over the king. Finally, a skeptic might explain the popularity of strong legislatures in revolutionary America by pointing out that the constitutions were drawn up by the house of representatives in every state but Massachusetts, and the authors, not surprisingly, reserved for themselves a full measure of governmental authority.

In contrast to the constitutions of Virginia and Pennsylvania, the frame of government drawn up in Massachusetts by John Adams, in 1780, provided a balance between the upper house, or senate, the house of representatives, and the office of governor. The first was designed to represent property, and its members were apportioned according to the wealth of each county (with results not much different from a distribution based on population); the lower house represented the people; the governor hopefully provided an element of firm authority; and the judiciary was largely independent of domination from either the legislature or the governor. Each branch was enjoined in the state's Declaration of Rights from meddling in the affairs of the other branches, "to the end that it may be a government of laws and not of men."

The appearance of a strong executive in the Massachusetts constitution is probably best accounted for by the fact that the document was not drafted and adopted until 1780, five years after the breakdown of royal government in the Bay State. In the interim, the provisional government was in effect simply the old General Court carrying on under the royal charter without any executive branch at all. The inhabitants probably came to appreciate the value of an effective governor, while the passage of time somewhat allayed their fears of executive government generated by such governors as Thomas Hutchinson and Thomas Gage. Furthermore, the Massachusetts constitution was drawn up by a special convention, not the legislature itself. It is interesting to note that during the decade after1780, many states that had followed the lead of Virginia and Pennsylvania summoned conventions to rewrite their constitutions, granting the executive branch broader powers.

As the historian Robert R. Palmer has pointed out in *The Age of the Democratic Revolution*, the most distinctive contribution that the American Revolution made to the world was in finding a practical means by which to put into effect so many of the political ideas shared by enlightened peoples of the late eighteenth century. The ideas of natural liberty and equality, of government by consent of the governed, of political representation, of independence from foreign domination, of the separation of powers — none of these ideas originated in America. Rather, America's unique contribution lay in the belief that the power to constitute government rested in *the people*. *The people* authorized a constitutional convention, delegated to its members the power to draft a constitution, and then passed judgment on its results. The convention created a government in the name of the people, dissolved, and its members joined the rest of the people in coming under the authority of that government. In the words of Palmer: "Having made law, /the people/ came under law. They put themselves voluntarily under restraint. At the same time, they put restraint upon government." Two levels of law now operated within the American policy: constitutional law, which could only be made or changed by the people, and statute law, which could be made and altered within constitutional limits, by the legislature. The means by which the people exercised constituent power remained America's unique contribution to political practice, a procedure that even the French at the height of their Revolution twenty years later found impossible to duplicate.

The Confederation, 1781-87

With stable government established in each of the states, Americans turned to the task of restoring their economy even before the end of hostilities with Great Britain. The transition from war to peace is always difficult, but in the 1780s, Americans were, in addition, moving from their former position within the mercantilist empire to one of economic independence. It is no wonder, then, that the level of prosperity enjoyed by many Americans as colonists did not immediately return with the ending of hostilities. The war itself had many effects, mostly harmful, on the young nation's economy. First, much of the materiel of war came from abroad, and therefore the profit from its manufacture enriched foreigners, not Americans. Second, the problem of public debt itself was badly handled by most states and by the Continental Congress. Bills of credit amounting to nearly five hundred million dollars in face value were issued by state and national governments as circulating currency, and runaway inflation brought chaos to many segments of the country's economy. Not until Robert Morris established a system of hard money, with the help of a French loan near the close of the war, was a stable currency re-established. Meanwhile, however, merchants and tradesmen, whose business required a dependable system of credit, suffered. When the Congress failed to redeem its bond issues, those shipowners who had patriotically bought government bonds were deprived of the capital they needed to replace vessels lost during the war. Increased taxation levied by debt-ridden state governments added to the fixed costs of every businessman. Farmers were particularly hard hit because land bore a disproportionate share of the tax burden in most states. At the same time, the wartime boom in agricultural produce came to an abrupt end. Purchasing power declined as many farmers went into debt, and by 1782, much of the nation was in the throes of a postwar depression.

What made economic life in the 1780s particularly difficult for the merchants was the fact that they no longer could enjoy a favored place within the empire. It is a credit to many patriotic merchants that they supported the cause of independence despite the uncertain future of their personal fortunes. Now in 1782 they faced the task of finding a place in the competitive commercial world without the benefit of monopoly markets in England and the West Indies, of bounties, and of generous terms of credit. Hopes for a treaty of commercial reciprocity between the two countries faded when Lord Shelburne and other ministers friendly to America were replaced in 1782 by vindictive men like Lord Sheffield. British commercial policy toward America was thereafter hammered out in a series of unilateral Orders in Council. Their author was William Knox, who, as a subminister under Lord North, had long been a foe to the colonial cause. Under these orders, no American vessels could trade with the British West Indies at all, and even British vessels could carry only a limited list of American products to those islands. Sheffield and Knox hoped that the loyal colonies of British North America, like Nova Scotia, would be able to replace New England as the principal suppliers of the West Indies. The fact of the matter was that these provinces could not even support themselves, and the British Caribbean possessions, therefore, suffered even more from their government's policy than did the United States.

While commerce was slow to recover from postwar depression, signs of future prosperity were, nevertheless, apparent. Individual vessels made voyages to new ports previously closed to Americans. Salem vessels made the first calls at Sumatra for pepper; New York and Massachusetts ships found their way to China; other Americans established commercial relations with less exotic ports in the Baltic and Mediterranean. Trade with England once more became the cornerstone of American commerce. Although faced with competition from British vessels flooding northern ports with English goods, merchants could still send tobacco, indigo, rice, and naval stores to markets in Great Britain. For this reason, prosperity returned rather quickly to the southern states. Other economic activities made their appearance in the decade after the war, including the first textile factories in New England, paper mills, nail factories, and iron foundries in several states. Banks and insurance companies were established to provide their essential services, and new turnpikes and toll bridges were built. These all became popular investments for the gradually accumulating capital of the nation's more successful entrepreneurs. Slowly the young nation groped its way through the dark first years of its existence. No one expected economic prosperity to be an early fruit of independence, and for the most part, Americans bore their hardships with patience.

For years, historians have debated whether the American Revolution aimed at social upheaval as well as political independence. Most recent commentators doubt that the patriots of 1776 had any major social reforms in mind, and they are hard pressed to cite examples of social change. There were some cases where the spirit of political liberty was applicable to social matters, as for example the abolition of slavery in most of the northern states and prohibition on the importation of slaves in most of the southern states as well. The disestablishment of the Anglican Church in New York, Virginia, and other states also reflected the spirit of freedom, but it should be noted that in New England, Congregational churches continued to receive public support. The pluralism that has since been characteristic of American religious life blossomed in the years following the Revolution. Methodist, Catholic, Presbyterian, and Lutheran churches all flourished beside older sects in the unfettered environment of the new nation.

In one sense, the fate of the Loyalists is another example of social change produced by the war, although few patriots saw the Revolution primarily as a class war against Loyalists. Many Tories found it necessary to leave the country, and in most cases their real estate was confiscated. The amount of land involved was not great, however, and the new titleholders were often as wealthy as the old. More significant, though no more by design, was the vacuum created among the mercantile circles of New York, Boston, and Philadelphia.

Successful merchants from the out-ports, like the Cabots of Beverly, Massachusetts, moved to the cities to take the emigrés' places and left the way open for upward mobility in their former homes. While most Loyalists remained in exile in England or Canada, those who returned rarely encountered anything more hostile than petty social discourtesy. The reinstatement of some was marked by election to public office, such as the choice of Loyalist Cadwallader Colden as mayor of New York.

One of the most significant developments of the Confederation period was the opening up of the trans-Appalachian west. In 1763, the British had prohibited settlement beyond the mountains and, in a series of treaties, tried to reserve these areas for the Indians. The Quebec Act of 1774 further discouraged Americans from the region by tying it governmentally to Canada. The quest for cheap, fertile land was so great that even before the end of hostilities, Americans followed the trail of Daniel Boone through the mountain passes and into the bluegrass region of Kentucky and the valleys of Tennessee. In 1784, these settlers formed the state of Franklin and applied for admission to the Confederation but were turned down. The search for new lands also took men north into Vermont and east into Maine.

The movement west was not always the result of spontaneous action by individuals, for the role of land speculators was important. Competition between two companies for western lands, claimed by Virginia, held up final ratification of the Articles of Confederation until, in 1781, Maryland was finally persuaded that no one group would get an unfair advantage. Land speculation was the most popular get-rich-quick scheme during the first decades of the young nation. State and national governments as well as individuals looked westward for a source of revenue, and corrupt bargains, involving millions of acres of prime land, were accepted by legislators whose conflicts of interest would make those of a modern-day official look insignificant. But the land companies played an important role as middlemen in the early settlement of the trans-Appalachian west and made land available in relatively small tracts to individual settlers.

In 1780, the Continental Congress announced that federal lands in the west would ultimately become states admissible into the Union along with the original thirteen. The principle of territorial government preceding statehood was introduced by Jefferson's Ordinance of 1785, and in the following year provision was made for the systematic survey of these lands. The New England town system was adopted as the model, with townships six miles square. One section (640 acres) in each township was reserved for the support of education while the other thirty-five sections were sold at auction. In the Confederation period's most significant act, the Northwest Ordinance of 1787, the Congress prohibited slavery from the Old Northwest and guaranteed the orderly expansion of democratic government into the vast interior of the continent.

The Problem of Federal Government

During the spring of 1776, as Americans debated the merits of independence, they had little opportunity to discuss the kind of central authority, if any, that should unite the thirteen colonies under one government. Thomas Paine did not go into the question in *Common Sense*, and not until 7 June 1776 — when Richard Henry Lee moved adoption of his three-part resolution concerning independence, foreign alliances, and confederation — was the subject discussed in the Congress. At the same time that Thomas Jefferson was made chairman of a committee to draft a declaration of independence, John Dickinson headed a group to draw up a frame of government uniting the independent states. But the Congress gave Dickinson's draft only intermittent attention, and it was not adopted with final alterations until November 1777.

General reluctance to rush into national union resulted from two factors. First, leaders of the revolutionary generation were brought up as Virginians, New Yorkers, and Pennsylvanians, and only secondarily considered themselves Americans. Their interest in self-rule did not go much beyond expanding the powers of their colonial legislatures and protecting them from an encroaching ministry and Parliament. Secondly, there was no tradition of union among the American colonies. Previous proposals of voluntary confederation, like the New England Confederation of 1641-76, or the Albany Plan of Union of 1754, were of limited purpose and in no sense provided a precedent for federal government. Nor did the authoritarian Dominion of New England (1685-91) illustrate the benefits of union. Both the Stamp Act Congress and the First Continental Congress met only briefly to deal with specific crises, and it was not until the

Second Continental Congress convened, in May 1775, that delegates from all the American colonies joined in a body sitting continuously and deciding issues as they came along.

Time was on the side of confederation, however. Not only was cooperation among the colonies a military necessity, but the activity of the Congress also generated a national unity of its own. So too did the existence of a Continental army. Likewise the passage of time dispelled, at least temporarily, some of the stronger suspicions between regions and some of the fears concerning a permanent federal government. And so the delegates to the Congress turned their thoughts to the problem of a union among the states. Federalism, the division of political power between individual component states, on the one hand, and a central authority, on the other, was known to eighteenth-century statesmen more in theory than in actuality. Switzerland was a federal union, and so was Holland, and several examples could be found in classical and early European history, but these countries were small, while the American states were spread out along a 1,500-mile coast line and reached hundreds of miles into the interior. The basic question was whether the central authority should act directly on the citizens of the member states or only through the governments of those states. In other words, was the nation to be a union of people or a union of states?

In his draft of a confederation, John Dickinson proposed that each state have votes in the Congress proportionate to its population. In rejecting that innovation in favor of continuing the "one state, one vote" principle, the Congress in effect decided that the confederation was to be one of equal states whose power derived from the governments of those states rather than directly from their peoples. Article II proclaimed that "each state retains its sovereignty, freedom, and independence, and every power, jurisdiction, and right, which is not...expressly delegated to the United States." The new government was to go into effect only when ratified by the legislatures of all the states and could be amended only by unanimous agreement among them.

The new central government was weak not only because it had little authority of its own, but also because it had neither executive nor judicial branches. In short, the Articles of Confederation did little more than legitimize the various powers already assumed by the Continental Congress. These included the authority to make war, manage foreign affairs, deal with the Indians, borrow money and circulate currency, and provide a forum for disputes between states. American colonists almost without exception had long conceded these powers to the British Parliament, a body in which they had no representation at all! It was Parliament's claim to the right of other powers, after all — the collection of revenue, alteration of charters, interference in judicial processes, and the regulation of some aspects of the economy — to which Americans had objected. Not surprisingly, these were among the very powers they now denied the new central government.

Despite weaknesses, the Articles of Confederation settled a number of basic questions. Most obviously they confirmed that all the states would be joined in a single, continuing union under republican principles. The possibility of several regional confederacies or the establishment of a constitutional monarchy, for instance, was ruled out. The Articles provided for growth by the possible addition of Canada and of other new states. By reserving foreign policy matters to the federal government, and by the requirement that the inhabitants of each state be granted the privileges and immunities of all the other states, the Articles also in effect created an American citizenship. Under ideal circumstances, the Confederation might well have lasted until the mid-nineteenth century. But the period 1781-87 was far from ideal, as we have seen, and the Confederation government was constructed too rigidly to cope with the numerous crises facing the new nation.

In order fully to recover from the postwar depression, those segments of the American economy most likely to provide dynamic growth, such as maritime commerce, market agriculture, and manufacturing, all required governmental encouragement. Merchants and planters wanted commercial treaties to establish foreign markets, while manufacturers sought protection from foreign competition. Most of all, a national economy required a government that could establish a uniform system of customs duties among the major ports, develop lines of internal transportation, and encourage the investment of capital in industry. Certainly the majority of Americans, who engaged in bare subsistence agriculture, could survive without such a government. But those Americans with vision believed that future generations deserved more than survival, and they came to realize that government, under the Articles of Confederation, was unable to provide the help necessary for economic growth.

Two western problems also remained beyond possible solution by the weak Confederation. One was Great Britain's refusal to evacuate some of its strategic forts at Niagara, Detroit, and elsewhere in the west. The British justified this violation of the Treaty of Paris on the grounds that the Americans had failed to carry out their obligations in respect to prewar debts and Loyalists' confiscated properties. Actually, the British wanted to maintain their control over the region's valuable fur trade, and until they abandoned the posts in 1796, after Jay's Treaty, American sovereignty in the Northwest Territory was seriously impeded. The other problem stemmed from Spain's influence among the Cherokees and other Indians of the southwest, effectively discouraging American settlement there. Furthermore, Spain denied use of the Mississippi to inhabitants west of the mountains and constantly intrigued to annex the southwestern region to its own Louisiana. It would require a stronger national government than the Confederation to persuade Great Britain and Spain to respect their treaty obligations and to encourage the American states themselves to live up to the terms of the Treaty of Paris.

The movement toward a revision of the federal government began rather inauspiciously with a dispute between Virginia and Maryland about jurisdiction over the Chesapeake Bay fisheries. While the interested parties settled the argument on their own, Virginia was prompted to sponsor a convention to discuss the general difficulties facing American commerce. Delegates from only five states actually attended the resulting session held at Annapolis in September 1786. Realizing that such a small group could take little significant action itself, the members decided instead to call for a new convention empowered to strengthen the central government. The Congress agreed to authorize such a body to meet at Philadelphia in May 1787 for the purpose of amending the Articles of Confederation.

As the Congress debated the proposal of the Annapolis Convention, the most serious crisis yet of the Confederation period came to a head in Massachusetts. The uprising in the summer of 1786 known as Shays' Rebellion grew out of the plight of the farmers on whom the state's poll and real estate taxes bore heavily. With the end of wartime prosperity in 1782, farmers in the central and western counties fell into debt, and many were faced with the loss of their farms. Relief measures such as paper money and land banks were consistently blocked by mercantile interests dominating the state Senate. Finally, in the summer of 1786, groups of desperate farmers gathered at county seats to prevent the courts from sitting. Militia broke up the crowds and, in January 1787, dispersed a band of one thousand farmers which, under the leadership of war veteran Daniel Shays, had attacked the arsenal at Springfield. The authorities had sense enough to deal lightly with the offenders, and the legislature adopted several measures for their relief.

The significance of Shays' Rebellion lay in the impact it made in the minds of political leaders throughout the country. While everyone recognized that Massachusetts had little real difficulty restoring order, observers everywhere were impressed by the fact that the Confederation Congress was helpless to assist any state government in the preservation of peace within its borders. Political leaders like Virginia's James Madison were sensitive about this problem particularly because critics had long predicted that federated republics would be too weak to maintain internal authority. Americans whose political views ranged from the conservatism of George Washington and John Adams to the more democratic outlook of Sam Adams took alarm together at the implications of Shays' Rebellion. More than any other single factor, the farmers of western Massachusetts brought to a head the movement toward a revision of the national government. Within weeks after the Congress acted favorably on the proposal of the Annapolis Convention, all states but Rhode Island had selected their delegates to the forthcoming meeting at Philadelphia.

The Federal Constitution

The men who gathered at Philadelphia in late May included the most intelligent and experienced leaders of the young nation. Many of the patriots who had played important roles in the events of the preceding two decades were present: George Washington, Benjamin Franklin, James Wilson, John Dickinson, and George Mason. Among the missing were Thomas Jefferson and John Adams, both serving as ministers abroad; also absent were Samuel Adams and Patrick Henry, neither of whom had distinguished himself as a statesman in the years since independence. Among the original fifty-five delegates were many lawyers, college graduates, and men of property. If the nation's plain-dirt farmers had none of their own as delegates, it was because the state legislatures making the appointments found few ordinary farmers prepared for such an assignment. Most of the delegates arrived with certain common assumptions about the state of affairs under the Articles of Confederation. The basic republican principle of that government was inviolate; no one except perhaps Alexander Hamilton seriously considered any other form. So too did the federal concept meet with approval, although many delegates believed the balance of power between state and national levels needed alteration. There was also widespread belief that the central government required additional powers, such as authority to levy taxes, to regulate interstate commerce, and to enforce the acts of the Congress itself. Finally, and most important, it was quickly assumed by most delegates that they should draft a new constitution altogether rather than simply to propose a series of amendments to the Articles. With these basic agreements, the delegates settled down to a summer of hard work.

As expected, the work of the convention consisted mainly of hammering out compromises between positions already taken by various groups of delegates. The fact that these compromises could be reached, and in a form that resulted in a logical end product, is one of the remarkable achievements of the convention. One important division was that between the large and small states. Another was between northern and southern states. Still another existed between those delegates eager to expand democracy and those more concerned with the establishment of stronger governmental authority. One by one, the issues separating these groups were settled. The plan proposed by Edmund Randolph of Virginia served as a useful point of departure, but it was sharply modified to provide for a senate in which all states had equal representation regardless of size. Sectional disputes concerning the slave trade, the regulation of commerce, and the levying of direct taxes were worked out. And while the conservatives dominated the convention, they did not take advantage of their position by forcing through wholesale restrictions against rule by the people. Rather, they adopted the principle of mixed government best represented by the Constitution of Massachusetts, wherein a balance was sought between the ancient principles of freedom and authority.

The resulting document owed much to the work of a relatively small number of delegates. James Madison, James Wilson, Edmund Randolph, Roger Sherman, and Gouverneur Morris deserve most of the credit, although even delegates like George Mason and Elbridge Gerry, both of whom refused to sign the finished product, made significant contributions. Washington and Franklin, while they did not participate in the actual debates, lent dignity and a high sense of purpose to the proceedings by their presence. Although an earlier generation of historians led by Charles Beard cast suspicion on the motives of those gathered at Philadelphia, current writers have found no evidence at all to substantiate the charge that the delegates were unduly moved by the hope of personal gain in their deliberations. On the contrary, more careful research than that undertaken by Beard has proved beyond question that there is no correlation between the kind of property held by delegates and the positions they took in the convention.

What a great majority of delegates did have in common, however, was a "continental viewpoint." Thirty-nine of the fifty-five men had served in the Congress, and nineteen were still congressmen as the Philadelphia Convention sat. They knew how low American prestige had sunk in foreign capitals, and they shared the frustration of struggling with their respective state legislatures. With varying degrees of consciousness, these men were spokesmen for an emerging American nationalism, born of the Revolution itself, and surging into prominence during the years following the Treaty of Paris. They also shared a faith in the principle that the central government, like the state governments, derived its powers from the people.

The government provided by the Constitutional Convention did have much in common with the structure it was soon to replace. Both the old and the new were republics, both were federal in principle, and both provided for the future growth of the union. It is in certain refinements of these principles that the significance of the new proposal is to be found. The government remained republican, to be sure, but now was added a strong executive branch and a system of federal courts. The resulting structure was, like the Articles of Confederation, federal in nature, but instead of being an appendage of the states collectively, the central government had its own sources of authority and worked in limited ways directly on the people without reference to their respective state governments at all. Thus the American was a citizen both of the United States and of his own state. This parallel federalism was an entirely new idea, and while events of nearly two centuries have since wrought changes, the basic principle has remained that the federal and state governments are each sovereign in their own designated spheres. At the same time the Constitution improved upon the provisions of the old Articles for the admission of new states into the Union, thus assuring the orderly growth of the federation into the foreseeable future.

The authors made certain that the new constitution would give the central government sufficient power to be effective. Article VI proclaimed the Constitution to be the "supreme law of the land," and bound all *state* judges, governors, and legislators, as well as federal officers, to uphold it, "anything in the constitution of laws of any state to the contrary notwithstanding." The federal judiciary was given full power to enforce the laws of the central government throughout the land. The Constitution retained the "full faith and credit" clause of the Articles and guaranteed that citizens of each state be entitled to the privileges and immunities of the other states. Among the powers granted the Congress was "to regulate commerce with foreign nations, and among the several states, and with the Indian tribes." Thus the new Congress could fashion a commercial policy for all the nation. And with its authority to raise a revenue, the federal government no longer had to beg from the individual states for necessary funds.

The delegates at Philadelphia had seen it as their responsibility to draw up a constitution that was not necessarily the best in theory, but one that was the best practical government for their fellow Americans. They never lost sight of the fact that their labor would be in vain if the resulting document was rejected by their constituents. The realization that some sixteen delegates refused to sign the completed document was a sobering one to its supporters. Their work was only partly done. The task of convincing other Americans that their handiwork provided the best form of government for their nation was the job they now faced.

The procedures for ratification of the Constitution were established at the Convention: upon the recommendation of the

Congress, each state was to call a convention of popularly elected delegates to discuss the proposal and by majority vote decide whether to accept or reject it. The principle of the people as constituent power was now established on the national level. When nine states gave their approval, the new government was to go into effect. Those in favor of ratification had already co-opted the positive name of "Federalist"; their opponents were thus left with the more awkward title of "Anti-Federalist." Other aspects of the debate gave the latter group considerable advantage, however. For one thing, the fact that each state was to discuss ratification for itself meant that the Anti-Federalists could use different arguments in different states with little risk of being called inconsistent. The Federalists, on the other hand, had naturally to defend the same proposal in all states, although they could emphasize particular features in different locales. The fact that ratification was by states rather than, for instance, by a national plebiscite, was theoretically a recognition of the importance of the states and would later be used to defend the principle of state sovereignty. Ironically, most commentators agree that the Constitution would have been rejected by such a nation-wide poll of citizens, and that it was only by winning over individual state conventions that the Federalists had a chance of success.

While varying slightly from state to state, the arguments of Anti-Federalists had much in common. First, they believed that the United States was too large a territory to be governed wisely by a single national authority. The principle of a confederation of republican state governments, as embodied in the Articles, was to them the only way such an extensive area could be managed. Second, most Anti-Federalists feared that the proposed strong national government would swallow up the state governments, riding roughshod over those economic and cultural differences that each state considered its unique quality and strength. Related to this was a third fear, that the national government was too aristocratic and that the liberty of the people would soon be destroyed. To support this claim, Anti-Federalists cited the indirect election of both President and Senate, the threat of a standing army, the failure to require annual elections and rotation in office for national positions, and particularly, the absence of a bill of rights. Other arguments heard in many state conventions appealed less to logic than to emotion. The delegates to the Constitutional Convention had exceeded their instructions; they had shrouded their proceedings in secrecy; and illegal methods of ratification were being used in some states, especially in Pennsylvania, the Anti-Federalists charged.

Federalists naturally made every effort to answer these arguments, both on the floor of ratifying conventions and in newspaper articles and pamphlets. The most famous series, later entitled *The Federalist,* was written for the crucial New York debate by James Madison, John Jay, and Alexander Hamilton. Here were the arguments for a more effective national government with powers to conduct foreign policy, regulate commerce, and establish a sound fiscal basis for itself and the nation as a whole. At the same time, Federalists everywhere were careful not to overemphasize the increased strength of a new national government and thus stir up the people's fears of centralized authority. In Massachusetts, Virginia, and elsewhere, the Federalists conceded that the absence of a bill of rights was an unfortunate oversight and agreed to proposals that such a document be added to the Constitution after ratification by the requisite number of states.

Although ratification went smoothly enough in the smaller states like New Jersey, Delaware, Connecticut, and Maryland, sometimes only after bitter battle and doubtful tactics was approval won in states like Pennsylvania, Massachusetts, and Virginia. Here the struggle was often waged more in personal than in ideological terms, with old patriots like Patrick Henry, Sam Adams, and Richard Henry Lee, fearful perhaps of losing some of the political influence they had enjoyed during the revolutionary generation. With ratification by New Hampshire in the spring of 1788, the Constitution was officially adopted, but not until Virginia and New York came over early that summer was the new government assured of operation.

At bottom, the differences between Federalists and Anti-Federalists were neither permanent nor very great. Much of the argument seemed acrimonious only because it was in the nature of political campaigning. Both sides believed in the essentials of American government — republicanism, a federal union preserving state authority within certain spheres, and liberty of the people. The Anti-Federalists simply doubted the willingness and ability of the Federalist leaders and their constitution to preserve these principles as well as they had been preserved under the Articles of Confederation and the state governments. The proof that the division was not very deep, at least by the standards of European internal political struggles, lies in the fact that the Anti-Federalists to a man proved to be good losers. Once the issue was settled, they followed the appeal of Patrick Henry to be "a peaceable citizen." The new system of government thus began in tolerably good spirit, without a disgruntled opposition baying at its heels.

The New Nation

In the spring of 1789 the first administration under the new Constitution took office. With George Washington the unanimous choice for president, and John Adams, Thomas Jefferson, and Alexander Hamilton all occupying important positions, the executive branch was dominated by those with a "continental viewpoint." The states similarly turned to nationalists in their choice of senators and representatives, and in most cases of governors as well. Within a decade, Americans would come to identify all that was glorious about their past and their future with the idea of Union. Without Union there could be no liberty. Indeed, by the early nineteenth century the Union in the minds of most Americans had become an end in itself.

But an effective government alone does not make a nation. Rather it is the attitude of the people toward themselves that is important. We have already noted that by the mid-eighteenth century Americans had begun to regard themselves as different from Englishmen. The events of the period 1764-89 accelerated this movement, and the attainment of political independence gave it new meaning, for independence from Great Britain was not confined to politics alone. In religious, cultural, and social spheres, Americans declared themselves separate from the institutions of the Old World. The Anglican, Presbyterian, and Methodist churches all established their own American organizations during the decade following independence. A spate of colleges appeared to answer the needs of the people for a higher education of their own. Most significant, a conscious search for cultural nationalism began during the 1780s. Noah Webster of Connecticut compiled an American dictionary, which altered the traditional spelling of a number of words and codified expressions that had originated in the colonies. Americans soon had their own geography, written by Jedidiah Morse, and a number of historical works appeared to present the young nation's past in suitable terms. Poets like Philip Freneau and Joel Barlow appealed to the basic patriotism of Americans in their writings, while artists like Charles Willson Peale and John Trumbull glorified national heroes and events on their canvases. All these efforts to express the spirit of the new nation would gain momentum in the coming decades. It was enough that voices of cultural nationalism were being raised at all during a period as preoccupied with political and economic matters. But in cultural as in other spheres, the men of the 1780s were not entirely innovators, for the process by which the European colonists and their descendants were becoming Americans had been going on since the founding of the first settlements 180 years before.

If one had told a young American parent of 1790 that his nation would barely last the lifetime of his newborn son, he would have been dismissed as an unpatriotic madman. For the idea of Union, conceived in 1774 as an expedient means to meet the threat of British tyranny, was well on its way to becoming an absolute American value. The Philadelphia convention demonstrated the lengths to which delegates from the various states and regions were willing to compromise "in order to form a more perfect union," to quote the preamble of the new Federal Constitution. Most of the regional distinctions posed no serious threat to the continuation of political union — what matter that New England tended to be Congregational and southern states Episcopalian, or that a Vermont farmer summoned his cows with a hearty "Boss!", while the Pennsylvanian bellowed "Sook!" Other differences raised more serious difficulties, however; New England's interest in overseas commerce contrasted with the southern states' greater concern for establishing control of the Mississippi and its tributaries. Most of these differences were sufficiently complementary, however, to become the grounds for workable compromise between the regions.

But there was one institution deeply rooted in the nation of 1790 that ultimately could neither be accepted nor ignored, neither dissolved nor compromised. The institution of slavery already cut across the American nation of 1790 like a geological fault lying just beneath the earth's crust. Union came in 1787 only because delegates from northern and middle states swapped whatever scruples they had about slavery for the promise of Union — a far higher goal on their scale of values than freedom for blacks. For while northerners and southerners may well have disagreed concerning the institution of slavery itself, white Americans of 1790 (save for the Quakers) were of one mind concerning the inferiority of blacks. And so the compromises and the bargains came rather easily for the founding fathers and their generation. Questions raised during the Revolution were put aside — questions such as "If all men were created equal, what about the black?" "If Americans were justified in resisting British slavery in 1776, what about their own black slaves?" "If the American environment was molding a new race of men from European stock, why was the African not accepted as an American?"

As we rightfully give recognition to our colonial ancestors for planting the roots of self-government, of economic opportunity, and of cultural independence, we must also recognize another aspect of our early heritage. In their belief that blacks were inferior to whites, in their treatment of fellow human beings as chattel, and in their acceptance of black slavery as part and parcel of their new nation, the founding fathers passed on to future generations of white Americans the dread disease of racism. The struggle waged by Americans of Indian, African, Mexican, and Asian heritage to free themselves from this most vicious and persistent of all tyrannies gives new meaning to the old idea of the American Revolution.

FURTHER READINGS

The most recent interpretation of Confederation period is Gordon S. Wood, *The Creation of the American Republic, 1776-1787* (Chapel Hill, 1969). Among the best surveys of the period are Merrill Jensen, *The Articles of Confederation...* (Madison, 1940) and *The New Nation: A History of the United States During the Confederation, 1781-1789* (New York, 1950). Allan Nevins, *The American States During and After the Revolution* (New York, 1924) is still useful. Robert R. Palmer, *The Age of Democratic Revolution: a Political History of Europe and America, 1760-1800, vol. 1: The Challenge* (Princeton, 1959) is a masterful overview that puts the American Revolution into the perspective of western civilization. More specialized studies of the whole period include Jackson T. Main, *The Social Structure of Revolutionary America* (Princeton, 1965); E. James Ferguson, *The Power of the Purse: A History of American Public Finance, 1776-1790* (Chapel Hill, 1961); Curtis P. Nettels, *The Emergence of a National Economy, 1775-1815* (New York, 1962); Elisha P. Douglass, *Rebels and Democrats: The Struggle for Equal Political Rights and Majority Rule during the American Revolution* (Chapel Hill, 1955); and Forrest McDonald, *E Pluribus Unum: The Formation of the American Republic, 1776-1790* (Boston, 1965). Among the many useful state studies of the period are Richard P. McCormick, *Experiment in Independence: New Jersey in the Critical Period, 1781-1789* (New Brunswick, 1950); Philip A. Crowl, *Maryland During and After the Revolution: A Political and Economic Study* (Baltimore, 1943); John A. Munroe, *Federalist Delaware, 1775-1815* (New Brunswick, 1954); and Oscar and Mary Handlin, *Commonwealth: Massachusetts, 1774-1861* (New York, 1947). For Shays' Rebellion, see Robert J. Taylor, *Western Massachusetts in the Revolution* (Providence, 1954). The drafting and ratification of the Federal Constitution has been the subject of much controversy among historians. The classic work, Charles Beard, *An Economic Interpretation of the Constitution of the United States* (New York, 1913), has been effectively attacked by Robert E. Brown, *Charles Beard and the Constitution* (Princeton, 1956) and by Forrest McDonald, *We the People: The Economic Origins of the Constitution* (Chicago, 1958). For the convention itself, see Clinton Rossiter, *1787: The Grand Convention* (New York, 1966). The struggle over ratification is discussed by Jackson T. Main, *The Anti-Federalists: Critics of the Constitution, 1781-1788* (Chapel Hill, 1961) and Robert A. Rutland, *The Ordeal of the Constitution: The Antifederalists and the Ratification Struggle of 1787-1788* (Norman, 1966). Three collections of interpretative essays that provide contrasting viewpoints are, Jack P. Greene, ed., *The Reinterpretation of the American Revolution, 1763-1789* (New York, 1968); Richard B. Morris, ed., *The American Revolution Reconsidered* (New York, 1967); and David L. Jacobson, ed., *Essays on the American Revolution* (New York, 1970).

Index